Theology of Creation

The Collected Essays of Peter Damian Fehlner, OFM Conv.

Volume 1:
Marian Metaphysics

Volume 2:
Systematic Mariology

Volume 3:
Franciscan Mariology—Francis, Clare, and Bonaventure

Volume 4:
Bonaventure, John Duns Scotus, and the Franciscan Tradition

Volume 5:
Ecclesiology and the Franciscan Charism

Volume 6:
St. Maximilian Kolbe

Volume 7:
Theology of Creation

Volume 8:
Studies Systematic and Critical

Theology of Creation

The Collected Essays of Peter Damian Fehlner, OFM Conv:
Volume 7

Peter Damian Fehlner,
OFM Conv.

EDITED BY
J. Isaac Goff

INTRODUCTION BY
Christiaan W. Kappes

WIPF & STOCK · Eugene, Oregon

THEOLOGY OF CREATION
Collected Essays of Peter Damian Fehlner, OFM Conv: Volume 7

Wipf & Stock
An Imprint of Wipf and Stock Publishers
199 W. 8th Ave., Suite 3
Eugene, OR 97401

www.wipfandstock.com

PAPERBACK ISBN: 978-1-5326-6395-6
HARDCOVER ISBN: 978-1-5326-6396-3
EBOOK ISBN: 978-1-5326-6397-0

10/16/23

Contents

Permissions

The publisher and editor wish to thank the following for permission to reuse previously published material:

Appendix 1: "Teilhard de Chardin Ambiguity by Design," originally appeared in *Homiletic and Pastoral Review* 50 (1960) 709–17.

Appendices 2–3: "Exchange on Teilhard de Chardin: Pro/Con," with Robert Francoeur, originally appeared in *Homiletic and Pastoral Review* 50 (1960) 34–47.

Abbreviations

AAS	*Acta Apostolicae Sedis*
Brev	Bonaventure. *Breviloquium*. In vol. 5 of *Opera Omnia*, 201–91. Florence: Ad Claras Aquas, 1891.
Chr. mag.	Bonaventure. *Christus unus omnium magister*. In vol. 5 of Opera Omnia, 567–79. Florence: Ad Claras Aquas, 1891.
DH	Heinrich Denzinger, Peter Hünnermann, and Robert Fastiggi, eds. *Compendium of Creeds, Definitions, and Declarations on Matters of Faith and Morals*. San Francisco: Ignatius, 2012.
Hex.	Bonaventure. *Collationes in Hexaëmeron*. In vol. 5 of *Opera Omnia*, 329–454. Florence: Ad Claras Aquas, 1891.
I, II, III, IV Sent.	Bonaventure. *Commentarius in IV libros Sententiarum*. In vols. 1–4 of Opera Omnia. Florence: Ad Claras Aquas, 1882–89.
Itin.	Bonaventure. *Itinerarium mentis in Deum*. In vol. 5 of Opera Omnia, 295–313. Florence: Ad Claras Aquas, 1891.
Red. art.	Bonaventure. *De reductione artium in theologiam*. In vol. 5 of Opera Omnia, 319–25. Florence: Ad Claras Aquas, 1891.
ST	Thomas Aquinas. *Summa Theologiae*. Opera Omnia. Vols. 4–12. Rome: Typographia Polyglotta S.C. de Propaganda Fide, 1888–1903.

Abbreviations for Distinctions in Individual Texts

a.	articulus	fm.	fundamentum
ad	ad oppositum	n.	numerus
au.	articulus unicus	opp.	oppositum
c.	capitulum	prol.	prologus
col.	collatio	prooem.	prooemium
con.	contra	q.	quaestio
d.	distinctio	resp.	respondeo

Introduction

CHRISTIAAN W. KAPPES

As UNSETTLING AS IT is, the world is contingent. A standard dictionary definition of contingency as an adjective describing a noun might include some descriptions as follows: (1) to depend on another for existence, (2) to be liable to happen or not; uncertain; possible, (3) and to happen without a known cause. It is with the first two senses that we begin reflections on the philosophy and theology of science in the writings of Fr. Peter Damian Fehlner, OFM Conv. Blessed John Duns Scotus (1265/6–1308) vied for the first or second place on Fr. Peter's lips depending on the specifics of any given question of science, philosophy, or theology. Of course, if Bl. Duns Scotus were not deemed worthy as the first point of reference for Fr. Peter on any given question, then it would only mean that Saint Bonaventure of Bagnoregio (the preeminent doctor of Scotus's Franciscan Order) had already satisfactorily analyzed and issued his judgment on the issue at hand.

But what relevance can two medieval schoolmen or members of the academy of their day have for us today? Surprisingly, St. Bonaventure's and Bl. Duns Scotus's precision on questions of necessary and contingent being is timeless, that is, on one hand, there is what *must* exist and can be known by us; on the other hand, there is that which might or might not exist (*cui non repugnant esse*) and can to some degree be known by us. The reflections upon these two hands, one and the other, i.e., the universe as known by us, was partially fruit of the collective wisdom of the Catholic university system, often said to have been established formally around AD 1215 at the University of Paris. It was the wealth of translations from ancient Greek and medieval Arab philosophers that percolated through the filters of these subtle minds. By understanding how to contextualize a problem, to eliminate anything contrary to the principle of parsimony (the so-called Ockham's razor that was originally the *razor Scoti*), and to distinguish necessary truths from those that are of varying degrees of probability, modern

1

scientific trends (sometimes called in shorthand the scientific method) found a fertile womb for its birth and development.

In this volume, Fr. Fehlner simply chooses carefully his modes of expression and reflection on a non-necessary universe that reveals itself only partially and with great difficulty to the eyes of the scientist apart from any revelation by a divine being. The rewards, as the scientific age of modernity have shown, can be virtually limitless: progress in medicine, technology, and in the so-called hard sciences. What often escapes the educated non-specialist in philosophy, however, is the disturbing and psychologically discombobulating admission of how little we "know" in the sense of having permanent, unchanging ideas founded on self-revealing and undeniably clear beings that never change or throw us for a loop in the constantly moving and changing universe. The fact that science, as we call what we learn in general and in universal education, is always progressing and that new theories replace old ones and that old facts (or sometimes merely their interpretation) can be challenged so as to give worldwide recognition and prizes to innovators who are sometimes iconoclasts of olden nearly dogmatic prior systems or bodies of so-called science creates real problems in a reflective rational being's confidence about what actually can be said to be known, if all is in flux, or if all has the potential to be called into question and overturned by means of but one influential experiment.

It is important to emphasize this for the reader who may not realize that philosophy of science, in its heyday, enjoyed a series of celebrity thinkers reaching a certain degree of notoriety for their admission of these sorts of problems. A sort of trifecta can be said to have taken the prizes in the eyes of the world with the advent of the scientific publications of doctors Karl Popper, Thomas Kuhn, and Paul Feyerabend. These men of erudition, defenders of scientific achievement as they were, attempted to account for the chaotic world and history of science where it had enjoyed little internal stability since it was first heralded by Galileo Galilei in the seventeenth century and remains ever in a state of becoming (*in fieri*). These three eminent authors coincide with Fr. Peter's own training in a strange way; namely, the fundamental analyses of Scotus with respect to what can be known about the world of matter and about its causes requires a foundation in logic, and the ability to distinguish between what are often referred to as *a priori* concepts versus *a posteriori* inferences. The kind of infallibility and eternity enjoyed by postulates of geometry (no matter the time, place, or culture) can produce perfect definitions or descriptions of the necessary parts of a whole (for example the number of lines and the degrees of their formed angles in a triangle). This kind of subjective or personal certainty about triangles never risks being wrong and all triangles, whether mental, digital, or material, are truly triangles only to the extent that they conform to this infallible definition.

This kind of certitude is possible in so very few items in the changing, corrupting, and reproducing universe. *Science*, as it is now called in the "hard" or rigorous methodological sense, must content itself to find patterns of movement or repeatability and predictability in order to claim predominance over a rival explanation of the facts. Dr. Popper even proposed that an essential facet of a real hard science is its disposition or innate characteristic to be open to experimental falsification by means of testing. Because of how much *a priori* or assumed truths and projections and assumptions go into any one science and given the fact that a science like astronomy does not feel the burden to do all the work and prove all the postulates of theoretical physics before studying the actual movement of the material universe, we see that there are only so many things that any science has selected to falsify during its institutional history, whether at a university, or within the chronicles of some recognized institution. It is laudable and meritorious that these questions were rekindled with such verve and vim, culminating in Dr. Feyerabend's iconoclastic work: *Against Method*. Dr. Feyerabend exposed the myth of a unified, experimental science and any allegedly objective method whereby science has been historically done. His point was not to destroy the modern academe, nor to advocate for some new version of a flat earth, but it was to tear down idols and to try to impose some sort of anarchism in scientific religion so that the marketplace of ideas or intellectual polytheism might allow for the gods or idols of scientists to accept that which is truly most prominent, i.e., the god one who produces the greatest miracles. That is to say, only the science that delivers a product that the community of stakeholders agrees are useful and valuable is the true science. Sometimes it is the marketplace, or the academy, or the government that has the rights or force to make this judgment in this or that society, but the judgment is made only for a time and place, only to be potentially overturned in favor of a competitor in short order.

All of this returns us to the medieval academy, where many of the same principles were at work in a more technologically crude environment and yet produced a fruitful dialogue between science and religion, philosophy and Christianity, and reason and faith. The exceptional stylistic ease for reading and yet intentional subtly within Fr. Peter's exposition of matters dealing with the alleged dichotomies between faith and science would be lost even on the grammarian. Each verbal use of the subjunctive or indicative, each conditional or indicative phrase is chosen with an eye to what may thought to be the medieval equivalent of Kuhn, Popper, and Feyerabend, that is, of Bl. Duns Scotus. It is not an exaggeration to describe Scotism thus. Most recently, specialists in the field of philosophy and theology have drawn significant attention to Bl. Duns Scotus's anticipation of what are the standard features of reasoning about anything from parsimony to causality in a number of respected modern fields like astronomy and physics. Neither is it so hard for the English reader to accept Bl. Duns Scotus's utility to great thinkers in the realm of fledgling modern and contemporary scientific endeavors, for who can forget that the great American pragmatist Charles Sanders Pierce was utterly convinced of the rightness of Bl. Duns Scotus's *orthoskepsy* or right thinking in matters of reason as applied to working out solutions to practical problems in the real world?

Our contemporary prejudice is one that fails to appreciate the mythology of sweeping historical narratives from the past, which tended to portray the contemporary situation as the culmination of constant progress in human knowledge and technology such that the medieval thinker is necessarily doomed to puerile thought. The medieval university represented a culmination in the world of logic and reasoning that remained unequaled from the fourteenth century until Frege. The contingencies of human history, like war, pestilence, and revolutions can account for some of the vicissitudes of medieval learning and its obscurity. Other realities that affected the works of Bl. Duns Scotus and his allies often had to do with the inability to determine the true author of very messy manuscripts or parchments written by the hand of amanuenses or copyists of varying talent. Sometimes texts such as these are virtually destroyed by interpolations or by excisions or by being incorporated into other texts. Bl. Duns Scotus's authentic works were not so very accessible until modern criticism in the late nineteenth century allowed for an authentic edition of his *opera omnia*. Until the initiation of such a project beginning in 1950, it was only the fallible but faithful Franciscan tradition of handing on verbally theology in the *studia* (friaries) or a Franciscan university that preserved the tradition of selecting the best passages alleged to be from Bl. Duns Scotus in order to form the principles of his philosophy and theology. Much of this tradition was essentially justified by the critical, scientific work by the Scotus Commission and other groups of scholars who are now producing all his works in critical editions that are soon to complete his *opera omnia*.

Consequently, many of the logical and metaphysical ideas that are embraced in the aforementioned trifecta can be found, even if more inchoately, in Scotus's account of science properly so-called or originally Aristotelian science. However, Scotus also treats of themes overlapping with modern physics and his ideas were explicitly applied by him to issues of astronomy, to mention one of the sciences already discussed. In this vein, I recall one eminent professor of philosophy at a prestigious university in the United States publicly recounting the work of his colleague, also an eminent Scotist and head of the department of philosophy, that this professor's efforts and publications have been dedicated (at least in part) to showing the proto-modern or modern scientific principles of Scotus in field like *Physics*, not to mention his clear anticipation of formal logic applied by Scotus with mathematical precision.

Returning to the modern prejudice theme, the prejudice—so observed this eminent philosopher—is to nowadays dismiss the rediscovery of Bl. Duns Scotus since modern philosophy has—during its seven hundred years of meandering back and forth between various extremes—arrived at a point that not only equals but surpasses Bl. Duns Scotus in areas such as the discipline of formal logic and philosophy of science. While it would be wrong to deny that the last seven hundred years have added a considerable amount of reflection to these aforesaid areas, and while it is not wrong to celebrate the fact that Bl. Duns Scotus—as an individual—has been equaled and surpassed by a mass of professional philosophers and their technological aids in doing science with greater precision, the issue missed should be glaring for the person of faith: Fr. Peter's synthesis represents the very same principles and their application (*plus minusve*) as applied to the deposit of faith (insofar as it can be useful) in order to ferret out the contingent and the necessary, the probable and the impossible, from theology properly so-called. The result is that Fr. Peter's unassuming style and engagement with supposedly complex and difficult data proposed by a new kind of scientism challenging the ecclesiastical establishment of Catholicism—from the early 1900s (the so-called modernist crisis) until its culmination and response by Pius XII (in the 1940s and 1950s)—is not very threatening or particularly provocative for Fr. Peter. As difficult as it is to believe for someone not trained in the advanced logic of the fourteenth century and in the critical approach toward Aristotle's notion of science, Fr. Peter's approach to the dialogue between faith and science recognizes the crude and naïve optimism of the so-called scientific worldview of the 1900s.

I have already admitted, conceded, and endorsed celebrating the achievements in technology and interpretation of data that makes our lives so very livable nowadays, making them qualitatively the best they have ever been able to be in the chronicled history of mankind. Nevertheless, the modern scientist is very often unacquainted with the internal limits of thought and ideas, the notion of impossibility of squared-circles and the pure possibility of goat-stags and centaurs. Where a scientist might want to think nowadays that a squared-circle is just a question of manipulating the material universe as whimsically provable by an experiment, the medieval mind (and modern philosopher of science) is amused by the simplicity of the unfounded wishful thinking even among minds who are otherwise brilliant within their specialization. On the other hand, the pseudo-scientism of the age might make fun of medieval classifications of centaurs and goat-stags under the logical notions of subjective or (for the sake of simplicity) real beings, while, on the other hand, such a one's own scientific community is really trying to achieve such monstrosities in the laboratory. A century ago, the idea that a human could live indefinitely (like, for example, an Adam or an Eve) is now standard fare in research and university laboratories, where billions of dollars are being spent in research because the hope is no longer merely wishful thinking that "eternal life" is simply a question of genetics but that a tweak of the cycle of cellular reproduction shall naturally give us the Adams and Eves that were only a century ago laughed and scoffed at as pure impossibilities within the same domain of science. In all this, we could have avoided both hubris and simple-mindedness by remaining grounded in the philosophy of Bl. Duns Scotus and his like-minded tradition. I certainly do not mean that Bl. Duns Scotus & Co. (viz. the Franciscan school) would have acted like a prophetic anticipation of modern discoveries, as if making a Scotist into a modern psychic who claims to know the contingent future; rather, Bl. Duns Scotus would have prepared us to read effortlessly and consider unworriedly the nuts and bolts of any one scientific advance or discovery and to realize its limits in what we have actually achieved; not unlike the aforementioned trifecta who has more recently done so by its more culturally relevant and elaborate engagement with the public on the same topics in a cultural and scientific idiom that has proven popular. So, the perennial value of Fr. Peter's reflections on alleged scientism and on real science will strike one as surprisingly open and then exasperatingly non-committal to an alleged insight and advance in the intellectual and practical orders of so-called scientific truth. This is so because each advance is an advance by so-called interpretation of data or by a quantitative increase in data but each of which augmentation requires a subtle mind to propose a hypothesis or establish a theory by experiment that accounts for all data (but really, as Dr. Feyerabend more accurately notes—since no theory can account for all the data—a scientific theory should account only for more facts and more dependably predict contingent outcomes than its rivals).

It is under the aegis of Bl. Duns Scotus, then, that Fr. Peter can effortlessly assert: "Any scientific theory, set forth under the name 'creation science,' thus indicating a dimension of the object of science not entirely comprehensible by scientific means, becomes by definition 'unscientific.'" Definitions of disciplines that assume the falsifiability or, at least, the testable nature of the data, must by their very nature, exclude as non-scientific what has become popularly and precisely designated "creationism" or a theory that purports to inject assumptions and interpretations of the Book of Genesis into the admittedly already chaotic world (per doctors Popper and Feyerabend) of scientific paradigm and method. What is at play here, however, seems at first to be that the pious priest Fehlner, in agreement with the putatively impious doctors Kuhn and Popper, are together pitted *against creationists and Dr. Feyerabend*, whose *Against Method* apotheosizes the mythologies, stereotypes, and superstitions of real geniuses of science whose very non-scientific methods, fairies, and superstitions (often *not at all* divorced from their actual performance of science) are part and parcel of these genius worldviews that led to their celebrated discoveries or interpretations. But the opposition is only apparent, for as a hypothetically Fehlnerian hard scientist (would that there were such as these!) might casually remark: Only geometric and human entities (rational animals and their moral acts) can be perfectly defined. In the world of messy matter and approximated assertions, we require horseshoe and hand grenade round-about definitions of everything.

Because the published and officially established scientific community has the right and has exercised the right to provide *descriptions* of science and its methods within any one branch or discipline, creationism is *by definition* not science. Fr. Peter instinctively need not enter into whether the definition *should be changed* to include creationism, particularly because those advocating such an eponymous creationistic science do not, so far, typically realize that the best *description* of such a science needs to take into account analyzable causes in the universe, which are traditionally material, formal, final, and efficient (with the addition of exemplary causality in the Late Antique and Bonaventurian traditions). When creationism so-called does not even see the relevance of such discussion of the kinds of causality and their effects (and often unconsciously presumes only efficient and material causality in its own methodology), whereas ancient, medieval, and modern physics can speak a little more of the same language (with whatever limited degree of overlap), then the pro-creationist ostensible scientist exposes a *petitio principii* or classic logical and rhetorical blunder: Such a one attempts to assert that "a" fits into the class of "x" without knowing of what "x" is constituted. The creationist mistakes the accidental or happenstantial overlap of certain objects in studies (for example, matter as it functions in the universe as in astrophysics) with the only requirement of the science; namely, the creationist wants certain occult causes to be admitted *a priori* though the demonstration of their probability (or not) of what is only logically inferential a posteriori and this must be accepted by reasoned argument from *philosophical cosmology* (i.e., ancient *physics*) but said creationists are typically *not* philosophers of science and thus fail to realize the primitive and invalid nature of their *philosophical* arguments from within that proper discipline, which has for centuries perfected its arguments for these kinds of entities (God, angels, or miracles) by means of a disciplined analysis. Creationists wish a certain number of occult entities to be readily admitted, though neither testability (let alone falsifiability) can justify their claims. The net result is to mix traditionally separate claims of metaphysics and physics, theology and astronomy, into a hodgepodge based upon the conviction that the rights of faith should trump reason.

In Dr. Feyerabend's universe, this is supremely acceptable, provided that the results of such prejudices and stereotypes justify the quasi-superstitious method. The jury is out whether such demands for the inclusion of God and angels into primary and secondary causal chains leading to visible effects actually have resulted in improvements or benefits that have changed the way scientists arrive at results that are deemed useful to their funding entities, inventions, and—of course—to their adoring public.

For his part, any presumptive opposition between faith and science was long ago addressed and dismissed by Bl. Duns Scotus who clearly demarcated the realm of a theology separating the eternal (*theologia de necessariis*) from other revealed truths about God's freely chosen contingent universe (*theologia de contigentiis*), not to mention the purely natural field of philosophical theology that can prove the existence of a divine being independent of any prophecy or book of revealed truths (*theologia philosophica*). From the perspective of the complex matrix of thought of Bl. Duns Scotus, Fehlner shares much more in common with our aforementioned trifecta than with anything that contemporary fideism proposes for replacing the modern institutions of science with some sort of undisciplined reliance upon immaterial causes while yet proven unequal to the task of being disciplined in its definitions, let alone accounting for more data by its theorizing on the organization of the cosmos than its modern rivals. Still, in openness to the thesis of Dr. Feyerabend, one ought not proscribe creationists from the scientific community unless their prejudices and stereotypes prove to be obstacles to theories that explain more of the relevant facts. In other words, were creationists ever to become a dogmatic inquisition over scientific communities, the democracy of free science would thereby be destroyed. It is in the marketplace of ideas wherein the creationist is welcome and should be celebrated along with his predecessors if and only if creationist science provides a better advance in explaining the data than its competitors. Of course, according to the rule of parsimony enshrined by Bl. Duns Scotus, so-called creation science is for the most part behind on this score. Yet there is another subtle way to improve on this anarchism for a genius like Fr. Fehlner; his conclusion is to escape from the false either-or dichotomy or false disjunct of either creationism or scientism (so-called) and to enter into the world of the philosophy of science where eternal knowledge is elusive and discomforting ignorance the rule, but for the person of faith this can be comforting in another way since one knows that no true opposition can exist between entities that are not merely intrinsically reconcilable to each other but all of which are effects of one and the same author, the triune God who is the source and the luminosity for all truth that is seen in him by divine illumination or, if you will, by the univocal clarity of the concept of being that has its intelligibility principally in the godhead and then by participation gleaned more complexly in the creature. In effect, the lack of eternal and abiding knowledge in the material realm of the cosmos (that is, clear changeless and immediate perception with total transparency of everything that a material object is) and our best guesses (that are worthwhile advancing in science) lead us to depend ever more on the eternal truth capable of shedding light in the darkness, even if naturally reasoned theology is more like the twinkling of a star than the overwhelming rays of light that the contemplative realities of revealed and infused theology present to the mystics. Yet, even there, rare are the insights that God deigns to show even to these privileged souls into the contingent order of nature since it is relatively unimportant, as passible and destructible, in comparison to the truths of the necessary divine and immutable moral order of God.

Fr. Peter's exposition of the faith will strike the reader by its assertions, informed as they are by Bonaventurian and Scotist reflections, as very matter-of-fact and confident. For example, in his commentary on God as creator according to the Nicene-Constantinopolitan Creed, he asserts:

> All that exists other than God, the invisible world of angels as well as the visible world of matter, came to be originally neither by an emanation from the divine substance, nor by development or evolution entailing natural processes of pre-existing agents not divine, but came to be out of nothing by an act of the divine will.

This summary is simply the repetition of the end term of scholastic debates on whether angels or other creations are capable of creating, a debate and speculation in scholastic circles originally inspired by the discussion of the same in the mega theologian and doctor, St. Augustine of Hippo (d. 430). What the reader does not see are the intricate considerations of the tantalizing modes of creaturely cooperation in the process of creation, especially as reconsidered by the absorption of pagan, Greek learning—preeminently the *corpus Aristotelicum*—into the Parisian university curriculum as discussed and critiqued by Schoolmen from the generation immediately prior to Bonaventure until the Enlightenment when such debates and their conclusive arguments crystallized into formal manuals of theology that provide a reader with the pith of possible and probable with regard to creaturely power and action in respect to creating *ex nihilo* or creating forms to affect preexistent matter.

On this very matter, Fr. Peter address the *ad hoc* appeals by putative apologists and even more scientific thinkers such as Catholics who are philosophers and theologians who claim that "the thought of at least some of the fathers on the origin of the species (work of ordination) is not incompatible with, indeed would seem to suggest in others a kind of 'mitigated evolution.'" Again, we turn to the somewhat ample discourse on the topic in St. Augustine's *magnum opus* of the *De Trinitate*. The notion of a *ratio seminalis* or a matter-form being that has unrealized potentialities upon its creation is hardly *per se* an argument that opens itself to polygenism, particularly that which claims a multiplicity of simultaneous instances of lower forms of life independently developing into higher forms who happened all to coincide in their arrivals at their highest term (so far) in humans who are capable of interbreeding in virtue of quasi-miraculous coincidence of all developing at around the same time and in the same way as if an ordered process of evolution were a law of development in matter. Once again, such so-called mitigated evolution constitutes a theory of ambiguities from the perspectives of schoolmen who demand a rigorous and transparent description of alleged and asserted entities whose existence requires demonstration and evidence in the realm of the *a posteriori* of the physical universe.

The patristic literature, with its mainly Neo-Platonic (just as Bonaventure's physics) views on matter and its potency or dispositions is not overly mysterious. St. Augustine overtly refers to his Neo-Platonic and pagan predecessors, just as his predecessor St. Gregory of Nyssa (died c. 395) had studied when at the pagan academy at Athens. As with the later Schoolmen, St. Augustine was in search of a classification of causes that could account for the creation of species of beings without reference to an act of creation or an action whereby something new is introduced into a world when no material or principle can account for it other than a divine agent. Ultimately, St. Augustine excludes creaturely creation, even in co-operation with divine Providence, even though he went to pains to justify such exegesis since the primitive and popular readings of Scripture in his own day led many to suppose that creatures creating or co-creating was hardly impossible. The most obvious example for St. Augustine was the description in Exodus 7 of Pharaoh's magicians who seemed to duplicate nearly every miracle of Moses. This issue has been a topic of reflection for all Abrahamic religions that profess these privileges exclusive to an omnipotent being, viz., to create. For example, Jewish interpretation not only confronted the possibility of a demiurgic form of magic or the demiurgic operation of demons, but even the New Testament and the fathers deal with the issue and the Qur'an quite explicitly—when confronting the same problem of the magicians—make sure to attribute to the magicians a reliance on contraptions, for they merely simulate the creator of all. Accordingly, Fr. Fehlner's exclusion of *ad hoc* solutions that superficially treat a universal tradition of confronting and rejecting any creature's claims to bring something into being *ex nihilo* goes a step further to address St. Augustine's references to the potencies or possibilities of matter.

The question remains valid for modern science: "Can natural causes account for the development of the rational animal." St. Augustine and the schoolmen knew that, given the contingency and limited capacity of material being, ultimately the soul and its body needed to revert back to God as creative cause, just as all lower forms of life. However, St. Augustine—like modern scientists—was more sanguine about the human composite's ability to reproduce like from like or for a human form to be the productive principle of another like human soul. This is not the argument in modern scientific discussion. The question, from a scholastic perspective, is whether different species of souls (plant soul, dog soul, and monkey soul) can organize themselves or be reorganized by a series of material and inferior kinds of external beings into a higher form of life and thought. This question still retains its relevance in scientific literature that seeks to find the evidence that such a leap is possible in spite of the philosophical begging of the question or objection from causality that demands proof on the side of modern scientific experiments and observation not the vice versa (while the response of average scientist is merely to appeal to scientific advance as the proof or scientific virtue of hope—known scholastically as a mere wish—that one day the circle will be squared).

This debate is made more difficult by the general disagreement between and among individuals of all camps about how to define a species. The Scholastics of all sorts and sects would have agreed: There is no perfect definition accessible to us of a mule, or horse, or donkey, especially when—even in the rarest of cases—such an animal can interbreed and even produce fertile offspring. Speciation is an elusive categorization. Do we define the limits of speciation by the capacity for interbreeding? While it is attractive to use the descriptor of certain genetic markers to claim to have an accurate definition of a species, until the genome of any complex animal is completely mapped, the claims to use these criteria remain myth or science fiction. What exists now is an incomplete description of all the genetic material of any one complex being that results in endless argumentation about classification of plants and animals of whatever kind.

Even when there is a generic agreement about larger genera or generic classifications of animal phyla and kingdoms outside of the issue of speciation, these categories are actually dependent on modes of division and comparison based upon appearances and observable characteristics that find themselves somewhat strengthened by genetic testing and descriptors that are relatively new to taxonomy. In other words, we still rely on the imperfect compare and contrast of visible external phenomena and processes of reasoning about similarity and difference to classify one species and phylum from another. This taxonomy is more greatly acceptable with the advent of genetic testing that allows such categories to be verified better or adjusted according to more intricate and complex sets of differences but ultimately what makes one species of horse different from another is a matter of degree of difference and sameness that is accomplished by committee or decree, not by *a priori* certainty as in the manner that a triangle versus a square can be differentiated.

In this ultimately messy universe of the imprecise, faith in science and faith in God enjoys plenty of breathing space. Science fiction often puts unfounded hopes on non-being (squared circles) but with an admixture of real possible such that advances can actually be inspired by fantasy and fiction mixed with improbability and impossibility. On the other hand, faith is nowadays little respected (other than by philosophers like the atheist Dr. Feyerabend) as sources for scientific advance. Fr. Peter's own approach is less adventurous and consequently utterly sober. As he unequivocally states:

> We cannot say that revelation given us by God is a complete description of his work, but one that is sufficient to identify the character of his action so that we might understand how to use this world and our time in it to save our souls. Further, revelation does not give an equally clear definition of each species, such that we can in every instance of present observation, merely on the basis of theology, discern the limits of each species philosophically considered.

This is supremely sobering but also infuriating to fideism. The bravado and hubris that Fr. Peter wishes to avoid are unreasonably reasoned inferences that revelation should be used as a series of geometric or quasi-Pythagorean premises by which the key to the secrets of the universe unfolds. The superficial rationality and use of extensive scientific studies in dialogue with, by and large, the King James Version of an English text that is subjected to projections of what a Hebrew author may have meant in the Ancient Near East when doing modern science is a lucrative and esoteric venture nowadays.

Aristotle stated rightly at the onset of his *Metaphysics* that "by nature all humans desire to know." The feeling of unknowing in situations that are important for a person's subjective experience of existential meaning, purpose of life or death, and intrinsic value often drive such a one to cling in desperation to any form of pseudo-knowledge that gives one the feeling of power, if only psychologically, over a universe that is otherwise mysterious, terrifying, or opaque. The aversion for feeling insignificant or floundering in an infinite sea of ignorance that many moderns have regarding the mystery of life, as well as the greater mystery of death, drives many to exercise any form of sophistry and rhetoric that can provide a metaphysical consolation (in the words of Nietzsche) to avoid the feelings of insignificance, lack of purpose, or impending annihilation.

The superstition and fetishism that is now popular even among committed Christians can approach a dogmatic level whereby they seek to exclude other Christians from the pale of faith based upon their alleged insights into reality by their secret decoder ring key rendering to them alone the perfect interpretation of the universe by reading the unchangeable text of revelation or the Bible by means of the ever-changing and fluctuating similitudes to truth of modern science, albeit in a constant state of flux. Fr. Peter's Bonaventure and Bl. Duns Scotus easily resist the temptation to exercise cultish control, if only psychologically projective, over the elements of the universe and their laws, and admit what is possible and probable and what can be explained of matter and what remains opaque until special revelation to the intellect allows such a thing to be known. However, to those untrained in the world of scholasticism, let alone the supremely rational world of Bl. Duns Scotus, the assertion that Scotism provides an answer key to overcoming existential angst and grappling successfully with the overall ignorance that we must admit with respect to our knowledge of beings within the contingent order sounds itself too much like a sort of agnosticism that celebrates ignorance. Really, the careful and detailed admission of what can modestly be known with unchanging certainty in the overall experience of beings in this world provides sobriety to the human intellect not to overly imbibe in Nietzschean bacchanalia and enthusiasm in some sort of putatively dark order to our universe. The approach of St. Bonaventure, as ulteriorly perfected by Bl. Duns Scotus, dissolves a Nietzschean embrace of the so-called Dionysian enthusiasm for the ordered chaos about the terrible universe by accurately describing what order to the universe can be known and, then, by admitting the utility and desirability of the scientific, in the modern sense, for describing the receding horizon of matter and material beings whose mysteries will ever need to be unlocked since Plato's fundamental frustration remains ever-valid, even if mitigated in Aristotle's reactions to his master, namely, the material is unknowable by us in this state of life given our limited intellects and our inability to unlock its secrets due to our dependence on knowing the mental abstractions and ideas that speak only of what is able to be inferred from our mental puzzling about really present conglomerations of color in its various sizes and shapes, with its sensible activities and reception of our acts upon it.

A laundry list of the movements of a particle and its reaction with vats of water or chemicals does not mean we see it directly and all its properties as if a luminous ray of light exposing every dust particle to full view. We have dark and approximate inferences that we draw from numerous experiments that may undergo innumerable revisions only to be abandoned in the next stage of science whereby—as Newton was overturned by Einstein—our present state of scientific reality will be overturned by a future genius, if not less bombastically by a bureaucratic group of researchers with government grants who unenthusiastically but meticulously carry out thousands of tests that ultimately invalidate everything that was once considered the standard description of a particular material being in very restricted circumstances.

None of this drama undercuts or undermines science but merely prevents us from overindulging in our fantasy about its mystical properties. Like vitamins, too much of a healthy product is sometimes that very thing which can send us to the hospital. The lack of mental equilibrium from which a random scientist may suffer is often dismissed in favor of a presumed brilliance (depending on the field), much like we tend still to celebrate Bobby Fischer's genius in the chess world, despite his congratulations to Al-Qaeda about the destruction of the Twin Towers and hatred of the Jewish people, for his capacity to see the possibilities of pieces on a chessboard and to master his opponent who would try to tell him otherwise, has a strange spellbinding power that permits many of us to dismiss or forget moral monsters in favor of some singularly good or useful product in an otherwise disturbing existence.

Our collective and media-driven cognitive dissonance with respect to the real messiness and manifold superstitions common among mythologized geniuses of the past and present is something worthy of laughter, even though the human dignity of that person demands an invitation to each to heal such mental wounds and to embrace virtue should rationality still hold power to persuade. We should celebrate science for its legitimate achievements and for pushing us to think more profoundly about the material universe, though it has proven—for people of faith—to harbor the same erratic prejudices in diverse times and places that Bobby Fischer's genius mind and heart did against his own government and the Jewish people. Sobriety need not have destroyed Fischer's chess genius but the two combined into one person is rarely a stereotype common to our thought but we seemed tempted to interpret virtuously what would be in all others vice and monstrous psychopathy but for the non-moral attribute of genius.

Perhaps a rare example of virtue and true genius is exampled though in Bl. Duns Scotus. So, myopic ideas of the overly specialist scientist about religion are also just as liable to manifest the same fault lines as our well-known example of Bobby Fischer. We should hope that every scientist could make his hobby horse Bl. Duns Scotus so that the dialogue between faith and science could be fruitful and respectful, undistracted by the nugatory descriptions of faith that are nowadays the all too familiar products of modern mediocrity, not the genius of the medieval edifice of theology that can include and comfortably digest each and every scientific advance without the least threat to the integrity of the intellectual commitment to the necessary cause of the contingent universe known with certitude; who is also the object of faith whose choice from eternity of the present contingent order can be seen, even by us, as rational and good in its whole and each of its parts.

Fr. Peter's exposition provides us in lay language with some of the premises from Genesis, seen through the perennial theology of the fathers, which attests to what can humbly be asserted as the point of departure for the theologian to muse on the world of modern science and its hypotheses whose purpose is to account for the real laws by which material beings do what they do in this universe. Of course, as Adam is the pinnacle of the act of special creation by God in Genesis (whereby a soul or principle of organizing matter was infused, where—the moment prior—nothing whatsoever like it had ever existed), Fr. Peter's exposition of the medieval and modern magisterial world of discussion of science in dialogue with Genesis will seem modest after we have experienced an unsteady diet of feast and famine in the media-rich and information-poor world of modernity regarding the dialogue between faith and science. However, the reality is that Fr. Peter's authority relies upon understanding the limits of human reason, the content of revelation, and the utterly mysterious world of the material universe, whose secrets even the philosopher's stone is incapable of unlocking. Perchance, and by means of philosophical speculation, we can imagine the human intellect possibly coming to a real knowledge of creation but it would need to be by the deity himself revealing to us the very divine ideas that underline its choice, order, and constitution. Until then, we justly celebrate the ever-expanding number of achievements of the members of the scientific community who are not only able to make a real contribution to bettering the quality of each of our lives but who can help us by their humble and sometimes ingenious service to humanity by applying the semi-constants of their experiments and theories to our day to day lives to experience creation and even other rational beings as part of a great and intricate order of beautiful complexity wherein each has a fundamental and contributory place in respect of the grand whole.

1

In the Beginning[1]

Foreword (2011)

THE PRIMARY FOCUS OF the essay is not what might have been, particularly
in regard to the origin of the first man and first woman, but what in fact
God has done, why and how he has done this, in so far as he has made this
known. The assumption here, one based on the first article of the creed, is
that the question of origins deals with what we might in a very broad, but
true sense, call a historical fact, whose truth depends on what the Creator,
the only witness, has told us about what in fact actually occurred, not what
might have been but did not take place. All discussions of this theme must
begin, not with possibility, but fact. Until that fact is firmly established, all
arguments from "scientific" or "philosophic" possibility, whatever their the-
oretic consistency may or may not be, remain inconclusive: *a posse ad esse
non valet illatio* (arguments from possibility to fact are inconclusive). And
where such arguments directly contradict what in fact God did, whatever
else he might have done, they are simply erroneous. Evidently this teaching, certain and unchanging, has implications of a philosophical nature

1. [The unabridged text of the study reprinted here was composed in 1983, partially
published in 1988 in the Roman review *Christ to the World* 33 (1988) 56–72, 150–64,
237–48, and thereafter on various web-sites. It was updated in 1998, and Fehlner composed a new foreword in 2011, bringing it into relation with further developments in
his thought on the topic of origins as presented in the other essays in this volume. For
Fehlner, the study's "aim is not a defense of one or another version of what is called 'creationism' but simply to state the teaching of the church on the origin of the world and
of the species, in particular the origin of the human family—not via a natural process
of generation from a common ancestor shared with some animal species, but from a
unique and miraculous process of formation on the part of the Creator."

The translations of the Conciliar texts are taken from *Decrees of the Ecumenical
Councils*, 2 volumes edited by Norman P. Tanner S.J., Sheed & Ward and Georgetown
University Press, 1990, with the exception of: the English excerpt of the Nicene-Constantinopolitan Creed which is from the new translation of the Roman Missal; and the
translation of the Apostles' Creed is Fehlner's.]

concerning the radically contingent character of all existence other than the divine and how it can be recognized via the correct use of our reason both at the metaphysical and at the physical levels of understanding. But this aspect of the question of origins and its bearing on Christian philosophy are only touched upon in passing.

Since the composition of this essay the author has not found any reason to think this analysis of the state of the question from the perspective of divine revelation and the teaching of the church needs to be modified in essentials. The observations of the late pope, St. John Paul II, on several occasions, in particular in his address to the Pontifical Academy of Science in 1996, when in passing he said that evolution as an explanation for the origin of the human body is more than a *scientific hypothesis* and that this assertion might be squared with the teaching of the church in terms of "theistic evolution," as well as similar opinions expressed by his successor, Pope Benedict XVI, mostly before he was elected pope, are not doctrinal propositions binding in faith, but merely the personal opinions of these two Pontiffs, to be respected, but not to be treated as definitive acceptance by the church of some form of "moderate transformism" or theistic evolution as it is now called. Affirmations of this kind, whatever their worth as theological opinion, do not constitute a basis for calling into question points of doctrine which are certain, even if presently "unfashionable." In the case of conflict in theology between mere opinion and certain truths of faith, opinion must yield to certain doctrine. A significant point of doctrine involved here is this: whatever the explanation of how the Creator in fact miraculously formed the first human body (as principal and not merely primary cause), such an explanation, in order to enjoy theological credibility, must not contradict the certain teaching that no brute in any proper sense of the term begot Adam, the first man, much less the first woman Eve. The formation of Adam, both in regard to his body as well as his soul, according to tradition, is primarily a miraculous action, not a natural process subject to scientific explanation. Even if for the sake of argument, we admit the possibility that the Creator could have begun this miraculous formation of the first human body with already living matter, we have *a priori* already excluded the possibility of the process being an evolutionary form of reproduction rather than merely reproduction of the same species.

Even if for the sake of argument, we concede the plausibility of some form of theistic evolution as an explanation of the differentiation of animal species (a concession which does not include the fact of that having occurred), it does not follow that it is also a plausible explanation of the origin of the first human body. Plausibility in this case rests on the priority of likeness over difference. In the case of the human body, difference from rather than likeness to the animal body takes priority. And the difference centers above all in the personal character of the human body as part of a personalized nature composed of body and soul. For this reason, the formation both of the human body as well as the human soul is a work postulating a special intervention of the Creator. It is for this reason that the subsequent production of a human body in the descendants of Adam and Eve is called not a reproduction of the species, but the procreation of a person.

Generally speaking, explanations of the origin of Adam's body from an already existing living body, e.g., an ape, via a theory of theistic evolution stumble on this point. In part this is because the very concept of theistic evolution is not very precise. For the sake of argumentation, we may simply make use of the definition supporters of theistic evolution commonly give it: "continuous creation," seemingly a scholastic term. But as it is used to explain development in the context of a scientific notion of efficient causality, the original theological meaning of the term radically changes from that of indicating the sustenance in being which the Creator alone provides each of his creature secondary causes so as to permit each to act as a principal rather than merely instrumental cause within the limits of its own proper nature, to that of indicating conferral of an additional power so as to act beyond those limits. In the case of the origin of Adam's body, the exercise of natural powers of generation on the part of a brute so as to terminate not at reproduction of an animal species, but at a new species with a nature beyond the limits of the parent would by any normal grammatical and logical usage confer on the brute the title parent of Adam. Why is this not so?

According to theistic evolutionists, this is because of the infusion of a spiritual soul. The reply hardly solves the problem. A soul is created by God alone each time a human person is conceived. But its infusion into the body does not humanize that body; it presupposes that it is already human. The question of how the first human body of the first man from whom all other men descend was first humanized is not explained by appealing to the infusion of a spiritual soul, because the infusion of the soul supposes the body is already human. Whether the starting point of this humanization of the body of the first man was inanimate or living matter, the process of humanization was not merely a natural process sustained by "continuous creation," but a miraculous one, for the simple reason that the human body transcends the reproductive powers of mere animals. An evolutionary process either involves a created agent as principal cause, or it is not evolutionary in the scientific sense. Before theistic evolution can be cited in support of the possibility of an evolutionary origin of Adam's body, the dilemma entailed in combining the two terms: theistic and evolution, must be resolved. To date no one has convincingly done this.

Finally, supporters of theories of theistic evolution often support it in order to defend the intelligibility and finality of creation. These are surely valid preoccupations. What they often fail to note is how the original "scientific" notion of the evolution of the human body from an ancestor in common with brutes, does not in fact support the intelligibility and finality of the world from the point of view of church teaching, but rather from the point of view of modern pragmatism. Modern science is not primarily directed toward resolving questions concerning the essence, nature and finality of objects of our sense perception, but toward how to best use these objects to our advantage. Such science can indeed be conducted in ways quite contrary to the real meaning and end of the visible creation. Whether or not the intelligibility conferred on the study of origins in terms of theistic evolution (to the extent this is possible) coincides with that recognized by theology and Christian philosophy is highly dubious when the starting point of the discussion are concepts characteristic of empirical, mathematized science rather than of Christian metaphysics.

There is, however, one possibly positive fruit of attempts to resolve the many questions surrounding the definition of theistic evolution and its use in current theology. These attempts, however failed, call our attention to a need, not to question the validity of the traditional teaching of the church on the origin of the world and man in particular, but to turn our attention to the purpose of what in fact the Creator has done and how reasonable this is. I refer here to the relation between creation, redemption and the Incarnation. In the Franciscan school of theology, the thesis concerning the absolute primacy of Christ has prevailed. This means simply that both the world and the redemption of mankind were willed by the Creator in view of the incarnation, not the other way around. This means further that the intelligibility of the world as *de facto* God created it is to be found in its relation to the mystery of the Incarnation, one transcending our natural intellectual powers unaided by the light of faith.

In such a perspective understanding of the origin and nature of God's creation first requires that the more perfect be the point of reference for explaining the less perfect, not *vice versa*. The differences between Adam and the beasts can only be grasped when we cease comparing Adam first to the beast, but rather to that heavenly exemplar whose image Adam reflects in body as well as soul. Thus Genesis 2:18–20, clearly indicates that before the formation of Eve from his side Adam could not find any like to him, i.e., Adam in the visible creation is comparable only to the Creator. Adam is incomparable with the beasts, firstly because he does not descend from a common ancestor with them. The Creator intervened miraculously, not merely via a "continuous creation," to form Adam's body. For the human body is destined to be "temple of the Holy Spirit," anointed by the Spirit after the manner of that body formed for the Son of God by the Virgin Mother through the working of the Holy Spirit. No beastly body is so ordained, or can be so ordained.

From this stems the importance of one of the most ancient patristic types of the Virginal formation of the Second Adam's body: that of "virgin earth" from which the Creator in person formed the body of the first Adam. The virgin earth, not a "virgin simian," as starting point for the formation of the first Adam is a type of Mary and of the miraculous character touching not only the creation of the soul, but also the body of the Second Adam. Whatever the theoretical possibility of "theistic evolution," this traditional teaching simply excludes any other explanation of the origin of the first human body and the radical difference between human procreation and animal reproduction.

Where the Scotistic metaphysics underlying the Franciscan thesis is accepted, there comes as well an epistemology of empirical science quite different from the Kantian one so often employed as the undergirding of modern science. In a Kantian context, there is no question that "evolution" is considerably more than a hypothesis. It is the indispensable condition for a scientific understanding of the world, how it functions and what can be done with it. But in a Scotistic context such an evolutionary postulate not only is not necessary to grasp the temporal-historical dimension of the divine plan of salvation; it cannot be reconciled with the premises on which the divine plan rests. It is the divine plan: what God wills, which takes precedence over and provides the key to the intelligibility of the created. In a word, the unchangeable is the basis for change and the point of reference for understanding what is coming to be and how it can come to be. In this context evolution, theistic as well as atheistic, loses its appeal as a universal postulate of existence and appears as it really is: not something more than a hypothesis, but merely a mental fiction postulated by the agnostic epistemology of Kant as the basis of all genuine "science."

Finally, the liberation of empirical science from Kantian premises sets it in proper perspective: a very useful form of knowledge, but not *Knowledge* itself. Those questions touching primarily on the personal and spiritual and personal character of the human body, its nature and goals, transcend the limits of empirical science. In the natural order evolution or development of a kind does occur, but within limits defined by a certain stability, a kind of relative monotony when this change (microevolution) is contrasted with the kind of development directed by a rational or intelligent agent in the cultural order and with the adaptations of the natural order which are consequent on this development. There is no need to question the truth of Catholic tradition about the origins of the human family in order to carry out the divine command to multiply, fill and develop the earth in view of its ultimate purpose: the glory of the Incarnate Lord and his mystical body the church. Quite the contrary: seen in this context the traditional teaching rather than any form of evolutionism defined primarily in reference to the natural material order provides the most hopeful basis for intelligent and humane progress as servants of the Lord and not as claimants to a false equality with the Creator.

Preface (1983)

For a number of years questions have been arising concerning the teaching of the Catholic Church on the origin of the world, of the species, and especially of the bodies of the first man and of the first woman. Unfortunately, that teaching has, more often than not, been seriously misrepresented, sometimes to the point of being unrecognizable, and this by persons claiming to represent the authentic teaching of the church. Two frequently met distortions are:

1. The teaching of the church on creation and the origin of the world (teaching in the first article of the creed) has no bearing whatsoever on the matter of teaching about origins in either parochial or public schools.

2. The issue is a purely secular one, because the issue of origins is a purely scientific one and hence should be resolved on purely secular grounds without reference to Catholic belief and religious practice. The teaching of the church has nothing directly to contribute for the presentation of origins in parochial and public education. "How" the world came to be is a secular-scientific question, to be settled independently of religious considerations. But the church is interested in the outcome because her teaching concerns the person "Who" caused the world to come to be or evolve as it has. As this argument goes, the church is quite prepared to accept the "fact" of evolution as the means by which God made the world. This point of view is often known under the heading "theistic evolution," and when its promoters seek to reconcile the notion of a "Creator God" with the "fact" of evolution they have recourse to a form of reflection known as "process philosophy."

Superficially examined, the two distortions are quite contrary. The first makes religion and the teaching of the church a merely private, personal affair vis-à-vis the public, visible world. The second ends by making the deity immanent in the process of evolution. Both positions, however, even at a superficial level of examination, are directly opposed to the first article of the creed as it has always been understood by the church:

- that in virtue of creation there is nothing in the world independent of God and thus in some way without religious dimension; and

- that, in virtue of his title Creator, God is not immanent in the processes of the natural order.

This common opposition to the first and most basic article of Catholic belief rests on two assumptions shared by the proponents of these distortions. The first is a notion of science as completely autonomous. The intelligibility of the object of scientific study is totally comprehensible to science or not intelligible. Any scientific theory, set forth under the name "creation science," thus indicating a dimension of the object of science not entirely comprehensible by scientific means, becomes by definition "unscientific."

Secondly, the teaching of the church and the teachings of revelation have nothing to contribute to the understanding, *a parte rei* or objectively, of what science and philosophy study or of how this object came to be. Both assumptions are the direct opposite of the actual teaching of the church since the beginning of her existence.

The objective of this essay is a correct statement of the teaching of the church on the origin of the world and of the species, especially of the human species, and of the consistent policy based on this teaching and followed by the church in assessing the results of philosophic and scientific study of these questions.

The exposition comprises five divisions. The first deals with a number of preliminary considerations indispensable to a correct interpretation of the creedal formulae of the church. The next three are commentaries respectively on the three solemn definitions of the church's belief in creation (the ancient creeds, the oldest and most frequently used being that known as the Apostles' Creed); the second being the definition of the Fourth Lateran Council, and the third being the definition of the First Vatican Council. A final section will treat the development of that teaching since Vatican I to the present. The conclusion will indicate application to the matter of teaching about origins in parochial and public schools.

Preliminaries

Belief in the Creator

The starting point of theology is our knowledge of God. Theology begins, writes St. Bonaventure,[2] where philosophy, including all branches of natural intellectual endeavor, metaphysics, science or natural philosophy (as it was called by St. Bonaventure) leaves off (i.e., with God). Natural knowledge begins with the visible, the objects of the senses, and through their investigation and study, arrives at a knowledge and understanding of God, their maker. Such knowledge of God cannot but be indirect, mediate, and very limited, especially when contrasted with that knowledge of God which begins with God, the invisible, the changeless, and from the knowledge of him Who is Creator proceeds to a study of his creation, which is all else that is. For this kind of study St. Bonaventure reserves the name theology.

This reflection of St. Bonaventure makes clear why belief in the Creator is the first and basic article of the creed, the first truth revealed in Scripture.[3] At once it assures both an unambiguous, distinct, clear, accurate notion of God who can and will save his people, and a sound criterion for the correct interpretation of all those signs pointing to the Creator and to the possibility of some greater work on his part. So long as a person is in fact mistaken on either or both of these points, so long will his salvation be endangered, so long will his true temporal welfare be impeded. Thus, from the beginning of her existence the Catholic Church has insisted on an accurate exposition of the first article of the creed as absolutely fundamental to her teaching mission and to the cultivation of theology.

The Content of this Teaching

God

There is but one true God, not merely the first, but the only God, unlike any other being, although all others, to the extent that they are, are like him. He is all powerful, all knowing, all good. Whatever can be done, he can do; and whatever he cannot do, cannot be. What is possible is what he knows to be possible, and what is not known to him is neither intelligible nor possible. And what actually comes to be outside him comes to be because he wills it freely, as he wills it to be, or simply is not. This *"Fiat"*—let it be, and it comes

---

2. *Brev.*, p. 1, c. 1, n. 3.

3. Gen 1:1.

to be—is called a creative act, as distinct from the natural processes and actions of creatures, as is the Creator from creatures. Only God creates by a simple act of his will, without assistance (instruments), and without acting on any antecedent matter. God makes out of nothing. This notion of Creator reveals God to be utterly independent and sovereign, the beginning or source of all else, without beginning,[4] an eternal, necessary, infinite ocean of perfection; all else that is has a beginning in dependence on another, a beginning in time, and thus is shown to be finite and not divine.

Creation

All that exists other than God, the invisible world of angels as well as the visible world of matter, came to be originally neither by an emanation from the divine substance, nor by development or evolution entailing natural processes of pre-existing agents not divine, but came to be out of nothing by an act of the divine will. Not every single individual existing now or in the past or in the future was made directly out of nothing in this way, nor is every change in the world to be explained directly in terms of creation. Nonetheless, before anything at all could exist or change, something was made by God out of nothing.

Not only did this creative act give existence to the world; it provided the world order and intelligibility, and this in two ways:

- by constituting the essences or species of the natural agents acting within the world, and

- by establishing certain patterns, rhythms, and laws according to which these natures act on or are acted on by each other.

This order and intelligibility define the limits of the created order, and of each created agent, limits which can be modified temporarily or permanently only by the Creator's direct intervention, otherwise known as a miracle. Within those limits created agents can be the source of change and development, for better or for worse.

At each of these points, the world as a whole, the essences of things, and the overall rhythms or laws of nature, the impress of the Creator and his creative act can be discerned and at the same time distinguished from the creature and his natural actions. For neither the Creator nor his distinctive mode of acting *ad extra* is continuous with, uniform, and

4. John 1:1.

comparable with the natural order and the processes which presuppose the creative action of God.

Summary

From the foregoing, it is quite evident that the Catholic understanding of the first article of the creed includes a revelation of truths pertinent to all creation, and not only to the Creator. How many and to what extent these truths provide knowledge not otherwise accessible to the human mind, or merely confirm what could be known naturally, are separate questions. So too it is clear that a careful study of God's creation (the world) should lead to a knowledge not only of God as Creator, but to a realization of the world as created. Whether in fact without the help of revelation the unaided human intellect ever could come to such a clear realization of the true character of the objects of our senses, or even to a faint realization of the notion of "being created," has often been answered negatively; but whatever the difficulties, or whatever final form the demonstration takes, the Creator can and should be known from the fact that this world, and what is in it, is created, finite.

Source of this Teaching

In exercising her teaching office, the Catholic Church does not claim the power to effect new revelations of divine mysteries, but only to set forth clearly, accurately, and consistently the "deposit of faith" entrusted to her by her founder. The source, then, of this teaching concerning creation and the Creator is revelation, as this is contained in the divinely inspired books of Scripture and tradition of the church. Further the church claims a divine guidance and protection from error in expounding the truths of salvation.

This does not preclude, on the part of philosophers and scientists, study of those points of revelation falling in one way or another within the scope of their disciplines. And just as faith can be of great help in the advancement of knowledge in all areas, so natural study can also serve to confirm and deepen the understanding of revelation and to help in distinguishing what is revealed from mere hasty inferences of the uninformed.

None of this is possible without universal recognition of the epistemological dimensions of questions concerning the origin of the world, and especially of mankind. What these dimensions are and what principles govern their adjustment and coordination will become apparent at several points in this exposition.

Terminology

Every intellectual discipline develops a vocabulary and usage distinctive of its subject matter and method of study. Correct definition of terms at the outset, especially in a matter such as the question of origins, is indispensable to the fair appreciation of the teaching of the church and of the theology resting on her authority.

Creative Act

The creative act is an action of God alone by which something which did not exist at all is made to exist. Strictly speaking, no process or passage from one state to another is involved, because no *terminus a quo* existed. Such a creative act may be contrasted with the divine processions in which one divine person proceeds from another, but which is not a process of movement or change, because in this "procession" the divine nature of the person proceeding neither comes to be, nor in any way is changed or divided, but is simply communicated from one person to another. Productive acts of creatures entail the management of instruments and the preexistence of matter on which to act. This implies a real process and passage of time in the production of the *terminus ad quem,* not existing prior to the process and change, both in the agent and in its effect.

Primary and Secondary Agents

God alone is said to be the primary cause, because all other causes presuppose his creative action in some way in order to exist and continue to exist so as to act. All other agents are known as secondary causes (i.e., creatures).

Equivocal and Univocal Causes

The Creator in the traditional terminology is said to be an "equivocal Cause," not because he acts deceptively, but because none of the effects he produces is fully like him, or need be exactly like each other. Thus, the Creator is capable of making a variety of species, each different from its maker and from each other in degree of perfection. A "univocal" cause is said to be one which produces effects always identical in nature with their cause. Rational creatures to a certain extent are "equivocal" causes to the extent they are capable of artistic work. Only the Creator is an "equivocal" cause without limitation. This point is an important one in assessing the relative stability of the order of nature and of the possibility of a miracle. The Creator, in the teaching of the church, most certainly established a relatively stable system of nature. Within those limits rational creatures are capable of directing a certain development of the world; but only the Creator is capable of modifying those limits temporarily or permanently, or of totally annihilating his work.

Two points pertinent to modern theories of upward evolution of the species may be noted:

1. Such a production entailing the modification not of accidental qualities, but of the substance and essential properties of the lower species requires as principal agent of change, a rational agent, an equivocal cause. An example of this is man, made out of the slime of the earth. A univocal cause by definition is incapable of producing such results, nor has any such agent, as is normally postulated in modern evolutionary theory, ever been observed to have done such. No "kind" or species not endowed with intelligence and freedom (i.e., a rational agent) is capable of modifying a species.

2. Apart from the "inorganic" world, no rational agent except the Creator is capable of changing a species essentially, but only accidentally, as for instance in stockbreeding, and this only within limits pre-determined by the Creator in establishing "each according to its kind."[5]

Principal and Instrumental Cause

The principal cause is the agent directly responsible for the specific effect produced, and is contrasted with instrumental cause, the agent responsible only in a subordinate way. Principal cause is not to be confused with primary cause, as is so often the case in explanations of origins known as theistic evolution. When a creature acts as principal cause of some effect, God is also involved as the primary cause conserving and concurring with that action. When, however, God is said to be Creator, he and he alone is the principal cause. When he is said to work a miracle, he may or may not utilize an instrumental cause, he may or may not act on pre-existing creatures. Although in some cases a miracle may appear to be like a natural process, it is in fact not a natural process at all, because the principal agent is not a natural agent, and

5. Gen 1:25. The *ratio seminalis* of St. Augustine, with the many different interpretations it has undergone since, was an attempt to explain the work of six days in reference to this biblical text.

therefore, the process is not uniform or measurable in those terms. For this reason, the term evolution, to avoid ambiguities and equivocations, should be restricted to natural processes wherein the principal agent is a creature. In the work of creation, the six days of Genesis, the church has always understood God to be the principal Agent, although each of his actions during that period may not have been creative in the strictest sense, but only in the broader sense of miraculous. He may have used instruments already created, or acted himself on pre-existent matter as in the case of Adam's body "from the slime of the earth." In any case, although individual creatures once created may have acted before the end of the sixth day when God "rested," they did so directly under the creative power of God, and only after completion of the entire work did the world begin to function with a relative autonomy in the sense of secondary, principal causality.

The importance of this distinction can be illustrated with the popular objection to the creation of the heavenly bodies in a single day of twenty-four hours. It is claimed in the objection that the formation of these bodies would have postulated a duration of enormous length, since such is the time required for light from these bodies to reach the earth at present, and that light was observed by the first man on his appearance (according to Genesis). The objection, however, begs the question. It assumes as certain what in fact the proponents of evolutionary theory should prove, that the processes now observed in the transmission of light from the heavenly bodies to earth—and the duration needed to traverse the distance between them—are the same by which they were made to shine initially. Where the Creator is the principal cause, there is no reason why he cannot do all this without the aid of natural processes and with or without any duration pleasing him and appropriate to his ends (twenty-four hours as Genesis tells us). Nor should it be said that the appearance of long "light-years" is a deception. Appearances are deceptive only where no key to their interpretation is provided. Thus, what looks like bread and smells like wine is bread and wine except where those elements have been "transubstantiated" into the body and blood of Christ by the consecratory action of a priest. There the appearances of bread and wine, real enough, indicate not bread and wine, but the body and blood of the Savior. This is known because God has told us so, that such power has been given to an ordained priest. So too in this case, the Creator, being the only witness to what happened in the beginning, has told us he made the stars and made them shine within a period of twenty-four hours, thus providing a key to the interpretation of the appearances "in the beginning."

Thus, the divine creative act is distinguished from his conservative act, both of which, though identical in God with his power, have different terms outside God. The second conserving act presupposes the completion of the "founding" of the world, and is directed to its relatively autonomous operation. The first is a reflection of what Catholic theologians subsequently called God's absolute powers, by which he not only made the world, but can destroy it, modify it, or temporarily interrupt its ordinary rhythms, as in the case of a miracle. The full extent of this power we cannot know simply from what he has already done, for he can always do something more. The second reflects his ordered power and is known from nature and the laws of nature discerned in creation.

The Apostles' Creed

Texts

Credo in Deum, Patrem omnipotentem, Creatorem caeli et terrae. . . .	I believe in God, the Father almighty, Creator of heaven and earth. . . [Apostles' Creed].
Credo in unum Deum Patrem omnipotentem, factorem caeli et terrae, visibilium omnium et invisibilium. . . .	I believe in one God, the Father almighty, maker of heaven and earth, of all things visible and invisible [Nicene-Constantinopolitan Creed, 4th century].

Textual Observations

Creator-Maker

The terms are synonyms when predicated of God. When he creates, he indeed produces an effect outside himself utterly dependent for its existence and nature on that productive act. The divine making is different from the productive act of the creature precisely because it is creative.

Uniqueness

Only God can make in a creative way, because he alone is omnipotent. Therefore, all things, invisible as well as visible, owe their existence and nature to this unique kind of productivity. The natures and actions of the created order will reflect partly the nature and action of the Creator; but the unique character of the Creator and his creative act cannot be defined in terms of that natural order and the processes stemming from created agents. Creation as an act of God is incomparable, discontinuous with, and different from natural activities in which it is reflected.

Sources of the Creedal Formulae

Some dogmas of Catholic faith are only made explicit, or given a definitive formulation after the passage of some time. An example of this is the Immaculate Conception of the Mother of God. Unlike some of these other dogmas, this article of faith, which is in the creed, appeared, as it were, fully elaborated with the church herself. The key elements, always regarded as synthesized in the classic form of the ancient symbols of faith, can easily be located in the recorded teaching of Christ and his apostles. Thus, the importance always assigned this article by the church for the foundation not only of Catholic theology, but of Christian philosophy and science, is rooted in the stress laid on this point by the Son of God through Whom all things were made, and without whom nothing that came to be was made.[6] Several examples will make this clear.

In the Beginning

"In the beginning (ἐν ἀρχῇ, *in principio*) was the Word and the Word was with God. . . ."[7] The "beginning" of the prologue of the Gospel according to St. John, the beginning which is without beginning (eternal) is contrasted with the "beginning" of Genesis 1:1, which refers to the world which is not eternal (infinite). The Word or Son of God, only begotten God,[8] comes from the Father not by a creative act, but by an act of generation as eternal as the Father. Thus, the Word conceived in the womb of the Virgin virginally is not to be confused with a creature dependent on and subordinate to the Creator, but identified as the one who before his beginning in time at the moment of his conception, pre-existed as the equal of the Father from eternity, and as the one through whom what he later became was made.

Elsewhere in the Gospel according to St. John, our Lord, the Founder of the church, and her teacher, is clearly recorded as defining the difference between Creator-creature, eternity-time, creative act-natural act,[9] and

6. John 1:3.

7. John 1:1.

8. John 1:14, 18.

9. John 17:5: ". . . Glorify Me with Thyself, with the glory that I had with Thee before the world existed."

asserting the possession of creative power or omnipotence, alone capable of effecting the resurrection of a human corpse by himself as the Word made flesh[10] for which resurrection the teaching of the church has always required the exercise of a power capable of drafting out of nothing, the power of working a miracle, a power belonging to God alone.[11] The constant belief of the church in the reality of Christ's physical miracles (e.g., walking on water, multiplication of loaves, transfiguration) entails a belief in the source of their possibility and inner intelligibility, in the power of the Creator to modify and correct for higher ends the created order and its laws originally established by him. And this power, in virtue of his divinity, was possessed by the Son of Mary

Adam and Eve

Not only does the cosmos as a whole, before it begins to develop with a certain apparent autonomy, have a beginning in time which is the immediate effect of a creative act of God, but the principal work of the sixth day, Adam and Eve, has a specific beginning on the sixth day and not before. It is not ascribed to the antecedent action of principal causes as merely creatures, but to the direct principal action and intervention of the Creator, touching not only both the material as well as spiritual components of that nature defined as human, but also the differentiation of male and female. In the Gospel according to St. Matthew (19:4), Christ refers to this specific beginning of man and woman as the basis of the distinctive, unchangeable (i.e., non-evolving) nature of marriage. This fundamental difference between the human and non-human among living creatures is present not only in the soul as in its root, but also in the human body, differentiating it from that of any other animal, however perfect. This difference

- is the basis of the human person's special likeness to God among all creatures and the root of his personal dignity;

- accounts for the distinctive, unchangeable character of marriage, giving to the marriage contract its sacred character, even among non-Christians; and

- is established directly by the Creator through the use of his distinctive power to create.

---

10. John 10:18: "No one take My life from Me, but I lay It down Myself, and will take It up again" (i.e., make my corpse live again).

11. Also, Matt 25:34.

However, the particulars of this action are described, it is not the equivalent of a natural process, as this is observable in the interaction of created agents already constituted *in esse*. In this century it is a point made by Pius XII, but little noted by recent commentators on the theology of human origins.

Nature, Grace, and Glory

There are parallels between the intervention of Creator *qua* Creator in the order of nature, of grace, and of glory. St. Paul, in the letter to the Ephesians,[12] formulates the principle explaining the nature of that link which correlates these three orders, a principle for the rest illustrated graphically in the many miracles of our Lord. The power at work now in the Christian (the grace received in baptismal regeneration), he writes, is the same that was at work in Christ Jesus raising him from the dead (order of glory). This power (δύναμις, *virtus*) is nothing other than the divine omnipotence by which all things were created (order of nature). The difference between the creative act, prerequisite for the foundation of the world and subsequent activity within it, is the exact measure of the difference between the action of God prerequisite for the establishment of the orders of grace and glory and their coordination, and the activities within them subsequent to their foundation. Pelagianism, the radical denial of the difference between grace and nature, results from a failure to acknowledge this precise difference.

The denial of the need for grace in order to act in a salutary manner, for a supernatural end, leads logically to a denial of any need for an omnipotent "Fiat" to originate the world and each of the species within it. However different from pantheism (polytheism, syncretism) that Pelagianism may seem, it rests on the same intellectual and psychological assumptions as does pantheism, the equation of the creature and the "created will" with the Creator and the divine will.

Relative Uniformity of Nature

St. Peter in his second letter[13] solves the objection of those who deny the possibility of the life to come, of the resurrection, of the coming of Christ in glory, and of a new heaven and a new earth, on the grounds that the world has always functioned in the same way in the past, and therefore will

12. Eph 1:18–23.
13. 2 Pet 3:3–13.

always function in the same manner in the future. St. Peter simply denies the truth of the assumption made by the skeptic doubting the realism of Christian hope as do those who call it an opiate today. The uniformity we presently observe in the world is not absolute and provides no basis for extrapolating into the past or into the future without limit and without taking account of God's power to modify the form of the world and the order prevailing among the actions of creatures. In fact, the Creator has modified that order at least once since completing his original creative work. He did this at the time of the universal flood, and will do so again by fire at the time of Christ's coming in glory. The basis for this relative uniformity of the laws of nature is to be located in the difference between a creative-miraculous act and one merely natural. Neither the original existence of the world, nor the constitution of its original order can be explained in terms of merely natural activity by extrapolating from the nature of that activity presently observed. Quite clearly, one of the key methods employed by evolutionists to prove an event no longer observable to scientists, viz., the uniformity of nature and the assumed continuity between the mode of origin of the species and of the world and the present, apparently uniform mode of acting within that world, conflicts with a constant church teaching and the possibility of miracles (physical in particular).

Summary

The creedal formula for creation, seen against its scriptural backdrop, quite explicitly contains the following points:

1. The one and only God, utterly incomparable, is the Creator of all else; the entire cosmos for this reason has a beginning in time. It is not eternal-infinite.

2. Not only is the Creator solely responsible for the existence of the world, but it is his distinctive action principally that gives order to the world in establishing the distinct natures or species in their essence and in establishing the laws or structures governing the subsequent activities of created agents.

3. Underlying these propositions (i.e., the relative and conditional uniformity of the laws of nature) are suppositions, a denial of which is itself a religious assertion, untrue factually as well as theologically, and because untrue, idolatrous.

Exposition and Use in the Catholic Tradition

The church's early tradition consistently demonstrates these same conclusions: that God created and principally caused the world and its order. These constitute his work (six days of Genesis), as contrasted with the work of creatures acting as principal causes, only after the prerequisite work of establishing and ordering had been completed by the Creator. These points have been amply demonstrated in a very careful study of E. Testa.[14]

Polemical Uses

The polemical uses to which the fathers of the church put this article of the creed likewise confirm these points. Thus,

1. The first article of the Creed clearly excludes any form of polytheism whose central tenet is not the denial of God's existence, but the denial of his uniqueness, both in nature and in operation. The doctrine of creation quite unequivocally secures not only the correct notion of divinity, but likewise the correct use of those evidences in this world pointing to the existence of the only God.

2. The first article excludes any form of Manicheism in bringing all things, even the lowest material being, under the Lordship of God, thus securing the basis for the reality of matter[15] and its goodness, because it is made by God. Not only metaphysical dualism, but skepticism concerning the reality of matter and the objectivity of the objects of the senses, is thereby excluded.

3. So too metaphysical dualism's exact contrary, pantheism, the ancient theory explaining the origin of the world by way of an emanation or evolving from the substance of God, is excluded by reason of the

14. Testa, "La Creazione," 5–68.

15. In the early church this skepticism about the reality of matter was known as "Docetism," and was associated with the heresy which claimed that in the incarnation God only appeared in the flesh, but did not in fact assume a real flesh or material body as his own, and that Mary only appeared to form in her womb a real, substantial human body. Mary, these early heretics claimed, was not a real mother and this was the true sense of "virginal" motherhood. Subsequently, such views were found in various forms of monophysite theory denying any real distinction in Christ between his divine and human nature, because the human nature was mere appearance. Skepticism of this kind reappeared in the writings of the Anglican Bishop G. Berkeley on the spiritual as solely real, a view exactly the contrary of those claiming only matter was real. All these claims ultimately end in some form of pantheism identifying created and uncreated, material and spiritual.

character of the creative act: not a natural process with a *terminus a quo*, but a simple act of the will, discontinuous with its effect.

4. In the exact parallel drawn by many fathers between the formation of the body of the first man from the slime of the earth and the raising of the dead body of each person from the tomb, two phenomena are identified as being both effected directly by the omnipotence of God, starting not from nothing, but from something inert, and incapable, except by the direct exertion of the divine power in a uniquely divine action (miracle) of developing into a body capable of vivification by a spirit (soul).

5. Throughout the history of the church a close connection between the first article of the creed and the dogma of the Incarnation is noticeable. For instance, at the time of the Arian controversy, St. Athanasius held that Arius' view of the Word as an exalted creature, but merely a creature, could not be correct. For the Word is the one through whom all else was made, and only a divine person is capable of a creative act in the proper sense.

So too the ancient modalism (and its modern counterpart, Unitarianism) which denied the real distinction between Father and Son has always tended to deny, and almost always in practice has denied, that the "one God is the Creator of all," and has espoused a religious system that can only be described as syncretistic. That is undoubtedly the root reason for the consistent sympathy to be found between various forms of modalism and Pelagianism across the centuries, a sympathy which John Henry Newman in his classic study of Arianism[16] notes to have first appeared in the views and practices of the Judaizers of St. Paul's time.

Once this is realized, it comes as no surprise to discover modern evolutionary theory denying the first article of the creed to be closely allied with modern versions of ancient Christological heresies in the promotion of syncretistic mysticism.

Speculative Discussion

Some twentieth century writers[17] claim that the thought of at least some of the Fathers on the origin of the species (work of ordination) is not

---

16. Newman, *Arians*, ch. 1, section 1.

17. Messenger, *Evolution and Geology* (1939), and *Theology and Evolution* (1949). For the general background of *ratio seminalis* in St. Augustine, see Portalié, *Thought of St. Augustine* (1960), and Gilson, *Philosophy of St. Augustine* (1960).

incompatible with, indeed would seem to suggest in other words a kind of "mitigated evolution." By this is meant an explanation of the *ratio seminalis,* or the essence of any species, as endowed with special powers such as to enable it to become in an individual instance something different (more perfect—a new, higher species) from what it was. The most famous fathers cited are St. Gregory of Nyssa in the East and St. Augustine in the West. And because their authority is frequently adduced to justify a merely figurative interpretation of Genesis on the origin of the bodies of the first man and woman in such ways as to permit a believer to hold a completely natural explanation of the origin of the human body and one or another form of polygenism as the origin of the human race, it is appropriate to indicate here why in general this interpretation is incorrect.

First, the term "mitigated evolution" is ambiguous. In modern usage evolution indicates a process of development arising out of the inherent natural powers of the subject developing. The evolution "discovered" in some church fathers is said to be mitigated, because the powers by which such development occurred during the Hexaëmeron are not natural, but special, for this occasion. It is difficult to see how these special powers differ from the miraculous. In fact, a natural sequence is being explained not in terms of natural powers, but supernatural endowments of the subject developing, so that what makes the critical difference between lower species and emergence of the higher is not the natural power of the lower species, but the power of God using this. In St. Augustine, certainly, the point is clear that he is not talking about evolution in the modern sense, for in opting for a figurative interpretation of "day" in Genesis, he does not intend to promote the idea of long eras of development, but that of instantaneous creation and ordering where "day" indicates merely logical sequence. Far from assigning a certain fluidity to the notion of species, Augustine intended, as St. Bonaventure saw so clearly, to defend the fixity indispensable to the intelligibility of any essence by making these all the direct work of God.

Second, the ancients, not only Christians and Jews but nonbelievers as well, were generally not familiar with the modern idea of the more perfect evolving from the less perfect. The ancient pantheism, with which the fathers were familiar, asserted the evolution of the less perfect from the more perfect, ultimately from the divine. This approach is particularly obvious in the ancient discussion of the descent of man from the gods. The closer a man approached the condition of the beast, the farther he had fallen from his original condition. The rejection by the church of pantheism is not the equivalent of an opening to evolution. Rather it is an assertion of a special "formative" act on God's part, rather than a natural generative action of some creature at the origin of man. Only in baptism could a man call God his Father, as does the Word, and then only by adoption, not by nature as does the Word.[18] In discussing this "creative" act of God in respect to human nature and by extension to other species, neither St. Gregory nor St. Augustine deny the common teaching that the formation of the first man and first woman is principally a divine work rather than natural and the source of the special likeness of God to Adam and to Adam in all his descendants.

Third, the discussion of such fathers is related not to the theory of evolution as expounded in modern science:

- How much concerning the origin of the world and of the species within it can be learned from its present operation?

But to certain questions of an epistemological character:

- How exactly and fully does revelation describe the formative work of God where that involved a sequence?
- How precisely is the essence of each species formed by God defined in revelation?
- How much knowledge of the present operation of creatures and form of the world can be derived from revelation directly?

St. Bonaventure

On these points raised by the fathers, the church has permitted and still permits a certain amount of discussion, on the condition that the discussion not call into question those points certain in the teaching of the church and which the unanimous witness of the fathers attests as the correct meaning of revelation. The assessment of St. Bonaventure in the thirteenth century is certainly a balanced one. We cannot say that revelation given us by God is a complete description of his work, but one that is sufficient to identify the character of his action so that we might understand how to use this world and our time in it to save our souls. Further, revelation does not give an equally clear definition of each species, such that we can in every instance of present observation, merely on the basis of theology, discern the limits of each species philosophically considered. In some instances, in particular that of human nature, a great deal more bearing on the essence of man is given than for other species, precisely because this knowledge is so intimately bound up with questions of salvation. Finally, revelation contributes only by indirection to the resolution of

18. The excellent study of Édouard des Places, *Syngeneia* (1964).

a great many questions of natural philosophy (science today).[19] In a word, it is not a substitute for the development of scientific knowledge, any more than the revelation of certain truths concerning the natural knowledge of God is a substitute for, or a resolution of, all questions bearing on the construction of this or that proof for God's existence.

Attempts within the past fifty years have been made to show in St. Thomas[20] and in John Duns Scotus[21] a certain opening to evolution, but without success, since in the judgment of most scholars the position of these two theologians does not differ from that of St. Bonaventure. Indeed, according to some (W. Hoeres) the metaphysical theology of Scotus in those questions of Christology (primacy of Christ) most often alleged today to provide a basis for theistic evolution represents an approach diametrically opposed to any form of evolutionary theory, particularly the theistic.[22]

On the particular point of the literal or merely figurative interpretation of the six days, St. Bonaventure acknowledges that the church has never condemned St. Augustine's view, creation of all as it were in a day. But what St. Bonaventure notes[23] in opting for the literal interpretation of day in the first chapter of Genesis has been commonly overlooked in modern times. The *ratio seminalis* of St. Augustine is the equivalent of essence, not embryo. It is the same when the world began to operate on its own as it is now. Only God can make it, change it, annihilate it. And thus, how long it actually took God to make these species, only God can answer, because no one else was there to observe. It might have taken a day, or two hundred days, etc., says Bonaventure, but the only evidence we have is what God has told us. For Bonaventure, the philosophical and epistemological points Augustine wishes to defend can be made just as well or better by holding for six days of twenty-four hours; and for Bonaventure there is no other convincing evidence pointing to a merely figurative meaning. Finally, the choice of six days by God to complete his work of creation provides a solid objective basis for the subsequent rhythms of history. The structure of the seven-day week, of the lunar and solar year, provide a very exact, regular, intelligible backdrop for the unfolding of the divine plan of salvation.

These reflections of St. Bonaventure also illustrate the very ancient basis for a distinction crucial to the evaluation of evolutionary theory, particularly

19. *Brev.*, p. 2, c. 5.

20. Messenger.

21. Wildier, *Teilhard de Chardin* (1968). For the anti-evolutionary interpretation cf. Hoeres, *Kritik* (1969); Solaguren, "El Cristocentrismo," 131–43. Cf. also, Carol, *Why Jesus Christ* (1986).

22. Doran, *De corporis Adami*; Doran, "St. Thomas," 382–95.

23. *Brev.*, p. 2, c. 2.

in respect to Christian belief. The distinction is between "fact" and truth on the one hand, and hypothesis on the other. Evolution is neither a truth immediately evident, nor a fact directly observed or attested by witnesses who have observed it, but a hypothesis constructed so as to resolve questions whose resolution is otherwise not possible to the human mind. Hypothesizing, in whatever the discipline, in every instance begins with observed or attested facts, and concludes with some kind of verification. Speculation of this kind may serve to deepen the understanding of the facts at its starting point or may serve to identify errors in observation. But what it cannot do is provide the grounds for simply rejecting as false or mythical the observed or attested facts providing its starting point.

Theories of the origin of the world or of the species within it, no different from any other form of hypothesizing, are subject to the same rules. In case of direct conflict between hypothesis and fact, observed or attested, it is the hypothesis, not the fact, which must be abandoned. In the case of unduplicatable origins no longer subject to observation, revelation attests to certain facts and truths which constitute a prime test of the validity of any hypothesis on origins. Such an hypothesis will be rejected either:

- because revelation provides a direct answer to every possible question that might be raised concerning the origin of the world or of the species, or

- because *a priori* science and philosophy can contribute nothing to elucidate such questions.

Any hypothesis on origins will be rejected because in each instance it directly contradicts certain facts attested by revelation and the teaching of the church.

In the subsequent sections of this essay, evolutionary theory will be shown repeatedly to stand in direct conflict with certain facts, attested by revelation and by the church, as basic to salvation. This evolutionary theory has emerged slowly and in various ways since the late middle ages. In each instance where the church perceives that conflict, the theory (not the truths of revelation) is rejected so consistently that one might justly surmise from this alone that theories of evolution, whatever scientific or philosophic claims might be made for them, are radically flawed as an attempt to answer questions primarily theological. In those cases where evolutionary theory claims scientific or philosophic support it is possible to demonstrate the falsity of such claims. That is certainly of great importance to the theologian, though not the primary basis for his evaluation of such theories.

Patristic Consensus

E. Testa,[24] after a detailed study of the teaching of the fathers on the origin of the world as set forth in Genesis, concludes that the negative response of the Pontifical Biblical Commission[25] to the question: whether the literal historical sense of the first chapters of Genesis can be called in question when the facts narrated touch the foundations of Christian religion, is an accurate resumé of the unanimous witness to the mind of the church from the beginning. These facts are:

- the creation of the entire universe in the beginning of time by God;
- the special creation of the first man;
- the formation of the first woman from the first man by God;
- the unity of the human race; and
- the initial happiness of our first parents in the state of original justice.

All of these facts figure in the teaching of the Fathers and in the liturgy. Some of them, directly or indirectly, figure in the official condemnations of the heresies, particularly Christological, heresies such as Apollinarianism, Nestorianism and monophysitism, and in the condemnation of Pelagianism. In all of these, certain facts concerning the origin and nature of man figure prominently, although only the condemnation of Pelaganism directly and solemnly affirms the unity of the human family through descent from a single pair formed directly by the Creator. In the condemnation of Christological errors, such definitions and attributes of human nature as the simplicity and integrity of the soul, the substantial unity of soul and body, are derived not primarily from philosophical reflection, but from the deposit of faith. In all this, the key point is not what man has in common with other creatures, but how he differs from others. This provides the correct basis for understanding what occurred when the Word hypostatically assumed a human nature. In every instance, God's direct formative action accounts for that difference; each Christological error ultimately rests on a denial of that difference and its source. The church claims a sound anthropology because she claims to know how God made man.

---

24. "La Creazione," 68.
25. *DH* 3512–19.

Summary

It is against these specifics that any philosophical or scientific theory of origins must be measured. The church in ancient times never denied that natural knowledge could contribute to the understanding of this world and of its origins. But in the case of conflict, the truths of revelation could not be "reinterpreted" to fit the new theory; rather the theory, including theological speculation, had to be adjusted to the facts of revelation certified by the church. Although the church has not formally pronounced on all exegetical questions surrounding the interpretation of Genesis, she reserves to herself the right to make final decisions. Whether, however, any modern theories of evolution can ever be reconciled with those points clearly and irreversibly defined by the church in this matter is another question. Some, the church has already indicated, cannot. But the basis on which this evaluation is made had already been clearly affirmed long before theories of evolution posed problems.

Lateran IV

Text

Firmiter credimus et simpliciter confitemur, quod unus solus est verus Deus unum . . . universorum principium: creator omnium visibilium et invisibilium, spiritualium et corporalium: qui sua omnipotenti virtute simul ab initio temporis utramque de nihilo condidit creaturam, spiritualem et corporalem, angelicam videlicet et mundanam: ac deinde humanam, quasi communem ex spiritu et corpore constitutam. Diabolus enim et alii daemones a Deo quidem natura creati sunt boni, sed ipsi per se facti sunt mali. Homo vero diaboli suggestione peccavit. (c. 1, De Fide Catholica).

We firmly believe and simply confess that there is only one true God . . . one principle of all things, creator of all things invisible and visible, spiritual and corporeal; who by his almighty power at the beginning of time created from nothing both spiritual and corporeal creatures, that is to say angelic and earthly, and then created human beings composed as it were of both spirit and body in common. The devil and other demons were created by God naturally good, but they became evil by their own doing. Man, however, sinned at the prompting of the devil.

Textual Observations

In comparison with the ancient creedal formularies this solemn definition identifies the invisible and visible respectively with spiritual-angelic and corporal-earthly, both established originally out of nothing at the beginning of time; then at the end of God's creative work he established the human, both body and soul united in a single nature. It is not said expressly that man was established out of nothing, but the word used, *condidit*, clearly indicates that God alone formed man. Moral evil only entered each created order, invisible first and then visible, after God had completed its establishment. This occurred after angels and men had begun to exercise responsibility within their respective created order.

Context

The definition of creation in the Fourth Lateran Council is in fact a repetition of the first article of the ancient creeds with additions constituting not a development of doctrine (for these points were already explicitly understood as forming the content of the creedal formularies), but a more precise formulation in view of certain errors of the time bearing directly on the origin of the world and in a particular way on the origin and nature of man.

According to St. Bonaventure,[26] the ancient dogma was so stated in order to make clear that three approaches to the question of origins, thought by many at the time to be compatible with Christian faith, were in fact utterly contrary to it. These were:

1. The eternity of the world, as proposed by many Aristotelians—thus the definition states the world was created in the beginning of time to make clear the exact meaning of finitude.

2. The subtraction of the visible-corporal world from the power of God, and the identification of moral evil with material existence, the position of the Manichees of the middle ages—thus the insistence on creation of matter by God *ex nihilo,* and the location of the source of sin in a free choice not in conformity with the divine law.

3. The limitation of God's omnipotence by making the exercise of his power dependent on the cooperation of instruments, the position of the medieval Neo-Platonists, a position akin to that of the emanationists of old and the theistic evolutionists today—hence the phrase "God alone" to describe who establishes and how he establishes his creation.

---

26. *Brev.,* p. 2, c. 1.

New Perspectives

The second and third errors, widespread at the beginning of the thirteenth century, did not however represent positions not dealt with by the church in centuries past. Often enough evolution is considered a "modern" theory, in all its forms linked popularly to the name of Darwin, and a theory with which, as with science in general, the church must come to terms. From the foregoing section of this essay, it should be clear that the remote basis of evolutionary theory had been familiar to the church from her beginning. Indeed, that beginning is inseparably tied to the first article of the creed, so that an attack on one is inevitably an attack on the other. For the founder of the church, the organizer of her clergy, the great high priest of her confession, is the Word through Whom all things are created. That basis, the old Manicheism and the old pantheism, was once again anathematized in the second and third errors proscribed by Lateran IV.

The roots of the "modern" theory of evolution, in so far as "modern" indicates a relatively novel form for a very hoary theory, are to be discovered, not in the eighteenth and nineteenth centuries, but in the thirteenth century with the appearance of "Latin Aristotelianism," a mode of interpreting Aristotle so as to make of Aristotelian thought an apt instrument for a radical repudiation of the entire Catholic faith and tradition. As St. Bonaventure saw so clearly, the cornerstone of this position was the denial of the dogma of creation as incompatible with an intellectual affirmation of the eternity of the world, in effect a thoroughgoing secularism.

There is no doubt but that the rediscovery of Aristotle in the West triggered an intellectual ferment constituting a challenge to Catholic theology, not hitherto dealt with directly, and centering on the first article of the creed, on origins, so that the conflict between secularism and Catholicism as contrary ways of life centered intellectually on the problem of the eternity of the world versus creation in time.

According to many modern interpreters of Aristotle, but also according to many in the thirteenth century, including St. Bonaventure,[27] Aristotle neither had any idea of the Christian notion of creation *ex nihilo*, nor did he ever raise the question of the origin of the world. He simply took the world for granted, as always existing, eternally imperfect, eternally perfectible. The unmoved mover by its immobility made motion possible, but was not understood by Aristotle to be the maker of the world. For in such a perspective the origin of the world is simply not a question, because a non-existent origin needs no explanation. Only when this perspective is

---

27. *II Sent.*, d. 1, a. 1, q. 2.

confronted by the dogma of creation does the question arise for such a philosophy. So long as the eternity of the world is maintained, so long will this question be resolved in a non-creationistic form.

As brilliant as Aristotle's thought was and is, it had major defects whose consequences, when uncorrected, are seldom appreciated by those who reject the Christian doctrine of creation and its relevance to the conduct of science. Fr. Stanley Jaki in *The Road of Science and the Ways to God* has noted that Greek science was a monumental achievement of the human intellect, but was stillborn because it lacked the knowledge of creation. Modern science, he claims, really began in the thirteenth century with the development of a Christian philosophy based on the notion of the world as created-finite and God as the infinite Creator; and to the extent that a scientist engages fruitfully in the cultivation of his discipline, even when he consciously rejects creation, he acts on a philosophy of science and methodology only possible on the assumption of creation as true. But to the extent a scientist works on the assumption of an eternal, radically infinite world, to that extent his work becomes progressively more fruitless because unrelated to the real world, which is the object of scientific study, a world in fact finite and temporal, not infinite and eternal.

Corrected, Aristotelian thought could and would prove useful to the further development of Christian thought, as the works of St. Thomas Aquinas and the Blessed John Duns Scotus demonstrate. But the needed correction, as St. Bonaventure saw so clearly, was a major one touching a point crucial to the determination of the final character of Aristotelian thought, closed or open to Christian faith, and therefore of its utility for believers and, as many historians of science hold, its utility for science as well.

Uncorrected, in the hands of those bent on the destruction of the Christian faith and the Catholic way of life, it became a potent instrument for undermining intellectual confidence in the first article of the Creed, because it provided in intellectual rather than religious form an alternative to the dogma of creation (with its philosophical and scientific correlatives) as a solution to the problem of origins. This is the first proximate root of modern evolutionary theory, a root despite its intellectual format, neither purely nor primarily intellectual and scientific, but religious, because the question of origins both thematically and historically is a religious question.

A second root of "modern" evolutionary theory in the thirteenth century, and of the secularism based on it, is to be found in Joachimism and the peculiar mystique of "progress" which it popularized during the thirteenth century and which has not disappeared from western culture since. Originally a theology of history proposed by the unworldly Abbot Joachim to explain and justify a program of reform and renewal of the

church, it was condemned at the Fourth Lateran Council as involving notions inimical to a sound understanding of the Trinity and of the nature of
the church. Its subsequent development showed it to be a potent catalyst
of ardent revolutionary fervor.

The progression, by which in this theory of history was to be explained,
provided a basis for an expectation of the imminent advent of the kingdom
of the Holy Spirit amid the inauguration of a time of peace and prosperity
wondrously contrasting with the misery and corruption of the present age
of the clerical kingdom known as the "canonical" or institutional church.
But like so many projects of the unworldly, this one lost sight of the difference between the temporal and the eternal, the secular and the spiritual,
and thus, in its own way of explaining the end of the world, eliminated
the difference between created and uncreated which Latin Aristotelianism
did by means of its theory of an eternal world as an explanation of the
world's origin. The results are not surprising. Religious and secular progress came to be identified; the reality of the object of Christian hope (a life
after death) eventually became confused with earthly progress. Unlimited
human progress and perfectibility on earth promised by human science
and achieved by human technology could be rationalized as the ultimate
hope and inspiration of human activity. And from the marriage of progress
with the theory of an eternal world came the modern notion of unending
evolution toward a better and better future in this world.

Since that time a certain number of characteristics have attached themselves to this kind of thought and are of considerable interest because they
tend to be present wherever evolutionary thought predominates at present.

1. The religious practice inspired by this kind of thought is strongly indif-
   ferent to dogma and highly syncretistic, seeking to reduce particular
   religions to a higher synthesis and very often giving to this synthesis a
   certain number of Christic trappings.

2. Movements impregnated with this kind of thought are radically anti-
   clerical in a violent manner, because firstly the existence of Catholic
   clergy, in particular the pope, is seen as an obstacle to religious progress and renewal, and secondly as an obstacle to intellectual freedom
   and moral spontaneity. In this framework the destruction of the clerical church is the necessary condition for progress or evolution. Indeed,
   this kind of principled and militant anti-clericalism throughout the
   history of the church has invariably been the *sine qua non* for any plausible identification of the spiritual with the temporal (idolization of the
   present world and denial of the world to come).

3. Such movements are endowed with a very potent totalitarian instinct, sometimes described as communistic, in the medieval period very evident among some groups of Franciscan spirituals, and after their condemnation, among the so-called *fraticelli* of the middle ages and various communistic groups at the time of the Protestant reformation.

The distinctive "anti-Creationism" of the thirteenth century involved in particular false concepts of human nature, justified by an intellectual system entailing complete independence from revelation and church authority, and inspired by an ideology or spirituality, totalitarian at root. Hence, from this time forward, official pronouncements of the church dealing with the question of origins place a particular stress on two points:

- a correct notion not only of what man should do, but what man is by nature in virtue of what his Creator has made him directly; and

- a correct assessment of the natural abilities of the human intellect vis-à-vis the exercise of faith in assenting to the truths revealed by God and proclaimed authentically by the church.

Magisterial Statements on Human Nature

Because of these factors the question of the origin of the world quickly came to center on the question of the origin and nature of man. While this may initially have been on the minds of all those departing from the tradition of the church, in fact there are but two starting points for any such discussion of human origins:

- creationistic or

- pantheistic, today often designated as evolutionary.

Further, as in earlier times, any departure from a creationistic standpoint invariably entailed serious Christological deviations. It is interesting to note in the texts that follow, that with the exception of the origin of the body of the first male human, every characteristic feature of modern evolutionary hypotheses concerning human origins was explicitly condemned between the Fourth Lateran Council and the Council of Trent.

Innocent III

Innocent III wrote *Gaudeamur in Domino* to the Bishop of Tiberias in Palestine, 1201. Polygamy is forbidden by the natural law, and monogamy is of the very nature of marriage, he affirmed, because of the manner in which the Creator formed the first woman, Eve, from the side of the first man. The narrative is taken in the literal sense, and as pertinent to the truths of salvation, just as the Biblical Commission in 1909 remarked concerning the same verse. The letter of Pope Innocent III is not a solemn definition; it does reflect quite clearly the consistent mind of the church on this verse from her foundation to the present. It also says that this understanding is not contingent on philosophical or scientific analysis, but on a theological tradition stemming from Christ.[28]

Council of Vienne (1311)

The ancient damnations of Apollinarianism (i.e., that in the incarnation the divinity of the Word replaces the rational part of the soul, and thus forms a substantial unity with the body), are repeated and so formulated as to exclude the erroneous views of a Franciscan, Peter of John Olivi. The council declared that the one intellectual soul, *qua* intellectual, is the form of the body of Christ conceived in the womb of the Virgin, just as it is in every other human nature. To hold, as Olivi seems to have taught, that the soul only informs the body by way of some power less than intellectual would be to open the way to a denial of the essential difference between the human body and that of the brute. The council further insisted that the soul of Christ is individual, not the common mind dear to the medieval pantheist throughout the thirteenth century and which in fact the divinity becomes in all forms of Apollinarianism.

The source of the teaching of the Council of Vienne on the human soul and its relation to the body ultimately rests on the church's traditional understanding of the origin of the first man's body and soul. Each was made specially by the Creator and then united by him to form a single man, who is not God, but a creature, a creature different however from any other in his special likeness to God.

28. Motherway, "The Creation of Eve," 97–116.

Fifth Lateran Council (1513)

Against the views of the Neo-Aristotelians of the Renaissance this Council defined the immortality of each human soul, the possibility of natural demonstration thereof (details unspecified) and the direct creation of the souls of not only the first man and first woman but of each and every descendant of Adam and Eve.

This creative act is to be understood in the sense of creation *ex nihilo*. The direct formation of the first human bodies by God has never been understood by the church as a creation *ex nihilo*, because the scriptures describe that uniquely divine action in respect to the first human bodies as on something pre-existent; for Adam the slime of the earth, for Eve a rib from Adam's side.

The Council of Trent

The Council of Trent, in the decree on original sin,[29] defined the unity of the entire human family as one of descent from one man and one woman made directly by God, and that in virtue of that descent and only in virtue of descent by procreation, one is a human being. Further, in virtue of that descent, original sin is a matter of inheritance, not of imitation of the sin of Adam.

No theory of polygenism is reconcilable with this belief, as both popes Pius XII and Paul VI clearly noted. The theory in principle is a denial of facts (that there was but a single couple and not multiple couples, owing its existence principally and directly to the Creator, from which couple all other human beings descend); and these facts, known as true on the authority of God, cannot be disproven.

Implicitly, this decree of the Council of Trent constitutes an affirmation of the literal sense of Genesis in those passages dealing with the individuality of Adam and Eve and of the unity of the human family.

Epistemological Considerations

The very obvious challenge to the first article of the creed represented in the position of medieval Latin Aristotelianism regarding the origins of the world (at once a continuation of the ancient Pantheism and an anticipation of key features of modern Evolutionism), in conjunction with

29. Session V, 1546.

the ideals of reform, progress and perfectibility of the human condition by human effort, exerted a strong magnetism over the human mind and spirit. Equally potent were the epistemological factors associated with this challenge, recognized as such both by the church and by her opponents as basic to the resolution of the questions raised.

Warnings and Prohibitions Against the Use of Aristotle

Throughout the first half of the thirteenth century the popes issued a series of warnings, and in some instances prohibitions against the use of the works of Aristotle as a basic textbook of philosophy in the school of arts of the University of Paris, and against the danger of using new terminology and concepts drawn from philosophy as a means of determining and interpreting the sense of revelation in preference to those criteria based on sacred tradition and Scripture.[30] St. Bonaventure[31] discusses theological methods and the dangers attendant on the use of merely natural knowledge apart from a divinely appointed authority as a primary criterion for the resolution of theological questions, of which the interpretation of the divinely inspired books of the Bible is one.

These warnings are not a condemnation of Aristotle, nor a denial of the possible utility of philosophical, and by extension scientific knowledge within theology, much less an attempt to control and manipulate philosophical and scientific research and reflection. Rather they indicate that until the valid insights of Aristotle, or any other scholar, are detached from a secular bias placing no limits on the freedom and prowess of man to know all naturally, a bias ultimately resting on the denial of creation and of the very possibility of faith, that mode of speculation, particularly when applied to questions touching the origin of the world, of man, and of the nature of the incarnation, employed as the initial model for forming the intellectual habits of youth, is dangerous to faith.

There appear here the rudiments of a policy subsequently developed and applied with great consistency by the church in questions involving not only theology, but other intellectual disciplines. Statements directly contrary to revealed truth are condemned as such. Hypotheses of a philosophical and scientific character are not judged directly in terms of the methodology employed, but in view of the assumptions governing any equitable and balanced use of the human intellect. These are rated, as it were, as safe and sound, or unsafe, in terms of what is known by faith to be beyond question.

30. Grabmann, *I divieti ecclesiastici*; Pope Gregory IX, *Ab Aegyptiis Argentea*, 1228.
31. *Hex.*, col. 19.

Like his modern counterpart, the secular intellectual of the middle ages regarded such a policy as obscurantist in principle. But however inept the administration of such a policy by ecclesiastics might become in certain cases, the policy can only be regarded as obscurantist in principle on the assumption that revelation and theology have nothing to contribute to the understanding of that which in other ways is the subject matter of philosophy and science. This is especially the case with speculation concerning the existence and nature of God, the origin of the world and of the species, in particular human, within it.

This policy, entailing in principle a radical compatibility and mutual support between the truths of faith and the results of genuine science (in the medieval sense, including what since has come to be designated under the headings philosophy, science and art), made two assumptions, whose affirmation or denial has inextricably been linked to the affirmation or denial of creation.

1. Truth is objectively one. Contradictories cannot simultaneously be true. Hence revelation and reason, to the extent they give distinct but authentic access to the truth, cannot be at odds. Apparent contradictions arise either from the thinker's abuse of faith or from the abuse of reason. Truth is eternal and immutable; otherwise, it would not be one.

2. Methods or procedures for the use of human intelligence in grasping the truth are multiple. One method, theological or scientific, is not capable of comprehending all there is to know, or even all there is to know about one object (e.g., the material world, or human nature). Because the Truth is one, these methods are coordinated one to the other and subordinated to (centered on) that one science providing the most direct access to the Truth itself, the study of revelation.

Effective avoidance of the practical import of this policy, whatever the reason, postulated the denial of these two assumptions. This is exactly what occurred during the thirteenth and early fourteenth centuries.

The Two-Truth Theory

During the Middle Ages, those who adopted the secular stance in intellectual and religious matters, but who also wished in some way to retain their link with Catholicism without acknowledging such a choice, precluded any such link and devised a rationalization of their position, later termed the "two-truth" theory. To avoid choosing between flatly contradictory statements, only one of which could be true, it was stated that what might be true theologically, could simultaneously be false philosophically (or historically, or scientifically), or vice-versa. Such a position could not be acknowledged as legitimate for anyone calling himself a Catholic, for it quite obviously entails a skepticism or intellectual relativism incompatible with the Catholic view of truth, and dogma in particular, as unchanging.

Between this theory and the mode of reasoning of Christian proponents of evolution attempting to reconcile the "fact" of evolution with the data recorded in Genesis there is a curious similarity. It is claimed that the facts of Genesis are true as theological symbols, a kind of code for transcendent religious truths, but false historically and scientifically.

But it is just this claim concerning key data of Genesis that the church has consistently denied throughout her history. They are not symbolically but literally true. To be included among the data so interpreted are both facts and essences (e.g., human nature).

On this point, many thorough evolutionists have always concurred. Consistency does not permit the synthesis represented by what is today termed "theistic evolution." One must choose between the dogma of creation or all-embracing evolutionary perspective as the starting point for any discussion and resolution of the questions of cosmic and human origins.

Nominalism

One of the characteristic features of this fourteenth and fifteenth century movement among Catholic philosophers and theologians was the refusal to concede to universal concepts a status greater than that of a generalization (a purely mental construct). Concepts never rise above the level of mental tags and symbols, and hence of themselves can provide no sure avenue to the understanding of the extra-mental real. For example, the concept of a species (e.g., human nature as a rational animal) tells the thinker nothing absolutely certain and unchanging about human nature outside the mind.

The implications of such a position for certainty and objectivity of human understanding are reducible to two:

- either such certainty concerning the reality and stability of the outer world is imposed by authority (Fideism); or

- the only certainty is that nothing is certain—reality is an unending flux.

Any attempt to reason on such an assumption tends to identify the real with the objects of the senses, always in flux, since the essence of things, even material things, not distinctly and directly perceived by the senses, are but mental constructs. Access to the truth, then, in so far as truth designates the real outside the mind, is the exclusive prerogative of the "scientific method," by definition the method appropriate to the study of the sensible. Thus, any theory of science radically nominalist will also be evolutionary, because the objects of the senses are constantly changing. Change or evolution rather than form or substance as the fundamental characteristic of the real will conversely be described in such a context as scientific and reasonable, whereas creationism, however presented, cannot appear, *a priori*, as anything but fideistic, authoritarian, and unscientific.

It is just this theory of science which Fr. Stanley Jaki claims is as unscientific as it is anti-Christian and anti-creationistic. Further consideration of the support which nominalism has always provided for theories of legal Positivism and arbitrary voluntarism confirms the radically arbitrary character of any theory of science based on nominalist assumptions, and the importance of distinguishing science as a genuine intellectual endeavor of the human mind from explanations of the nature of that endeavor. So too, it is important from a Catholic point of view to question whether evolutionary thought has ever been scientific in any but the sense of being part of a theory of science whose root assumptions are incompatible with what Pope Paul VI in his creed[32] considers an integral part of Catholic belief: the human mind's ability to form universal concepts by which objective knowledge about the essences of things is derived.[33]

The Galileo Case

Once the rejection in the sixteenth century of the authority and traditional policies of the magisterium of the church had become sufficiently widespread, it was possible to use technical advances made possible by the cultivation of science as a kind of marvelous or miraculous confirmation of the theory of science set forth by scientists and philosophers at odds with the Magisterium and the traditional teaching of the church and as a proof of

32. *Credo of the People of God*, Introduction, n. 5, 649–55.

33. Also Sermonti and Fondi, *Dopo Darwin*, 104–12. On a related point, Pope Paul, in the encyclical letter *Mysterium Fidei* (1965) makes the following observation: "These [dogmatic] formulas—like the others that the church used to propose the dogmas of faith—express concepts that are not tied to a certain specific form of human culture, or to a certain level of scientific progress, or to one or another theological school. Instead, they set forth what the human mind grasps of reality through necessary and universal experience and what it expresses in apt and exact words, whether it be in ordinary or more refined language. For this reason, these formulas are adapted to all men of all times and all places" (n. 24).

the Obscurantism and childishness of faith. The case of Galileo has become a landmark in the illustration of such a point of view.

There are many questionable aspects of the Galileo case, touching both parties in the dispute:

- the conduct of certain ecclesiastics,

- the narrowness of certain theologians and scholars (but by no means all supported the final decision),

- the unscrupulous use made of human failings by the propagandists of Secularism, buoyed by the alleged triumph of modern science liberated from the dogmatic Obscurantism of the church.

Whatever the truth about the alleged failings of some ecclesiastics involved in the trial, the final decision, in so far as it involves questions of doctrine and of the relations between revelation and reason as sources of knowledge, was consistent with tradition. Hence, it is not correct to make of the decision a kind of dilemma; either support the decision and maintain intellectual narrowness, or repudiate it and in effect capitulate to modernism's major assumption that truth is a coefficient of the current culture and subject to evolution proportionate to the progress of science.

In so far as the two decisions in the Galileo case touched matters of belief, two points were involved:

1. The astronomical theories of Galileo touched points also mentioned in Scripture. His views, propounded as proven fact, would seem to render Scriptural reference to the immobility of the earth either false or meaningless. Thus the decision to place the works of Galileo on the Index of Forbidden Books, and to forbid him to publish anything more, was not a condemnation of scientific theorizing as such, or this theory of Galileo in particular, but only an insistence that it be held merely as a theory, until such time as the church should have resolved the exegetical questions; and not to publicize the same in circumstances where it might easily be taken as proven fact by the uninformed to the detriment of their faith. One may discuss whether this was the best manner to handle the pastoral problem; but it hardly constitutes intellectual tyranny. And just as Galileo's celestial mechanics were not condemned, neither were Aristotle's canonized.

2. The immediate concern of the church was not the justification of astronomical theory, but the guardianship of the deposit of faith and of its correct interpretation.[34] Revelation does contain references to

34. Council of Trent, Session 4.

what seems to be a fact: the immobility of the earth. The Fathers of the church, as St. Robert Bellarmine noted, also seem to attest this as a fact pertaining to the mystery of salvation. If the heliocentric theory is true, then, as St. Robert observed, our understanding of these passages must be reexamined to discover the faulty interpretation, but it is not permissible to say God has stated something factually false by way of the literal sense of Scripture or engaged in pious deception. But if this theory is merely a possible hypothesis which could be true, but also false, it is not a sufficient basis, according to St. Robert, for doubting the literal sense of Scripture attested by the Fathers, but only of saying we do not know how to reconcile the two points. In passing, it may be remarked that there are still serious scholars willing to make a case for the geocentric theory.

Despite the polemics surrounding this affair, the decision in essence illustrates a policy, and the basis for that policy, on the part of the church in dealing with subjects, at once a matter of revelation and of reason, already in evidence in the thirteenth century, and which will appear again in subsequent centuries.

All the factors subsequently involved in the Evolutionism condemned by the First Vatican Council and by Pope Pius XII in the encyclical *Humani Generis,* as is apparent from the foregoing, were already familiar to the church long before the time of Hegel and Darwin, and were rejected as incompatible with the truths of revelation which the church professed the Apostles to have received from her founder, Savior, and teacher, Jesus Christ. All that is missing is the name "evolution" and the designation of such thinking as "scientific."

Vatican I

As the Fourth Lateran Council anticipated key elements in the medieval challenge to the first article of the Creed, so too the First Vatican Council performed the same service for the church in modern times.

Texts:

Dogmatic Constitution Dei Filius

Hic solus verus Deus bonitate sua et omnipotenti virtute non ad augendam suam beatitudinem nec ad acquirendam, sed ad manifestandam perfectionem suam per bona, quae creaturis impertitur, liberrimo consilio "simul ab initio temporis utramque de nihilo condidit creaturam, spiritualem et corporalem, angelicam videlicet et mundanam ac deinde humanam quasi communem ex spiritu et corpore constitutam."[c. 1]

This one true God, by his goodness and almighty power, not with the intention of increasing his happiness, nor indeed of obtaining happiness, but in order to manifest his perfection by the good things which he bestows on what he creates, by an absolutely free plan, "together from the beginning of time brought into being from nothing the twofold created order, that is the spiritual and the bodily, the angelic and the earthly, and thereafter the human which is, in a way, common to both since it is composed of spirit and body" [See Lateran Council IV, const. 1.].

Eadem sancta mater Ecclesia tenet et docet, Deum, rerum omnium principium et finem, naturali humanae rationis lumine e rebus creatis certo cognosci posse. . . attamen placuisse eius sapientiae et bonitati, alia eaque supernaturali via se ipsum ac aeterna voluntatis suae decreta humano generi revelare. . . . [c. 2]

The same holy mother church holds and teaches that God, the source and end of all things, can be known with certainty from the consideration of created things, by the natural power of human reason. . . it was, however, pleasing to his wisdom and goodness to reveal himself and the eternal laws of his will to the human race by another, and that a supernatural, way. . . .

Hoc quoque perpetuus Ecclesiae catholicae consensus tenuit et tenet, duplicem esse ordinem cognitionis non solum principio, sed objecto etiam distinctum: principio quidem, quia in altero naturali ratione et altero fide divina cognoscimus; objecto autem, quia praeter ea, ad quae naturalis ratio pertingere potest, credenda nobis proponuntur mysteria in Deo abscondita, quae, nisi revelata divinitus, innote scere non possunt. [c. 4]

The perpetual agreement of the Catholic Church has maintained and maintains this too: that there is a twofold order of knowledge, distinct not only as regards its source, but also as regards its object. With regard to the source, we know at the one level by natural reason, at the other level by divine faith. With regard to the object, besides those things to which natural reason can attain, there are proposed for our belief mysteries hidden in God which, unless they are divinely revealed, are incapable of being known.

Porro, Ecclesia, quae una cum apostolico munere docendi mandatum accepit fidei depositum custodiendi, jus etiam et officium divinitus habet falsi nominis scientiam proscribendi, ne quis decipiatur per philosophiam et inanem fallaciam. [c. 4]

Furthermore the church which, together with its apostolic office of teaching, has received the charge of preserving the deposit of faith, has by divine appointment the right and duty of condemning what wrongly passes for knowledge, lest anyone be led astray by philosophy and empty deceit [See Col 2:8].

Neque solum fides et ratio inter se dissidere numquam possunt, sed opem quoque sibi mutuam ferunt, cum recta ratio fidei fundamenta demonstret eiusque lumine illustrata rerum divinarum scientiam excolat, fides vero rationem ab erroribus liberet ac tueatur eam que multiplici cognitione instruat. Quapropter tantum abest, ut Ecclesia humanarum artium et disciplinarum culturae obsistat, ut hanc multis modis iuvet atque promoveat. Non enim commoda ab iis adhominum vitam dimanantia aut ignorat aut despicit. . . . Nec sane ipsa vetat, huiusmodi disciplinae in suo quaeque ambitu propriis utantur principiis et propria methodo; sed justam hanc libertatem agnoscens, id sedulo cavet, ne divinae doctrinae repugnando errores in se suscipiant, aut fines proprios transgressae ea, quae sunt fidei, occupent et perturbent. Neque enim fidei doctrina, quam Deus revelavit, velut philosophicum inventum proposita est humanis ingeniis perficienda, sed tanquam divinum depositum Christi Sponsae tradita, fideliter custodienda et infallibiliter declaranda. Hinc sacrorum quo que dogmatum is sensus perpetuo est retinendus, quem semel declaravit sancta mater Ecclesia, nec umquam ab eo sensu altioris intelligentiae specie et nomine recedendum. "Crescat igitur. . . et multum vehementerque proficiat, tam singulorum quam omnium, tam unius hominis quam totius Ecclesiae, aetatum ac saeculorum gradibus, intelligentia, scientia, sapientia: sed in suo dumtaxat genere, in eodem scilicet dogmate, eodem sensu eademque sententia." [c. 4]

Not only can faith and reason never be at odds with one another but they mutually support each other, for on the one hand right reason established the foundations of the faith and, illuminated by its light, develops the science of divine things; on the other hand, faith delivers reason from errors and protects it and furnishes it with knowledge of many kinds. Hence, so far is the church from hindering the development of human arts and studies, that in fact she assists and promotes them in many ways. For she is neither ignorant nor contemptuous of the advantages which derive from this source for human life. . . . Nor does the church forbid these studies to employ, each within its own area, its own proper principles and method: but while she admits this just freedom, she takes particular care that they do not become infected with errors by conflicting with divine teaching, or, by going beyond their proper limits, intrude upon what belongs to faith and engender confusion. For the doctrine of the faith which God has revealed is put forward not as some philosophical discovery capable of being perfected by human intelligence, but as a divine deposit committed to the spouse of Christ to be faithfully protected and infallibly promulgated. Hence, too, that meaning of the sacred dogmas is ever to be maintained which has once been declared by holy mother church, and there must never be any abandonment of this sense under the pretext or in the name of a more profound understanding. "May understanding, knowledge and wisdom increase as ages and centuries roll along, and greatly and vigorously flourish, in each and all, in the individual and the whole church: but this only in its own proper kind, that is to say, in the same doctrine, the same sense, and the same understanding" [Vincent of Lerins, *Commonitorium*, 28 (PL 50, 668)].

Commentary

First Text

The first text is a repetition of the solemn definition of the Fourth Lateran Council, with an additional reference to the nature of that creative act, a free act of God's will, rooted in his goodness and omnipotence, and motivated not by a desire for gain, but one of generosity. Both as to its motive as well as to its character the creative act is distinctive of God and is the basis for condemning in the canons of the Dogmatic Constitution, *Dei Filius*, the following errors:

- that the one God is not the Creator of all else (c. 1, canon 1);

- that the substance of God is identical with the world (c. 1, canon 3);

- that finite beings evolved from the substance of God (c. 1, canon 4);

- that through its evolution or manifestation the divine substance becomes all things, or a part of some things (c. 1, canon 4); and

- that the world and everything in it, spiritual as well as material, was not produced by God *ex nihilo secundum totam suam substantiam* (i.e., in its every part) (c. 1, canon 4).

The first anathema excluded from Catholic belief the view (deism) that one can subtract the world from dependence on God, either in existence or perdurance or both, and still claim belief in God, and by implication claim that belief in God tells one nothing about the existence and nature of those subjects forming the direct object of philosophic and/or scientific study.

The second, third, and fourth anathemas exclude various forms of pantheism, both the ancient form (psychological monism) claiming the world emanated from God or that God became a part of certain things and the more modern form (Hegelianism) claiming the world becomes God because it is the manifestation or evolution of the divine substance, as compatible with Catholic belief.

The fifth anathema cited here clearly indicates that the world also studied by natural reason in various ways, and the natural development characteristic of the world as a whole and each of its parts, presupposes a creative action of God touching not simply the first moment of the world's existence, but the entire work of six days by which the species in the philosophical sense were established and the universe given an orderly, intelligible form. Any theory that claims to explain the origin of the world, or of the species, exclusively in terms of natural processes (evolution) is by that very fact opposed to Catholic belief. The essences of finite species, and the essential structure of world order are not the fruit of the activity of those species, but their necessary prerequisite, only possible in virtue of a distinctive, divine productive action.

Second Text

The second text is a corollary of the first.

Precisely because the things of this world can be recognized in their existence and essence as created through the use of the human power to know naturally therefore God can naturally be known as the one, true God who is Creator. But precisely because his creation is finite, there is much more about him, and about the designs of his will, that cannot be known naturally. All this can only be known from a supernatural revelation.

The teaching of the church, and the revelation which it claims to declare, contains in addition to truths knowable only by revelation and faith, truths accessible to reason as well, and asserts that it is a part of Catholic faith to profess this. The first of these truths is that the world created by God reflects in its nature and activities the perfections of its Creator, and that these most basic aspects even of the humblest material object can be recognized as such. To deny on principle that either philosophy or science cannot eventually point to such is incompatible with Catholic faith.

Third Text

This text indicates the basis for distinguishing between the orders of natural and revealed knowledge, in terms of which these two cognitive orders are correlated, avoiding at once fideism (the denial of the possibility of achieving any certitude in the use of the intellect naturally, whether philosophically or scientifically) and rationalism (the denial of the very possibility of faith).

Fourth Text

This text makes clear the right of the church to proscribe not merely errors concerning the content of revelation, whether this pertains to mysteries of faith or to truths of the natural order, but to unmask those epistemological errors *falsi nominis scientiae* parading in the guise of legitimate philosophy or science. These the faithful must not only avoid, but recognize for what they are: denials of the faith of the church, and therefore false religion.

Fifth Text

The final texts set forth the belief of the church concerning the relations between faith and the cultivation of the intellect:

- in principle, the cultivation of faith and reason will be mutually beneficial, because the same Creator is the source of both;

- the ecclesiastical magisterium does not interfere with or attempt to supervise the internal development of any discipline in accord with its proper method and nature;

- that the magisterium is concerned that in the name of a specious academic freedom (*falsi nominis scientiae*) these disciplines should incorporate views which are false, because directly contrary to revelation, or that in the cultivation of these disciplines reason should come to occupy the place of faith; and

- that although reason can contribute to the progressive elucidation of the deposit of faith entrusted to the church, the primary criterion must remain the church's past unchanging and inerrant declarations whose sense may not be altered in view of the "progress of science."

Thus are anathematized (chapter 4, canons 2–3) two positions very much bound up in the controversy over evolution, scientific as well as philosophical: that it is possible to enjoy such liberty in the use of the human intellect that one can hold as true what is directly opposed to the belief of the church (e.g., that the world is eternally evolving) and that the church may not proscribe such a position; and that the progress of science constitutes grounds for interpreting the articles of faith in a way different from the traditional meaning assigned them (e.g., polygenism in place of monogenism), in respect to the texts of Genesis on Adam and Eve.

Evolution in the Light of Contemporary Church Teaching

The statements of the ecclesiastical magisterium over the last hundred years dealing with the questions of the origin of the world, and of the human species in particular, occasioned by theories of evolution, do not contain any elements not previously set forth in earlier times as the teaching of the church, but are, rather, representations of those aspects in view of theories apparently independent of or directly contradictory of those resting on the origin of the world and of all in it in terms of creation. It is often objected that the earlier teaching has no normative value in the current discussion, because it reflects merely a primitive and immature level of scientific culture, and that the church can only form an assessment of these points after and in the light of a resolution of the scientific questions. That, however is precisely the point which the teaching of Vatican I denies. The church claims to know something about God as Creator and about the world as creation, quite independently both of philosophy and of science. Even if the cultivation of philosophy and science can contribute in some way to the clarification of our understanding of the Creator and his work, the faith of the church does not depend or wait upon this development, or upon the authority which philosophy and science can give to the results of their respective research.

Vatican I

In this regard the First Vatican Council teachings on creation, on the nature of revelation and faith, and their relations to philosophy and science provide an excellent recapitulation of the mind of the church over the centuries in respect to two key issues (pantheism and rationalism) at the center of the controversy over evolution and Catholic faith. Any scientific explanation of origins that entails either the one or the other or both is directly opposed to Catholic belief, indeed is not only false but false religion, and according to the teachings of Vatican I is not only opposed to faith, but in the opposition undermines the health of the intellect. Key signs of such positions are the affirmation of the eternity of the world, the infinity of the universe, the exclusive right of science to evaluate theories of evolution and explanations of the origin of the species, and the inability of the church and believers to know anything about the origin of the world apart from scientific speculation.

Subsequent declarations of the church are but elaborations of particular points within this frame of reference, occasioned by claims made for evolutionary pantheism (of Hegel for instance) as scientific; and because scientific, rendering impossible any longer a literal interpretation of Genesis and many other parts of Scripture, particularly those dealing with contingent facts of an historical kind and the unchanging character of the human species as constituted by the Creator directly.

Inextricably linked to these claims, as Pope Pius XII would point out in his encyclical *Humani Generis,* are theories of doctrinal development utterly relativistic (historicist) and utterly subversive of the genuine teaching of Christ and of the church as coming from Christ and the apostles.

Theistic Evolution Disfavored

It is little wonder, then, that attempts by Catholics (St. G. Mivart, M.D. Leroy, J.A. Zahm) in the closing years of the nineteenth century to reconcile acceptance of evolution, especially of the human body from the beast, with Catholic faith, met with disfavor, and that some of those authors' works were proscribed by high church authorities. No reasons were given for the judgment, but from the circumstances it is clear enough that the kind of evolutionary theory envisioned was Darwinian, and that such theory was not only linked to pantheistic and rationalistic modes of thought, but quite inseparable from such.

Such decisions were merely disciplinary, and by themselves provide no answer to the query: whether it is possible to construct and convincingly defend merely within the limits of science and on scientific grounds alone an evolutionary theory of origins. The response of the Biblical Commission in 1909[35] is quite important to the question, whether a Catholic is permitted to call into doubt the literal-historical sense of the facts narrated in the first three chapters of Genesis. Without such freedom the ability of a Catholic believer to construct and defend a plausible theory of evolution is greatly constricted, indeed many would say in effect non-existent. The decree of the Commission, summarizing the tradition attested by the fathers, states that in matters which directly touch the bases of the Christian religion a believer must interpret these facts in the literal-historical sense. Then examples are listed:

- the creation of the entire world at the beginning of time;
- the special creation of man and the formation of the first woman from the first man;
- the unity of the human race;
- the initial happiness of our first parents in the state of justice, integrity and immortality;
- the testing of Adam and Eve through a positive precept;
- the temptation and transgression under the influence of the devil;
- expulsion from the initial paradise; and promise of a Redeemer.[36]

Such an answer is perfectly coherent with the tradition of the church and the solemn definitions of the first article of the creed. If one believes in

35. *AAS* 1 (1909) 567–69.

36. *AAS* 1 (1909) pp. 567–69, reply to question 3.

a Creator God, on whose creative act rests the existence and intelligible order of the world, then this list is a mere specification of those "facts" made by creation and not evolution, and prerequisite to any subsequent development and the limits thereof. Nor is it any less coherent that such a listing should be made, not on scientific evidence in the first instance, but on authority, for the only basic and adequate proof of these facts is the historical witness of a competent observer—in this case only the Creator. Hence the sense of the narrative must be taken historically at these points; not to do so would be the equivalent of denying the traditional notion of creation as expounded by the church from her beginning.[37]

Literal Defined

What is meant by literal sense in this decree is relatively simple to grasp, but is much misunderstood. "Literal" can be defined in three ways when predicated of the sense of sacred Scripture, as contrasted with the accommodated, the spiritual, the figurative or metaphorical senses.

1. In the first case, the literal sense is the one intended by the sacred author (i.e., the Holy Spirit), whereas the accommodated sense is the further meaning the text has when applied (e.g., by a preacher in his sermon).

2. In the second case, literal indicates the direct, primary meaning of a passage intended by the inspired author (i.e., the human author), whereas the spiritual, allegorical, symbolic sense is a secondary one intended by the author of Scripture (i.e., the Holy Spirit), but only by way of the literal sense.

3. In the third case, literal has reference to the mode of expression and indicates the sense, expressed univocally, without metaphor or comparison, whether simply or complexly, popularly or technically.

Thus, what is literal in the second sense, that about which the decree of the Biblical Commission is concerned, may in some instances be expressed in a form that is either literal or figurative. A "literal" truth revealed by Genesis (e.g., the direct formation of the body of Eve from a part of the first man by God) might in part be expressed figuratively (i.e., "rib" as a metaphor for "part of man") or in a popular rather than technical style. But such formulations do not make the primary and literal meaning of the text any less true. To deny this, and insist that an historical fact, or a primary datum of the real

37. Council of Trent, session 4; Vatican I, *Dei Filius*, c. 2.

world can only be expressed in a certain style, or known by a trained scholar or scientist is not only to adopt a position radically skeptical of the objective truth and accuracy of Scripture, but of the direct knowledge of reality obtained by our senses. Thus, my knowledge that I am alive, that such and such moves, that so and so is human and not animal, that what I see is colored and not merely an illusion or subjective impression, is knowledge both true and accurate, though not fully accurate perhaps or fully understood, antecedent to further scientific or philosophic analysis in the proper sense. So, too, in the same way God can and does reveal something true and accurate about the origin of the world and of its structuring, especially of the origin of human nature, although this knowledge may not constitute full knowledge or be expressed always in a manner corresponding to the style and apparatus of a developed philosophy and science. Indeed, there are certain "facts" (e.g., the beginning of the world) that permit only a literal form of expression or are not true. Finally, it is also a possibility that certain primary truths concerning origins, like those truths directly accessible to anyone exercising his cognitive powers irrespective of his degree of education, are best expressed in a simple rather than complex manner.

These distinctions were commonplace in Catholic theology long before the controversies over evolution arose. Hence it cannot be said that they were devised only to escape the implications of modern science. Some fathers of the church (e.g., St. Gregory of Nyssa) observed that, although Moses was learned in the science of the Egyptians, he chose under the influence of the Spirit to write about the creative work of God in another style, accessible to all, not merely the learned, and by implication more appropriate initially to a discussion of a divine rather than natural activity.[38] Once noted, these distinctions enable one to perceive that the alleged reversal of stance toward evolution effected by Pius XII in his 1943 encyclical *Divino Afflante Spiritu* (from antipathy to sympathy for it) does not in fact exist.

The study of the literary forms of any part of Scripture of itself does not threaten the dogmas of the church. Such a threat is only verified when the student does not understand the difference in meaning attached to literal or thinks that in establishing the literal sense in the third case above, that this automatically and always resolves the question of literal sense in the second case. Thus, Pius XII in this encyclical, and Fr. Voste in his letter to Cardinal Suhard of Paris in 1948,[39] do encourage the study of the literary forms found in the ancient writings of the Old Testament, a study

---

38. Also St. Paul, in 1 Cor, chapters 1 and 2, where he contrasts the style of speech appropriate to philosophy and that appropriate to revealed theology: the first is relatively developed and polished, the second by contrast appears simple, unpolished, rough.

39. *DH* 3862–64.

not only not forbidden to Catholics, but one that can contribute to the further illustration of the revealed meaning, and to the correction of faulty interpretations of the literal sense.

But this hardly constitutes a revocation, express or tacit, of the decree of 1909, that a Catholic in virtue of conclusions pertaining to literary questions may not doubt that Genesis does literally convey facts of an historical character directly bearing on the resolution of the problem of origins. Nor does the fact that some Fathers and theologians of the past combined belief in the literal sense with expositions of a faulty kind, either in terms of literary form or philosophic-scientific study soundly based, invalidate their accurate witness to the revealed, literal sense. Thus, this encyclical hardly implies that the earlier teaching of the church on origins was "fundamentalistic" and in need of correction, where fundamentalism denotes not merely adherence to fundamentals but the imposition of explanations of these resting on insufficient knowledge. In the case of church teachings, it is the faulty interpretation of this by individuals, not the teaching itself, that sometimes requires correction. The difference has been recognized by the church from ancient times.

Pope Pius XII

That this is a fair reading of the mind of Pope Pius XII in regard to the question of origins as set forth in the teaching of the church is quite evident in the address given by this Pope to the Pontifical Academy of Sciences two years before the encyclical *Divino Afflante Spiritu*.[40] In this address the pope makes the following points:

1. The starting point for any discussion of the question of origins is not the similarity, but the difference between the Creator and the creature, between human nature (including the human body) and the rest of creation.

2. What principally and primarily accounts for the difference is the distinctive productive action of the Creator (creative and/or miraculous) and not a natural process.

3. In the case of the initial existence of the world (at the beginning of time) only that creative action of God accounts for the difference and therefore the partial resemblance of creation to the Creator, and the possibility of knowing God from a study of the visible world.

40. Pius XII, "Address . . . Academy of Sciences," 504–12.

4. In the case of the bodies of the first man and woman, as well as of their souls, it is the direct divine intervention which accounts for the specific difference between human beings and the rest of creation.

5. Antecedently to the formation of Adam and Eve the heavens and the earth were ordered by the direct intervention of God culminating in the appearance of the first man and woman.

6. Science as well as philosophy may be able to contribute to the further understanding of what is principally the work of God as a whole (the Hexaëmeron) but only by respecting these truths. To date, he concludes, none of the sciences has contributed anything certain and definitive to the knowledge of origins already possessed from revelation and set forth by the church.

In this address Pius XII mentions the age of the world in terms of millions of years. The question of the age of the world was merely incidental to the theme he was discussing, and in no way constitutes magisterial resolution of the question bearing on the age of the world or of the measuring of "day" in the Genesis account of the work of God, any more than St. Augustine's views on this point have represented more than a merely personal opinion. The church has always permitted discussion of this point for Catholics, provided the final judgment was left to the church, a judgment to date not rendered. Nor does the church forbid holding a literal interpretation of "day."

Humani Generis (1950)

The pope returned to the subject of origins in his encyclical *Humani Generis* in 1950. The encyclical as a whole deals with questions touching the nature of theology and theological method. Because theories of evolution touch not only the particular question of origins but raise issues of theological method, the encyclical devotes considerable attention to this theme.

- Evolution as a basic mode of thought is condemned as directly opposed to those modes of reflection implied by Catholic faith. In this sense it is a form of rationalism underlying three contemporary errors: pantheistic totalitarianism, existential skepticism concerning the objectivity of philosophic knowledge of essences, and historicism or skepticism concerning the unchanging character of eternal truths and dogmas of the church. Any specific scientific hypothesis constructed on the basis of evolutionary thought is by that fact opposed to the truth, and therefore false. Not only is it false, but it is not scientific; rather it is a form of false religion parading as science because it is a direct denial of the truth of creation, at once the key to our understanding not only of God, but of the most basic truths about the world and ourselves.

- Evolution merely as a scientific hypothesis, on the assumption that one can be constructed apart from evolution as a theory of knowledge (the pope does not say whether this is impossible in every instance, only that so far it has not successfully been done) may be investigated by properly trained Catholic scholars, provided certain conditions are verified:

  - that such hypotheses are not used or proposed to explain the origin of the world in the beginning of time, a question already definitively settled on the basis of a strictly creative act of God;

  - that such hypotheses are not used or proposed to explain the origin of the human soul, a question already decided on the basis of a strict creative act of God;

  - that such hypotheses are not used or proposed to suggest that any member of the human family has any other origin except by way of carnal generation from a single couple formed immediately by God (condemnation of polygenism);

  - that such hypotheses, when the subject of discussion, are not disseminated indiscriminately among those unprepared to grasp the complexities involved and the precautions that must be taken in order not to deny certain points of truth;

  - and that in studying these hypotheses scientifically the reasons against, as well as for, a possible theory of evolution be presented with complete objectivity, in such a way as not to imply that scientific analysis by itself provides an adequate basis for resolving a point of revelation, or that any other authority but the church has the right to decide such questions definitively.[41]

- The encyclical permits Catholic scholars to propose, hypothetically, evolutionary explanations for the origin of the first human body (Adam's[42]) from pre-existent living matter, so long as these take account of the direct divine intervention principally involved in this process.

41. The Council of Trent, session 4, on authority and criteria for determining the inspired sense of Scripture.

42. Eve is not mentioned, but in view of the antecedent tradition should be regarded as excluded, if not mentioned explicitly.

The encyclical does not indicate what might be the eventual contribution of science to the understanding of the origin of the first human body, or the origin of any other material being mentioned in the revealed account of origins, nor does this encyclical deal with the question whether evolution, used to describe tenable and untenable hypotheses, is a term used in the same sense (univocally) in each case. The requirement that such theories account not only for the Creator as primary, but as principal cause in such a process, would indicate that such hypotheses differ significantly from those normally designated as such, because the latter do not make allowance for a miraculous element in the formation of the first man's body. From the point of view of this encyclical the permission to study human origins scientifically might just as well, or even more so, point to those hypotheses often known as "creation science" in the event evolutionary hypotheses fail to justify their scientific character. The encyclical does not take note of any doubt concerning the scientific character of evolution, even within the limits enjoined for its tentative investigation. Rather the encyclical assumes any such investigation and the formulation of its results will be strictly scientific. Should this not be the case, or further should it prove impossible, Catholic proponents of evolution as a "scientific" hypothesis could not appeal to *Humani Generis* for support. Indeed, a fair reading of the encyclical would entail abandonment of such hypotheses, as a kind of *falsi nominis scientiae* proscribed by Vatican I. Hence, *Humani Generis* is not, as so often claimed, a charter for evolutionism among Catholics. Rather the passage often cited to support this claim is essentially approval to examine the question of origins from a scientific standpoint, in so far as this is feasible. The limits traced in the encyclical serve to define "feasibility" in practice.

In any case those theories known as "theistic evolution," which attempt to explain the origin of the human body of Adam and Eve in terms of a purely natural process, and which more often than not, when extended in fully logical fashion, have defended the possibility of polygenism and of a notion of God, involving him in the process of creation as a subject of change himself, have met with the consistent disfavor of the church, and in the best known case, that of Pierre Teilhard de Chardin, public reprimand[43] preceded by numerous prohibitions to pursue such lines of thought or publish these.

---

43. The *Monitum* of 1962, declaring his works to contain heresy and errors dangerous to faith, reaffirmed in July, 1981,

Summation of the Teaching of Pius XII

The teaching of Pius XII should be regarded, not as a definition of points hitherto undeclared by the church, but as a clarification of issues in view of a double objective:

- establishing the limits of academic freedom, particularly scientific, to speculate vis-à-vis the exercise of faith;

- and rebutting the charge that the practice of faith, particularly the unconditional obedience entailed therein, is obscurantist in principle.

The guidelines provided both in regard to historicism (evolutionary episte-mology) and in regard to allegedly "scientific" theories of evolution for the origin of the first human body, if one is to judge from the comments of this pope's successors, are still valid, but have not been followed too faithfully by all Catholic scholars.

Two questions rarely raised in connection with *Humani Generis* are:

1. Are the "evolutionary" theories of human origin permitted as hypoth-eses of a strictly scientific kind under the conditions established by Pius XII, truly evolutionary?

2. Does any theory of evolution merit the appellation "scientific"?

One of the merits of "creation science" is to provide an excellent basis for a negative response to both, especially to the second. A negative response, while hardly an exhaustive and definitive resolution to all problems of bib-lical exegesis associated with the question of origins, will indeed tend to undermine and destroy the grounds for doubting the traditional teaching of the church on creation, and at the same time provide a positive impetus to science.

Pope Paul VI (1966)

Pope Paul VI, in an address[44] to theologians gathered in Rome to study the theme of original sin, made the following points:

1. The traditional dogma of original sin, unchanged, figures in the teach-ing of Vatican II at many points, and is to be taken seriously as a basic criterion for assessing the meaning of the documents of Vatican II.

---

44. Paul VI, Allocution, 649–55.

2. Polygenism, as repeatedly stated in the past, is incompatible with the teaching of the church on the state of original justice of our first parents and the origin of original sin.

3. If hypotheses of evolution touching the origin of the first human body, never the soul, proposed in accord with the still binding directive of Pius XII in *Humani Generis,* cannot be constructed plausibly without holding polygenism, then the hypothesis of evolution must be modified or abandoned as false, not the dogma changed to accommodate the hypothesis.

In the introduction to his *Credo of the People of God*[45] this same pope makes a very interesting observation germane to the discussion of origins. In addition to that knowledge of the real world available to men through observation and the cultivation of science, it is also possible for the human intellect to attain to an understanding of the essences, the *quid est* of those agents whose activities are observed. The pope states that the Catholic believer will always affirm the possibility of objective understanding on both counts. The reason is clearly stated in Vatican I: belief in God the Creator is the most realistic basis for strengthening the native powers of reason to know with certitude those aspects of reality within its grasp. Denial of the first article of the creed is the best way to undermine that intellectual confidence native to the human mind as a participation in the perfection of the divine intellect and its natural orientation to the truth.

The notion of species, of nature, employed at the level of observation is that of a generalization, subject to exceptions, to change and modification. There is nothing objectionable *per se* to the use of generalizations. But when such a notion of species is used exclusively in the construction of any theory of origins, as is the case with evolutionary theory, the modifications to which that "species" can be subjected appear unlimited. Indeed, evolutionary theory would seem impossible without the use of such a device to render ceaseless progression plausible. Catholic belief on the contrary implies that such modifications are not infinite, actually or possibly, but rather circumscribed within the limits of the species understood essentially, as a universal concept not admitting of exceptions, the same whatever the conditions of the subject in which it is found; and that any development of a species as in the scientific sense, without the intervention of a rational agent, always presupposes, and does not produce the species in the philosophic sense. These developments within the limits of each species, will not be continuous, but discontinuous with each other. The only question to be raised concerns the

45. Paul VI, *Credo,* 433–5n5.

possibility of a rational agent, other than the Creator, modifying these living species first established by the Creator. Catholic tradition replies in the negative; and scientific experiment tends to confirm this.

This observation of Paul VI,[46] which he claims to be an integral part of the teaching of the church, is a rejection of one of the positions commonly associated with the nominalist philosophy of the fourteenth century (William of Ockham and disciples) and especially that characteristic of Lockean empiricism and Kantian skepticism in the modern world. In the context of the *Credo* of Paul VI this observation provides the immediate background for understanding his teaching on contraception as intrinsically evil, and the invariability of human nature, as well as for the possibility of transubstantiation (in what sense the first is against nature, and therefore not within our power to change; in what sense with the second the species or accidents can remain unchanged, the substance of bread being totally changed into the body of Christ).

Contrary to theory fashionable since the days of Ockham, F. Bacon and J. Locke, science tends to confirm the importance of the universal. Change is not unlimited, but finite, and when observable within the world of living beings occurs within the well-defined limits of the species in the traditional Catholic sense of this term. Apparent exceptions at the level of observation are rather the result of imperfect understanding on the part of the observer, rather than the absence of anything objectively denoted by the term species or essence in the sense of "universal." Proponents of evolution have yet to demonstrate:

1. that their theories correspond to anything that is happening or in fact has happened, and that the traditional notion of species so integral to the dogma of creation and "literal" interpretation of Genesis, as in the thought of St. Bonaventure, is irrelevant to sound science.

2. Whatever the personal belief and philosophy of scientists, scientific practice tends to confirm the wisdom of the *Credo* of Paul VI.

Appraisal

It is not too difficult to appreciate the pertinence of this observation to the question of the origin of the species and of human nature in particular. Evolutionary theories stress the continuity of development between the species from the lower to the higher, as well as a sufficient duration to permit the

46. Cf. the related observation in Paul VI's *Mysterium Fidei*, n. 24.

operation of natural or artificial causes according to the laws governing these. Catholic belief stresses an essential discontinuity, which in the case of those essences, whose limits were fixed by the Creator and which cannot be modified by the intervention of natural or artificial agents of a finite power, only the divine omnipotence can transcend, and that without any prerequisite duration, long or short. In the case of the human body there is nothing implausible in the fact that God should have formed the first human body, beginning with inorganic matter rather than organic, and bringing it to such a degree of perfection that the soul especially created for it might be infused into it. The divine omnipotence (the principal agent) is not bound to act within the limits of a merely natural process. Nor is there anything mysterious about the fact that this action cannot be duplicated naturally, because it is not within the power of finite agents to deploy the power of the Creator.

Catholic teaching has never pretended in every instance of observable species, on the basis of revelation, to know what those outer limits are as fixed by the Creator. But that there are such limits, even at the level of inanimate existence, sound science as well as philosophy has tended to confirm in stressing the finite character of the world and all that is in it. There is, for example, a point beyond which particles of matter cannot further be split. Could this be done, annihilation of matter would occur. Annihilation: reduction to nothing, like creation: producing something out of nothing, in the teaching of the church, can only be accomplished by one who is omnipotent, viz., God. The created agent can only modify, for better or worse. Yet the origin and nature of these particles is neither self-explanatory, nor intelligible in terms of yet simpler elements. As the scale of being is ascended, the relative stability of essences is reflected in the inability of finite agents to effect their variation, except within recognizable limits, pre-existing and pre-requisite for the variations. The non-living agent does not naturally become a living being by itself; nor the plant an animal, nor even the humble fruit fly a horse fly. Plant and animal breeding may be useful to humans, but such breeding does not change the essential species with which the breeding begins.

In the case of human nature, and in particular the human body, the limits are even more precise and fixed, and have always been so regarded by the church. Any attempt to suggest, much less hold as certain, that the unborn child is less human essentially than the one born, that the uneducated, the senile, the retarded, etc., are less human essentially than the sophisticated, the alert, the socially productive specimen, has always been termed by the church as a pernicious error. Thus, she regards eugenics, genetic experimentation aimed at modifying human nature, divisions of human nature into subspecies based on physiological, cultural, linguistic, or similar grounds, as an immoral assumption of divine prerogative, and as an affront to the dignity of the human person. This belief in the unique stability of human nature from the first moment of conception is clearly linked to the belief of the church concerning the direct formation of the first man and first woman by the Creator, and that the only natural process capable of producing and accounting for the production of another human body is the human procreative process directly established by the Creator in forming the first two human beings as male and female. And just as clearly and inseparably this notion of the unchanging essence of the human species lies at the heart of the moral and sacramental orders as these appear characteristically in Catholic belief and practice.

Nor is it very difficult, with all due allowance for the stylistic characteristics of the Genesis narrative, to discover there unmistakable indications not only of the initial creative act of God at the beginning of time, but of that relative fixity and discontinuity of the species, most of all in the case of mankind, whose origin is the distinctive intervention of the Creator as principal cause, and whose truth forms the context and limits within which subsequent natural and artificial development can and should occur, until such time as the Creator should see fit to modify this order.

This is another way of saying the specifically more perfect cannot come from the less perfect naturally, but only through the intervention of a wise and free agent, and in certain cases that wise and free agent can only be the Creator-God. What might have seemed to be only a point of scholastic philosophy overly influenced by certain aspects of Aristotelian thought, is primarily a part of Catholic doctrine, rooted in revelation, just as "pre-scientific" in relation to the highly sophisticated reflection of Aristotle as it is in relation to modern science, and as such, providing a key to the mysteries met by science at its frontiers.

Pope John Paul II (1981)

John Paul II, in an address to the Pontifical Academy of Sciences,[47] briefly touched on the question of the origin of the cosmos in its epistemological and hermeneutical aspects. The address is not a doctrinal constitution in the strict sense; but simply a series of reflections on themes bearing on belief and science reiterating without further defining the tradition of the church on the points touched. Since it is widely being quoted as supportive of "theistic evolution" (a position as espoused by Pierre Teilhard de Chardin, only a few months earlier once again reproved as incompatible with Catholic tradition)

47. October 3, 1981 *AAS* 73 (1981) pp. 668–67.

and indicative of a modification of the earlier tradition, an examination of the pope's remarks follows.

The pope noted that revelation, especially the Genesis narrative, is not to be conceived as a kind of scientific encyclopedia providing direct and immediate answers to questions of a formally scientific nature. Revelation is no substitute for the work of scientific research in the unraveling of the secrets of nature. Revelation rather is a body of religious doctrine which, when it touches points concerning the cosmos, does so with the intention of teaching the correct relations between man and God, and between man and the universe. Other types of teaching about the universe are extraneous to the intentions of the Bible. Which and how many points of this religious doctrine are facts bearing on the subject of scientific teaching it is not the pope's purpose to discuss here; rather that purpose is to state the professed limits of revelation in these matters, and why its presentation as a whole does not coincide with that of modern science. But that at certain points revelation and science do meet and in part overlap he does not deny; indeed, one of these points of encounter is at the heart of these observations by the pope. Further, remarked the pope, this knowledge of the cosmos conveyed by revelation is not couched in the language of modern science, but rather in the terms commonly employed by contemporaries of the sacred authors when discussing religious questions involving the cosmos, still employed today, and often described as "popular" or "pre-scientific." It is clear from the tenor of the pope's remarks that such "popular" language is so employed in the Scriptures as to correct the errors of all times concerning the relations of God and the cosmos, and of man and the cosmos.

It would, however, be a gratuitous inference contrary to Catholic tradition that "popular" here means merely symbolic, and does not literally (in the sense of primary, direct content) convey any factual knowledge about the world and how it was made, because revelation is not a scientific textbook or does not speak in a scientific style. Quite the contrary, on at least one point discussed explicitly, the first origin of the cosmos, only a source other than science, in a language other than science, can communicate a true and factual answer. The aphorism used by the pope to summarize his first point: revelation teaches not how the world was made, but how to go to heaven, refers to the intentions of the sacred author, not the content of his message, which quite surely does teach us how the world was made "in the beginning" by creation. This discussion of the "limits of revealed knowledge" vis-à-vis the subject matter of science was not undertaken by the pope for its own sake, but in view of a second point, the limits of science and its proper correlation with revealed theology on the question of cosmic origins.

But before examining the second point, it is worth noting to what degree the knowledge of "how" the world was made entailed by the revelation of "how" to get to heaven (i.e., salvation, or the purpose of revelation) coincides with the knowledge of "how" the world was made presupposed for the progress of science. Because the knowledge of how to get to heaven does not require the kind of understanding of the world offered by science, that does not mean knowledge of salvation does not convey, indeed require, some knowledge of the origins of the world and of the human family, in some respects the only certain source of knowledge. The quarrel between evolutionism and creationism in part concerns whether or not that salvific knowledge coincides with the root suppositions of genuine science. The creationist affirms the coincidence; the evolutionist denies this. From a Catholic point of view, the evolutionary denial is "scientism," not science. Since theistic evolution shares this denial, its claims to support from Catholic faith and to be a support of Catholic faith are suspect.

In connection with these claims of theistic evolutionists for their particular version of evolutionism as radically religious, there is this curious point to be pondered. In times past, almost until the time of *Humani Generis,* the plausibility of evolution for the general public inclined to accept it, lay in its denial of final causality to the world and to the natural forces operative within it. The "why" of the world had no relevance to its "how." The approach was quite congenial to an atheism rooted in a thoroughgoing materialism and in the epistemological assumptions of the positivist school used to justify this approach.

But with the shaking of popular faith in the "necessary" laws of nature and with a realization of how little trust, much less absolute trust, could be placed in the *arbitrium* of scientists, exactly the contrary bias has come to support the plausibility of evolutionism over the past half-century. Evolution now appeals because it explains the finality of the world, because it provides a basis for apprehending the unity and continuity of existence and for forming an all-embracing synthesis of the real, ultimately appearing to satisfy the desire of the human mind for ultimates and to give concrete shape to the wildest mystical flights of human fantasy. Evolution, far from being atheistic, has become religious; far from being materialistic, it has become idealistic and spiritual. Unfortunately, either way, evolution is not true because the truth of God's existence excludes the possibility of materialism as an explanation of the universe; and the truth that God is a Creator-God excludes the possibility of a "mystical" pantheism as an explanation.

If theology is limited in what it can say about the world by the extent of revelation God has chosen to give us, science is also limited in its efforts to explore the intelligibility of its subject matter. These limits are nowhere more evident than in the inability of science, universally acknowledged, to provide any ultimate explanation of the origin of its subject matter, and therefore of its own rationale. For this answer the help of "pre-scientific" knowledge, metaphysics and revelation, is necessary. In support and illustration of his point the pope cites a passage from an address of Pope Pius XII[48] on the proofs for the existence of God in the light of modern science. In this address Pius XII, after noting the insoluble enigma constituted for the scientific mind by the question of ultimate origins, insoluble either in terms of an uncreated (infinite) world, or self-creating (evolutionary) world, stated that the scientific mind versed in the wisdom of metaphysics and revelation will indeed discover evidences in the world studied scientifically pointing to the true answer given by revelation: the *"Fiat"* of an omnipotent Creator. Pius XII discusses two of these pointers:

- the mutability and variability of the world and

- its finite character, reflected clearly in the law of entropy.

On at least two points these remarks of Pius XII, cited so recently by Pope John Paul II, constitute as it were a basic charter for creation science:

1. Science is not absolutely autonomous in the pursuit of its goals. It cannot be absolutely independent and self-sufficient in unraveling the intelligibility of its subject matter.

2. On at least one point, the origin of the cosmos, fundamental to all the rest, the doctrine of creation as traditionally expounded by the church (and not evolutionism) provides the clue, the key, the paradigm or context for discerning the sense of all the rest.

Clearly, two questions must be distinguished:

1. How much does revelation tell us about the subjects investigated by science?

2. How much can scientific investigation tell us about the subjects and facts contained in revelation, in particular about the origin of the cosmos and of the species?

To each question the Pope Pius XII's reply is quite traditional. To the first question he states relatively little, but that seeming little is more important than all the rest. To the second he replies perhaps something on some points, but on certain matters like the origin of the cosmos, he replies nothing at all, except in dependence on revelation.

48. Pontifical Academcy of Sciences, November 1951, *AAS* 44, 231–43.

Despite multiple claims to the contrary, the church in the last half century no more approves or permits "evolutionism" as the epistemological matrix for the thought of Catholics than in times past. While many specific theories proposed in "creation science" on purely scientific grounds hardly can be described as "canonized" by the church, or "certain" on scientific grounds, several of the epistemological and hermeneutical assumptions made by creationism coincide with the teaching of the church.

Objections Addressed

Objection is often made to the foregoing presentation of the teaching of the church on origins as false. The teaching of the church, it is alleged, not only has no interest in creation science but is quite opposed to it as a form of "literalism" or biblical "fundamentalism."

Some of the evidences adduced to support such an objection may be dismissed as selective reading, out of context, of the teaching of Pope Pius XII. To say that in permitting Catholics, for example, to study the problem of literary forms and hold conclusions not identical with those of the Fathers, this pope also permitted Catholics to depart from the literal sense of Scripture as attested by the fathers, to be the primary content of revelation, as in the case of Genesis or in the case of the infancy narratives on the virgin birth, simply is not true. In discussing the possibility of Catholics holding, merely as a scientific opinion, limited forms of evolution in reference to the first human body, this pope made it very clear that any presentation of such theory effectively giving "carte blanche" to science to decide the meaning of Scripture was not ever permitted to Catholics, and that in the event of conflict the theory, not the truth, is to be modified or abandoned. Further, this pope in *Humani Generis* did not permit Catholics to opt for an evolutionary "paradigm" accounting for the "fact" of evolution as distinct from the uncertainty of specific theories, in science or in any other area of intellectual endeavor; quite the contrary, he forbade this as irreconcilable with faith. And in every instance where such was done in contradiction to the directives of the pope, the finished result (e.g., the works of Teilhard) met with consistent reproof and prohibition as containing grievous errors contrary to revealed truth.

Four arguments are often adduced in support of the objection that the foregoing presentation is not a correct interpretation of the teaching of the church in respect to the matter of teaching about origins in either parochial or public schools.

Literalism

Argument: Catholics are not required to subscribe to biblical literalism but are required to ascribe only symbolic value to such descriptions regarding the transcendence of God, the dignity of man, and the on-going sustenance of the world.

Reply: A Catholic is not required to subscribe to biblical literalism, where "biblical literalism" assumes a naïve and uncritical correlation between the "facts" of revelation and particular exemplifications of these as they might be currently imagined on the one hand, or on the other highly sophisticated and abstract scientific speculation about the world of the senses. An equally naïve and uncritical counterpart of biblical literalism in this first sense is a kind of arrogant "scientific literalism" which assumes that scientific speculation alone provides an exact and realistic understanding of the objective world of the senses, and that if revelation provides any factual knowledge of the cosmos and of the species within it, it must be strictly in accord with the methods and terminology of "modern science." The repudiation of both forms of "literalism" described above is not the equivalent of a denial that any facts about the world are to be found in revelation.

Where "literalism" has reference to that factual content touching the work of the Creator, especially Adam and Eve, and its bearing on salvation, however simple, "pre-scientific," or metaphysical the style, there a Catholic is required on the basis of his faith to subscribe to a literal, or historical interpretation of the passages in question. Indeed, the entire tenor of Catholic tradition is that these facts in particular can only be expressed first in this manner, if they are subsequently to be discussed in any other fashion.

The oft-alleged opposition between the assertion of "biblical literalism" in the early decrees of the Pontifical Biblical Commission and its "repudiation" by Pius XII in his encyclical *Divino Afflante Spiritu* does not exist. For the encyclical of Pius XII has reference to literalism in the first sense above, where the decrees refer to literalism in the second sense.

Hence there is no need on the part of a Catholic to choose between an allegedly naïve Fideism (represented by the early decrees of the Biblical Commission) incapable of discerning the real from the imaginary and of appreciating the marvelous advances of "modern science," and a skeptical relativism (permitted by the encyclical of Pius XII) in respect to the interpretation of the facts traditionally believed revealed in Genesis. Why such a choice should seem to anyone inevitable, when in fact it is hardly such, is another question whose resolution is undoubtedly linked with metaphysical and epistemological assumptions incompatible with Catholic tradition and elsewhere mentioned in this essay.

Revelation and Science

Argument: Revelation contains a body of religious doctrine; therefore, it tells us nothing about the world as studied by science and neither does the magisterium of the church.

Reply: This observation begs the question. That revelation should be a "religious doctrine" does not mean it contains no information touching the subject matter of science, unless it is assumed science alone can comprehend and convey understanding of the visible world. That, however, is precisely the point at issue, which cannot be decided primarily on scientific grounds, but on others: the Catholic on one set of beliefs, the secular humanist on another. The church does not maintain revelation is a scientific textbook such as to provide exact parallels for every scientific question. At certain points, however, science and revelation meet, and at those points (e.g., the question of origins) revelation undoubtedly has something to say basic to scientific understanding and science.

Evolution as Paradigm

Argument: Evolution is not merely a scientific hypothesis touching one or another issue of scientific research, but a "paradigm" providing the context, assumptions and methods best calculated to justify the nature of science and of its characteristic procedures in studying the uniformity, continuity and similarity among all elements of its subject matter.

Reply: Good arguments can be adduced to show that evolution is simply not a scientific hypothesis. Hence the paradigm providing the context for scientific endeavors is something other than science. And it is just this assumption of "Evolutionism" as the universal "paradigm" that directly conflicts with the teaching of the church and constitutes an abuse of the limited permission of Pius XII to propose tentatively hypotheses of evolution within the limits of certain scientific questions and without questioning the decisions of the church in matters also touching revelation. Nor does the church concede this kind of autonomy to politics, economics, etc. Within the well-defined limits of each science, art or profession, the trained practitioner is free from the authority of the church. But that freedom does not mean license to define the limits of one's science independently of the Truth that is God, and the revelation he has entrusted to his church. Such a position is the equivalent of relativism in the intellectual order, and secularism in the practical.

Latitudinarianism

Argument: The Catholic is free to accept or reject evolution merely on scientific grounds, since matters of revelation are beyond proof or disproof scientifically and cannot be affected by scientific theory.

Reply: Such an affirmation is too broad and is equivalent to the fideism condemned by the First Vatican Council.[49] It renders *a priori* impossible that faith should seek understanding in human terms (theology) or that the intellect should seek faith (apologetics). Faith, in a word, becomes purely an arbitrary affair. While it is true reason cannot prove the mysteries of faith, it can certainly apprehend these. It is not an exercise in mystagogery.[50]

The opposite of the axiom cited in the objection is equally broad and the equivalent of rationalism: Scripture and revelation can neither affirm nor deny anything about the subject matter of philosophy and science; revelation can only interpret the religious meaning of whatever it is reason investigates. But this is what is precisely not the case with the dogma of creation in the teaching of the church. So, too, with many other truths of revelation which are mysteries of faith, and which are therefore not directly accessible to reason, but which like the virgin birth, the incarnation, the mystery of the real presence of the body and blood of the Savior in the Eucharist and the mysterious miracle, transubstantiation, by which this is effected, and other natural truths such as the immutability of human nature, the uniqueness of the human body, and the nature of human conception. All tell us something factual about the material, whose understanding is not irrelevant to the sound conduct of philosophy and science.

In summary, the objection is a thinly veiled presentation of science as self sufficient, a notion not at all evident scientifically no matter how many "authorities" are cited in its favor, but resting on assumptions of a "pre-scientific" and "religious" character, directly conflicting with the teaching of the Catholic Church.

49. *Dei Filius*, c. 4.

50. *Dei Filius*, c. 4 and canons 1–3 of the same chapter.

Theistic Evolution

Argument: It is claimed that the believer, by adopting a position generally called "theistic evolution," can drop those aspects of traditional "Creationism" as set forth in this essay, particularly the facts narrated in Genesis, which the evolutionist regards as unscientific and the critical historian as naïve, and hence not "literally" true. At the same time such a position permits the believer to retain a belief in God, which the agnostic or atheist rejects on the basis of evolution, *inter alia*. In such a synthesis religion is said to explain "who" made the world and "why," while science explains "how" he made it (by evolution). Religion deals with final causes, while science deals with efficient causes, processes and facts.

Reply: The Catholic believer cannot drop from his belief facts bearing on the origin of the physical world and its contents as well as on the origin of the human world as expounded in the revealed account of these origins without in fact also changing the nature of that belief, something not in his power. Hence, "theistic evolution" as a viable Catholic position is *a priori* inconsistent with its alleged relegation of the "how" of creation to study by science alone.

Further, the Catholic in subscribing to the first article of the creed affirms not only that God is and that he made the world, but how he made the world, and especially how he made the angelic and human species. It is precisely in affirming the difference between the uniquely divine activity (either creation *ex nihilo* or miracles), and those natural processes proper to different created species that the difference between infinite and finite natures is demonstrated. The operation of a created agent presupposes the prior existence of the world and of the species and cannot extend beyond these limits. The operation of the Creator does not. Any refusal to recognize the radical inadequacy of natural processes as an explanation for the origin of the world and the distinction of species must logically lead to a failure (Pantheism) to perceive the distinction between God and his creation. Pantheism clothed in the terminology of Christian theology becomes a particularly insidious form of syncretism.

Finally, from a scientific point of view "theistic evolution" appears an illogical compromise. Either natural processes provide an answer to the question of the origin of the world and of the distinction of the species in terms of efficient causality ("how") or they do not. In the first case theology has nothing at all to contribute to the resolution of the precise question raised, and the atheistic evolutionist is vindicated. Religion in any form is simply an aspect of subjective experience. In the second case, the tradition of Catholic belief, theology will have a great deal to contribute bearing not only on religion, but on the assumptions of philosophy and science, but this theology will not be "theistic evolution," for in the event that "evolution" cannot be verified, no amount of religious finality, however noble the ideals, will render it adequate or true.

Conclusions

Creation

The teaching of the church on origins from her beginning embraces a body of doctrine consistent and unvarying, not only as regards its general content and tenor, but the explicit formulation of its details as well. The one God is the only God, infinite and omnipotent, Who by his creative power not only made all else in the beginning of time, but ordered that creation, an ordering initially culminating in the formation of Adam and Eve. By the same power and with the same kind of action he is capable of modifying and perfecting the original creation, which in fact he has done in the work of salvation. The doctrine of creation, in general and in all its detail, is intimately bound up with the mystery of salvation. That is why no Catholic may call into question any aspect of the doctrine of creation which in fact the church believes is related to the mystery of salvation without also doubting that latter mystery.

While the church does not hold that God has revealed all that can be known about his creation, or of that which has been revealed, that the precise sense has in every instance been definitively explained by the church in the most explicit manner possible, certain points concerning the origin of the world and of the species within it have been so revealed and definitively explained by the church, either solemnly or in her ordinary magisterium, in such ways that they may not be questioned or subjected to modification to accommodate human theorizing.

1. The whole world was created by God *ex nihilo* in the beginning of time.

2. The essential structure or order of the world presupposed for any subsequent activity or development was established by God and admits of no exceptions, except those directly produced by divine intervention, such as that which the church claims will bring to pass the resurrection of the human body from an inorganic to an organic state, and the new heavens and earth at the end of time.

3. The nature of the first man and first woman was made directly by God, by forming the male body out of preexisting matter, the female body out of the body of the first man, by creating out of nothing a soul for each and then uniting soul to body as its form. At each of these three steps, formation of a body, creation of a soul, and infusion of soul into body, the principal agent is the Creator, not a creature; hence the process is not a natural development from one species to another, but a divine or miraculous action discontinuous with any possible, merely natural process. This discontinuity accounts for the distinctness and greatness of the human, and of each single human person in the whole of creation, and the special value of man before God.

4. God made only one man and one woman in this fashion. All others find their origin in descent from these two, human procreation through conception accounting for the origin of the body, divine creation of each soul *ex nihilo* for the origin of the soul and its infusion into the body conceived. Thus, there is but one historical human family, with but a single couple at its beginning, this couple owing existence directly and principally to God as Creator. Only in the second birth of baptism can a human person speak of being born of God.

Epistemology

The church holds that some truths about the creative work of God can be known only from revelation; others might also be known naturally (philosophically or scientifically). But in both cases what is known from revelation is known as true, even if in fact nothing more is learned about these points naturally. Further, on the basis of criteria essentially theological, one of which is the unanimous witness of tradition, the church holds that she alone has been authorized to decide definitively that a given point of doctrine pertains to matters of faith and morals and what the sense of revelation is on that point. On those points not yet so decided she permits the presentation of various opinions (e.g., the exact meaning of day in the work of six days) provided that none is presented as anything other than opinion subject to correction or rejection by the magisterium of the church.

Further, the church clearly distinguishes between the study of literary form and style and the determination of the meaning of Scripture in the theological sense. Precisely because the theological principles underlying the mystery of salvation rest on historical facts brought to pass by the free acts of the Creator *qua* Creator, that sense also includes historical facts certified by the magisterium of the church. One is free to discuss problems of styles and form, so long as certain truths declared as such by the church are not called into doubt, and the results of these studies as they bear on the meaning of revelation are subject to final evaluation by the church.

Culture and Revelation

While the principal concern of the teaching of the church is salvation, that teaching at many points is also concerned with the truths of the natural order. Revelation and the teaching of the church contain truths whose revelation is useful, indeed in some ways necessary for the balanced development of human culture, philosophic, scientific, artistic; and whose ignorance or facile denial is deleterious and destructive of the same. The church holds that this culture is best developed not apart from, much less in opposition to faith, but in harmony with it. This does not mean that the church believes either revelation or her own teaching provides ready-made answers to queries formulated within the limits of philosophy or science properly defined, or that she possesses the authority directly to intervene and supervise legitimate research within those limits. Rather she believes that in virtue of the deposit of faith entrusted to her she possesses an epistemology enabling her to formulate a sound policy for the discernment of those limits and the harmonization of intellectual effort in relation to him who is the way, the truth, and the life. In a word, if the church does not hold that a formally developed philosophy or science is to be found as such in revelation or in her teaching, she does hold that she is in a position to support in a very basic way the cultivation of one. Thus, she believes philosophy and science to be only relatively autonomous in respect to the attainment of their specific objects.

Evolution

In the matter of origins the church permits the proposal of theories of evolution as scientific explanations of the origin of the species (never of the world) in only a very restricted way, and on conditions reflecting what she otherwise knows to be the truth, in such wise that any such hypothesis only doubtfully merits the designation "evolutionary."

Further, because any theory of evolution, provided it can be detached from the pantheism and rationalism condemned by the church, touches points also contained in revelation and bearing on salvation, the church regards any proclamation of evolution as a fact on merely scientific grounds as a scientific statement which presumes to determine on merely human authority what can only be determined on divine. Thus, it becomes a scientific statement tantamount to a counter-religious argument not free of the rationalism condemned as false by the church. Nor can the difficulty be avoided by a facile distinction claiming for science the task of solving the "how" of origins and for religion the "who." It is precisely because the Catholic faith claims to explain not only who did it but how he did it (by creation) that we are able to distinguish the world as created from God as uncreated and infinite, and from our knowledge of the finite recognize not only the existence of God, but of the only God with whom all may be compared, but who is incomparable to anything else.

Evolution Exclusively Presented

Not all accept the teaching of the church. Dissenters consider dissent freedom to conduct their intellectual lives as they see fit. So long as such persons do not attempt to impose their views on believers, there exists no immediate conflict with the teaching of the church. But in the context of what is defined and proclaimed as a "neutral" school, the exclusive presentation of evolution as the only plausible explanation of cosmic and of human origins, or worse as a "fact" beyond doubt, belie the religious neutrality of the school. Such a presentation does conflict directly with the teaching of the church at many points, and is tantamount to indoctrination of a religious kind, one judged by the church to be false. Presentation of arguments for an evolutionary theory and against it and set forth in a truly scientific manner (and that is a very big question, for it is yet to be demonstrated conclusively that any theory of evolution can meet threshold requirements of science), for a creationistic theory and against it, is in principle fair, provided both can be presented merely as scientific hypotheses and appreciated as such by public and parochial students.

That, however, is a major proviso. There are those who maintain that however plausible an evolutionary hypothesis might seem, it does not stem from any scientific character of the theory, but rather from the religious-philosophical assumptions employed in such a theory as the matrix for the organization of a great deal of disparate phenomena. Similarly, there are those who maintain the difficulty, indeed the impossibility of separating "creation science" as a scientific hypothesis from the dogma of creation, a truth whose certainty is on revealed grounds beyond doubt and not to be confused with the merely hypothetical. The church cannot agree that a revealed truth may be taught on the same footing as a hypothesis which in fact is false, for such in fact would amount to a tacit acceptance of religious indifferentism. It may well be that the only workable solution is to eliminate the treatment of origins from a "neutral" school, since once the subject is introduced, it may become difficult or impossible for a public school to remain neutral.

Such a solution naturally underscores one of the essential and irremediable failures of the "neutral" public school: to assume that a balanced and basic education is possible without assent to religious-salvific truth. The only alternative in such a setting is to say nothing at all about the subject of origins, for the subject of origins cannot be treated definitively in a merely secular fashion. Yet no man can form a genuine philosophy of life without resolving such questions which are raised by the subject of origins.

Creation Science

Finally, if the teaching of the church, taken as a whole and examined throughout its history, indicates a native sympathy for the creation science approach, this sympathy is not the equivalent of a doctrinal canonization of creation science in its particulars. Creation science is not so much a "scientific" theory or demonstration as a set of assumptions forming a matrix and model for approaching certain primary questions of science, particularly where these tend to touch questions of origins. Once the matrix or model is accepted, then a great many other pieces of information can be organized coherently. But this coherence is hardly to be taken as a demonstration of creation, a truth by definition neither observable nor verifiable as the scientific method postulates.

But even if the creation science matrix or model is not scientifically demonstrable, neither can creation science be disproven scientifically, any more than evolutionary "science" can be verified scientifically. When science reaches the question of origins, then it must look elsewhere for the key to solutions, for the same reason that it must look outside itself for the theoretical justification of its first principles. Therein is recognized one of the recurring themes of Catholic tradition. Any human intellectual endeavor arrogating to itself absolute autonomy merits the Pauline epitaph: *falsi nominis scientiae,* and in fact is not science, but false religion decked out in the garb of intellectual respectability. Creation science surely looks to God and his revelation for the key. No form of "evolution science" has been shown to do the same; in the history of the church most theories of evolution have quite openly declared the contrary.

In dealing with the problems occasioned by the rise of evolutionism one need is to unmask false religions—usually pantheistic—disguised as "scientific" theory or "fact" beyond question. Another need is to indicate how sound science points to the truth about origins revealed by God in order to further our salvation, viz., the dogma of creation and the work of the six days, particularly the formation of Adam and Eve. On both counts creation science can be a very beneficial instrument, to be employed in all schools, both parochial and public (neutral), that have the true welfare of the child at heart.

2

Trojan Horses in the City of God

Evolutionism and Creationism as Explanations
of or as Sufficient Reason for the Origin of the
Species *Versus* Marianization: Recapitulation
and the Law of Perfect Freedom[1]

By Way of Preface

SINCE THE PUBLICATION OF Darwin's classic on the descent or origin of
the higher bisexual organisms, above all man, from lower and less perfect examples of organic life via an evolutionary generative process, whose
starting point was the less perfect species and terminus the more perfect,
debate has raged among all Christians, Catholics included, about the
compatibility, not of Darwin's evolutionary hypothesis, but of the generic
concept lending that idea however incorrectly formulated by him a certain
plausibility, indeed a certain affinity with Catholic theology.

What is called evolutionism and historicism has been condemned by
the church. From this it does not follow that history has been condemned.
We may raise a parallel consideration in reference to claims, first articulated
in the English-speaking world by John Henry Newman on the publication
of Darwin's anti-Christian classic, that while atheistic evolutionism is false,
the concept of evolution is radically positive and imbedded in Christian
tradition and revelation itself. Traditionalism is bad; tradition is eminently
good and holy. Pietism is to be shunned; piety cultivated. So, too, with the

---

1. This essay was first composed in 2003. Abridged versions of it have circulated
privately. The full version of the essay appears here for the first time. This was a work
still in progress at the death of the author. Certain ideas and formulations were still
being worked out and integrated into the intended final form of the essay. Bracketed
comments in block quotation format represent Fehlner's "notes to self" about sections
of the text with which he was not fully satisfied. —Ed.

notion of evolution in connection with the origin of the species. This is clearly the view of the reigning pontiff [John Paul II].

In the view of those who agree with the pope that this is a logical development of the guidelines sketched by Pius XII in *Humani generis* concerning the theoretical possibility of some kind of moderate transformism or theistic evolution to explain the formation of the body of Adam (male and female before the separation of Eve) and therefore by analogy the progressive or evolutionary differentiation of all organic species (between breaks bridged by intervention of the Creator), *evolution* is to be distinguished from *evolutionism* precisely because the latter expressly or implicitly excludes (a) an initial formation of the world as a whole out of nothing or immediate creation without a positive *terminus a quo* preceding the world or *terminus ad quem*, hence a production without process; and (b) the immediate creation of each single spiritual creature.

Evolution, on the other hand, which affirms both points, is not necessarily incompatible with the first article of the creed. It may not have happened (at least the fact cannot be established presently), but the differentiation of the species as described in revelation does not exclude a process, in which a less perfect reproducing actively contributes to the first appearance of a higher organic type. The hypothetical possibility of this is clearly allowed by revelation on the mediate creation of the first man (highest organic type). Was this a process involving already existing organic matter? This depends on how virgin earth or slime of the earth is understood: as an initial stage of development or recapitulation, or the final state. Biblical symbolism (virgin earth as a figure of the Immaculate) could be taken to favor the latter and so point to a certain fittingness of progressive creation or theistic evolution as a pre-stage of introduction of the spiritual into the material and the subsequent elevation of the human to the supernatural order, as an aspect of the obediential potency of creation for final recapitulation in the man-God via the mediation of the Immaculate. Whence, a long-standing Catholic sympathy for the underlying validity of evolution as the temporal-historic character of finite being converging on the recapitulation of all things in Christ, or the fusion of divine and creaturely activity in the return of all things to the Father after the initial creation of the world and of finite spirits.

In order to validate this point it is necessary, according to John Paul II, to identify breaks in the development or evolution of the world where the factor of elevation from a lower order of being and operation (or sphere) to a higher, from non-living to living, from vegetative to animal, from animal or pre-historical to human and historical, from natural to supernatural-salvific, entails a "break," viz., a point at which the active cooperation of the creature cannot reach its term unless there be a unique intervention (miracle in the broad sense) of the Creator to transcend the limits of finite activity, but with which the action of a lower sphere can be integrated into a higher, even that of the divine Trinity.

Such a view one finds in ancient Christianity, where creation "before" the first day is understood as a kind of *seminarium*, where all the various types or species were present incipiently as the fundamental point of departure, rather than the individual immediate creation of all organic species according to a certain order determined solely by the Creator, without any intrinsic relation to the activities of pre-existing created agents. This may be regarded as a basis of the possibility of the cooperation of the creature with the Creator in the perfection of the world in view of its final end, a position neatly opposed to that of Protestants supporting the theory of special creation as the origin of the species.

It is further confirmed by the stress St. Bonaventure lays on the rhythms of the cooperation of mankind in the work of "re-creation" prefigured in the work of the six days as a part of a process or temporal continuum culminating in the formation of the first man. Because the formation (plasticization) of Adam as male and female requires a unique intervention of the Creator, it does not follow that the pre-existing subject from which Adam was formed was merely passive in the process. Nor does it follow that the creation and infusion of the soul into the body thus formed could not also be the supernatural force transforming this process of hominization into one of humanization after the formation, not of another species, but rather of a person. An analogous case is found in the developmental process preceding human conception, initially biological, a process terminating in a procreative action bringing into existence a person, a reality greater than a species.

In this essay I wish to consider aspects of the history of the controversy among Catholics and their reasons for favoring some form of theistic evolution as the correct interpretation of Genesis. These Catholics understood theistic evolution, not in terms of efficient or final causality as is so often the case with theories of progressive creation, and much less as a direct answer to scientific questions. They rather favored theistic evolution as a theological principle touching the ontic constitution of the finite as *per se* temporal and as the hermeneutical *a priori* for any kind of subsequent empirical study of the natural order or physics in the traditional sense.

In general, *evolution*, as a valid concept, is an aspect of what is best described as *exemplary* or *personal* causality, ultimately centering not only on the Creator, but on his most perfect creature, the Immaculate Virgin, and the fruit of her womb, the Man-God. Closely connected with this and key to the resolution of key objections is the correlation of the biblical account of the process of origin of the first Adam as male and female with the theory of archetypes. There are *male* and *female*, as point of contact between the metaphysical notion of species as fixed essence and the empirical approach to types as only relatively fixed within a progressively more developed spiral. In this context *evolution* must be seen as an *analogical concept* closely related to those of elevation and recapitulation.

> [Terminological considerations: species and essence; genus and species in logic and in biology; macro and micro taken metaphysically and phenomenologically, or absolutely and relatively; origin of species and spheres; multiplication of individuals and procreation of persons; species and family; reproduction as means to preserve species and temporal limits of species existing autonomously in individuals; species as common nature and as universal; hominization and humanization (before and after conception, before and after formation of Adam's body, goal of all progressive specification; incorporation of specific perfections into Adam; immortality of persons and family). Evolution metaphysically as a condition of finite existence in the already, but not yet; evolutionary theory and special creation as misapplications of creation and evolution to limited questions; need to define evolution like creation independently of limited hypotheses in science or historical reconstructions.]

Autobiographical

When the author of these reflections began his systematic philosophical and theological study of the question of origins (the doctrine of creation) he came to be convinced of the correctness of the Scotistic line. Three basic points of this approach are central to the question of origins:

- In philosophy the radical possibility of demonstrating a Creator God (were it not for the fact of original sin, which makes the notion of a purely creative production *ex nihilo* difficult to grasp clearly), but not of demonstrating a creation in the beginning of time.

- In theology the importance of the distinction between the origin of the world as such (solely by creation) and the origin of organic species, or differentiation of kind rather than singulars within time, both before and after sin: by formation out of preexisting matter, in act, even if only minimally in the first moment, rather than purely potential, illustrated above all in the final, crowning work of the six days, the creation of Adam (and Eve), not *ex nihilo*, but out of a pre-existent and as proto-type of the "re-creation."

- In cosmology the importance of the seminal reasons (*rationes seminales*) of all organic species present from the first moment in the primordial matter, the enduring constant linking all parts of the visible creation from which derived the distinct species, to be correlated with the eternal reasons (*rationes seu ideae aeternae in arte aeterna Creatoris*), premises not unrelated to human artistry or poesis centering on inscape and instress (Hopkins), but in the Creator in the order of instress-inscape.

In the wake of *Humani Generis* he took up a defense of the tradition of the church. This defense held that on the question of the *origin* of the world one must reject *any* evolutionary thesis, e.g., Bergson-Teilhard. This is the case whether an evolutionary thesis was understood as an explanation of the "how" of the creative act, or as the *a priori* of any creative act. Both were seen as incompatible with the first article of the creed, because each was simply a form of pantheism. It is in this sense that his articles in criticism of Teilhard must be read.[2] On the question of whether *scientific hypotheses* of evolution, or the term "evolutionary" used to describe philosophically the characteristic of the first moment of time recurring in all successive moments are thereby rendered *per se* invalid, merely because their first popularizers were pantheists or atheists, the author took no final stand then, nor does he now.

The late Henri de Lubac always maintained that scientific hypotheses of evolution were not *a priori* invalidated simply because early promoters were heterodox in their theology or mistaken in their metaphysics. This realization poses a great difficulty for special creationists. For the theories of the special creations to be fully convincing, they must show that their understanding of special creation is in fact the case theologically. This is exactly what their appeal to the fathers and great scholastics fails to demonstrate. The falsity of any given theory called "theistic evolution" or moderate transformism does not *eo ipso* validate "special creation." For, as any careful study of the problem will reveal, these tags, on one side or the other, have no absolutely fixed connotation in relation to what they purport to explain. Thus, there is a considerable number of Catholic creationists, who, like their Protestant counterparts show a certain proclivity for methods reeking of the old Calvinism. With this affinity there is found a concomitant narrow-mindedness traditionally associated with this mindset as repulsive as the ideology more often than not accompanying various versions of theistic evolution.

2. Fehlner, "Teilhard," *CE* 7, appendix 1; Francoeur and Fehlner, "Exchange," *CE* 7, appendices 2 and 3.

Thus, regarding the question of the origin of the species, the author has believed that several distinctions are in order. First, scientific hypotheses of macroevolution qua scientific are not the direct interest of the church. Second, since these hypotheses are attempting to pronounce on processes which no longer occur, they can never be conclusive, one way or another. Third, even if *irrelevant* to current processes of change, they cannot thereby be shown *not* to have occurred in the past. Or, fourth, if relevant, that does *not* prove them to be the explanation of what occurred in the first differentiation of the species, a fact of history. Hence, the author insisted, a fifth distinction, on the theological (history of what the Creator did) and on the philosophical (study of the intrinsic or metaphysical possibility of what was done) study of origin of the species as enjoying a certain priority over the scientific.

Until about 1980, along with most Catholics, he leaned in favor of some form of moderate transformism, or theistic evolution, or progressive creationism as the basis of an explanation. This was not a purely natural transformism, but one specially endowed with supernatural powers by the Creator. Such seemed to better account for the graduated teleology to be noted in the teaching of revelation on time and history as well as modern and scholastic insights into development.

On becoming interested in the creationist movement, and its Catholic supporters, he sought to do justice to the weaknesses of theistic evolution in dealing with the supernatural element any Catholic version required. It was apparent that the latter element left the special creationism void of *any* really evolutionary dimension. Nonetheless, it also became apparent after a number of years that the special creationists who rejected any form of evolutionary theory to account for the origin of the species, tended to render the notion of the formation of Adam from the virgin earth meaningless and to approximate the Protestant-Calvinistic notion of *Creator solus* as absolutely the only agent actively involved in the subsequent re-creation and salvation of man.

This impasse led to his conviction that the entire problematic had to be rethought and an approach to a resolution formulated anew, both conceptually and linguistically independent of the present alternatives. The essay which follows strives to make clear the reasons for his diffidence with respect to *both* these alternatives (theistic evolutionism and special creationism) and how he believes a *tertium quid* can be elaborated.

The Problem of the Problematic.

The extended reflection of the debate in course for over a century among Catholics on the origin of the species between the supporters of theistic evolution and the supporters of special creation has been occasioned by the author's frustration in dialogue with both groups in explaining how his own approach, despite grounds of sympathy with major concerns of each, does not coincide with either. He has found supporters of theistic evolution as seemingly viewing their account of origins as the fundamental *a priori* for the study of the origins of the economy of salvation. This position is now held by the vast majority of theologians, including it seems John Paul II. Those on the other side of the debate view special creation as the only possible orthodox approach to the problem of the origin of the species in particular the human. In numbers they make up a small minority. Yet, they are extremely vocal and often censorious of their opposition, even of the Holy Father, as not orthodox.

In so far as the theological-philosophical-spiritual (ethical) concern of the special creationists is extremely important, while not agreeing with them on certain key issues, the author of this essay supported their critique of theistic evolution on the priority of the divine at the level of metaphysics. In some way all thought and action must begin absolutely with the divine, with the origin of the created absolutely (beginning or first moment "in time") in an exclusively divine creative act (efficiently) and a non-existent subject (nothing rather than matter) ordered to an end chosen by the Creator (source of significance and intelligibility of the contingent or non-necessary).

On the other hand, the author has found almost complete incomprehension by the special creationists of the metaphysical problems entailed in defining what is meant by a first moment or originating moment. This first is something radically new as opposed to nothing[3] or *nunc permanens*, yet it is also the first moment or *nunc fluens* of a series.[4] The temporal character (univocal in the first instance) basic to the duration of the material and organic and human spheres of existence is radically conditioned by this dynamic, immanent fluidity. This is distinct from the aeveternity characteristic of the duration of immaterial or spiritual creatures. The succession or continuity in angelic duration is better represented as discrete.[5]

3. Essential or vertical order between Creator and created.

4. Accidental, horizontal, linear order between moments in a continuum, real as well as notional.

5. A purely mathematical abstraction, connoting nothing directly in the real world outside the mind, a tool for critiquing or understanding what is extramental.

Succession and an Absolutely First Moment

Whence arises a primary problem, whose sufficient resolution is a prime goal of any study of the origin of the species. This problem concerns, as it were, the successive moments of the temporal duration, recapitulating the character of the absolutely first moment as something new in contrast to what preceded (new kind), yet not entirely new like the first moment (whose locus is nothing-the non-existent). This problem arises because duration's locus is something real, a moving continuum or time.[6] The modern concept of motion, beginning with the generation of Scotus and especially with Scotus, favors, indeed supports, the validity of the distinction between macro- and micro- graduated change, fundamental to all evolutionary theory, theistic as well as atheistic.

Non-Creation *A Priori* of Special Creationists

The second mode of change, microevolution, deals only with generation and corruption within a spatio-temporal context limited by a pre-determined and fixed type or species.[7]

Theories of special creation hold microevolution to set the limits of any real, developmental or graduated change for better (generation) or worse (corruption) after the initial creation, short of an exclusively creative re-intervention of the Creator accounting for the appearance of new and higher species, as well as spiritual creatures, such as angels and human souls. Its cosmological premise or *a priori* is the notion of motion conceived in terms of Aristotelian hylomorphism, in which all movement is essentially passive, dependent on the impulse of an already moving agent from without. This impulse is ultimately explained by a first "unmoved mover," whose immobility, not whose thought or love, is the source of all motion different from pure act (uncaused efficient cause). *Omne motum ab alio movetur*, is the Latin axiom summarizing this point of view of physics,[8] a theory which encases and relativizes the artificial and mechanical based on free choice or liberty of an *agens intelligens* within the limits of a radically stable natural order.

---

6. To give it its formal name as one of the two conditions under which it is perceived: spatial as a single substratum, temporal as a dynamic continuum.

7. Nature-*physis*, principle of operation.

8. According to Aristotle, the study of nature or motion.

Thomas and Scotus on Physics, Natural Theology
and the Ontological Proof

St. Thomas does not reject a physics or science of the natural order based on hylomorphism. However, he adapts the concept of unmoved mover so that as first cause *initiating* temporal duration, it no longer is an unknowing, unloving, impersonal it, but a personal Creator whose creative act is not a natural process, but as the church teaches a contingent, free, gratuitous personal choice owed to no one. But, importantly, the Angelic Doctor did *not* modify the notion of *subsequent* development or the graduated, temporal continuum (duration as time in the strict sense) as an accident of fixed types whose fixity is independent of development or appearance in a graduated series. Thus, Aristotle does not allow for what is called macroevolution, where stability of kind is *relativized by place in* a moving continuum and is *affected by activity from within* the continuum: its own and that of other species.

Scotus critiques this understanding. He held that the physics of Aristotle cannot easily be reconciled with the Christian notion of a Creator God. This approach to physics (in the Aristotelian sense) prioritized proofs for God's existence on the principle of cause and effect interpreted hylomorphically as valid apart from the ideal order. Scotus believed this prescinding from the ideal order leaves the proofs radically inconclusive. Phenomenologically speaking along Scotistic lines, in terms of intuitive cognition of the singular, the axiom should run thus: *non omne motum ab alio movetur.* This formulation contrary to Aristotelian physics affirms that not only God, but also created intellectual agents are an autonomous source of motion from within, not as physically pre-moved by another. Without the so-called ontological proof of God's existence from the idea of God, it is not possible to demonstrate the existence of a transcendent, Creator-personal God, in no way necessitated by the nature of things, even as abstract principles of created being, absolutely free and independent. Now it is this proof—rejected by St. Thomas as an illicit *transitus* from purely mental existence to the affirmation of extramental reality—which, at least indirectly, renders the concept of macroevolution plausible[9] when it is combined with the modern notion of motion as linear rather than circular, as active from within even prime matter, as a dynamic impulse, radically contingent, rather than a passive reaction to a predetermined impulse from without.

In a word, the Scotistic distinction between an *accidentally ordered series* and an *essentially ordered series* is highly relevant to the discussion

---

9. Even if it does not prove this to have occurred historically.

of the theoretical possibility of some kind of macroevolution, even if in fact none such ever occurred. An accidentally ordered series indicates a series whose formal notion does not immediately exclude the hypothetical possibility of an indeterminate regression *a parte ante*. In an essentially ordered series no such regression is possible. On the contrary, the very intelligibility of an essentially ordered series postulates a first *effectivum* without antecedent, on whom all other agents are secondary and dependent for their existence and operation. This serves also as the explanation of the Anselmian proof for the existence of a Creator. The limits of divine omnipotence cannot be positively stated by the finite mind, except to say that anything contradictory is impossible. This because a contradiction is simply nothing, and because, as infinite being, God cannot sin, cannot suffer and cannot act in any manner requiring corporeity.

Now, the Scotistic critique of Aristotelian-Thomistic physics does not immediately make Scotus a promoter of theistic evolution as an explanation of the origin of the species, nor does this critique immediately make apparent its importance as a question of theology and metaphysics, rather than of science, in which *per se* the church has no direct interest. However, if the modern notion of motion-movement is accepted (and no serious scientist would reject it), and, if the further prioritizing of the ontological argument in "natural theology" or better as the conclusion of metaphysics points up the centrality of the "critical question" as the *de facto* psychological and historical starting point of all reflection seeking the last or sufficient reason, speculative and practical, then it becomes clear why the problem of origin of the species is a test of the validity of any natural theology. This holds for all things existing—their origin and end—above all the human. The ontological argument, and its implications for origins, physics, and natural theology, takes on ever greater importance because the vast majority of theologians and Catholic philosophers in some way admit the validity of Kant's point concerning the "critical question."[10]

Scotus admits the validity of the ontological proof as a conclusion to the study, not of the physical possibility of what is actually functioning, but of metaphysical possibility centered on the principle of contradiction, identity, and sufficient reason. That study of the idea of univocal being provides direct access to the extramental that is essentially valid apart from any psychological-historical-social reference to the sensible and conceptual items occasioning it. Kant denies the validity of the proof and therefore of what Kantians call "onto-theology," precisely because it has no such

---

10. This includes even Thomists, like Gilson, who deny its epistemological conclusiveness.

real reference to the extramental apart from the sense data provoking it. For Kant, metaphysics is merely a study of the first idea (being) as a radical category or mental instrument permitting the possibility of discerning and/or organizing the content of science. Thus, for Kant, metaphysics is merely an instrument of hermeneutics.

Experience, Being, and the Evolutionary Context

Both the affirmation (Scotus) and the denial (Kant) of the ontological argument confirm in common that (1) our first notion of the existent (extramental) is intimately linked to a primary experience of consciousness as real (subjective, practical, free) and (2) objective (notional, determined, developing, both mentally and extramentally). Our knowledge of the act of existing and of the interrelation between its components in the real world (cause and effect within a graduated order) cannot be separated from the act of thinking, consciousness, and of freely acting (spontaneity-autonomy: Scotus; Newman; Hopkins) of which it is the reflection. Such an experience, even if not the immediate explanation of its origin and end,[11] cannot be understood except in terms, by definition, of an "evolutionary" or developmental context serving as the substratum (dynamically and symbolically) of higher forms of finite being. This especially includes the human person, whose being and history, for better or worse, is conditioned and reflected, even if not determined, by and in the temporal thrust of nature. Nature itself, in turn, is moving, or, better, spiraling under the direction of mankind in obedience to divine law, either to an ever more perfectly organized whole, or in disobedience to that divine law toward an ever more disorganized activity and eventual exhaustion.

What is meant here is not any particular scientific hypothesis of macroevolution,[12] whether true or false scientifically, whether supported by or contradicted by the laws of thermo-dynamics. Rather I have in mind that *a priori* premise of all reflection on time which permits an affirmation of the contingent and radically changing character of all nature (Bonaventure) and so the relatively and not absolutely stable character of any species, and the absolute liberty of the Creator to determine what is absolutely contradictory and only relatively so in relation to his always ordered (wise,

11. This is the temporal continuum in which this singular and personal experience is situated.

12. As bearing on the present state of time, or on any part of a given hypothesis, hypotheses of macroevolution may all be nothing more than mere possibilities.

befitting) exercise of his absolute power (omnipotence) in view of an end sovereignly selected by him (Scotus).

Without the hypothetical possibility of macroevolution understood as the emergence of distinct species from the activity of secondary causes, rather than merely variations on an already existent species or microevolution, it is impossible to maintain the following two points bound up with a Catholic affirmation of the first article of the creed. First, the central importance of the critical question. Second, the sovereign liberty of God, viz., the priority of defining grace in God before determining its relation to the natural order (concept of pure nature) rather than beginning with a concept of nature defined prior to grace. It is simply not true that the incompatibility of evolutionism with the doctrine of an initial creation *ex nihilo* renders every form of theistic evolution also incompatible with faith, unless one can show that the metaphysics of Scotus is contrary to faith.

Nonetheless, the term and concept of evolution as it presently is used in the phrase "theistic evolution" remains a radically flawed one, despite the undoubtedly valid insights it attempts to formulate. *Evolution* is open to interpretations in a pantheistic or ontologistic direction, as can be seen in some of its most popular forms, e.g., Bergson-Teilhard, Blondel-De Lubac. Even where allowance is made for the supernatural element indispensable for a Catholic version of the physical efficiency involved in accounting for the self-transformation of a lesser species into a higher, the supernatural seems either to be a *Deus ex machina*, or the entire process is not genuine evolution. Whence the need of a total reworking of the problematic and formulation of a third type of explanation, one taking account of the positive points of the other two theses, but avoiding their drawbacks.

> [Insert summary definition of problematic, pinpointing central issue: how exemplary metaphysics provides realistic *a priori* for empirical study of pre-history of progress since Adam to Christ, but not answers to scientific explanations of process: from immutability of species in mind of God to species subject to mutation in coming to be during *Hexaemeron*. The significance of plurality of forms, of a lower species being recapitulated as part of a higher. This is not merely passive material causality, it is a form of active exemplary causality, even when efficient cause is Creator alone, therefore a figurative, dynamic anticipation of the principle of cooperation of secondary causes with Creator-Savior in return, or evolution properly so called. Or again: theological interest in evolution bears not on science, but on the possibility of natural passing actively into supernatural.]

With these considerations as a backdrop let us see whether some sense can be made of the history of the debate so as to understand why the question of the origin of the species:

a. is theologically relevant; and

b. cannot be resolved unilaterally either in terms of special creationism because it tends to negate the basis for any kind of creaturely cooperation in the "re-creation" or return of all things to God, or in terms of theological evolutionism, because it does not account for the supernatural element in the process, and

c. is best resolved conceptually and linguistically in terms of the universal mediation of Our Lady, the Immaculate Conception.

This third alternative permitting a resolution of the apparent dilemma, either special creationism or theistic evolution, rests on the concept of *personal*, or *dynamic exemplary causality* behind the mediation of Jesus and Mary rather than on the preoccupation of both atheistic evolutionists and special creationists with physical causality, and the theistic evolutionists with final causality. Further, it is anchored not in an analysis of the accidental series, but in the divine counsels and the eternal predestination of Jesus and Mary as the basis for the possibility of the contingent, fully revealed not in the beginning (the already) or to be awaited in the future (the not yet), but as the absolute end in the middle of time, against which both already and not yet can be assessed.

Introduction

The First Article of the Creed and False Alternatives

At the time of the publication of Darwin's studies on evolution and the descent of the species, up until little more than a century ago, creation and evolution were regarded almost universally by Catholics and non-Catholics alike as mutually exclusive.[13] Belief in creation as traditionally set forth and explained in the Catholic creed *eo ipso* precluded:

1. an eternal world,

13. The initial and spontaneous perception of such opposition is reflected in the remark attributed to Coleridge on the first appearance of theories eventually entitled evolution of the species: "the theology of the orangutan as father of the human race, in substitution for the first chapter of Genesis." That this perception is not merely the fruit of ignorance is reflected in the exhortation of Pius XII to use great prudence in the study and discussion of evolutionary theory.

2. an origin of spiritual creatures (angels and human souls) by other than creation *ex nihilo*, and

3. an explanation of the differentiation and graduation of organic species in terms of merely natural processes.

The third point St. Thomas and St. Bonaventure discuss under the headings of origin, structure, and ornament of the world in the exclusively divine work of six days: the *Hexaemeron*.[14]

Both sides of the controversy assumed that an acceptance of the scientific hypothesis of evolution, as an explanation of the origin of the species, was also a demonstration that the origin of the spiritual and indeed of the entire world *could* be explained apart from the existence of a Creator God. Hence, the acceptance of evolution was taken as an affirmation that the above three points could be explained in terms of exclusively natural processes within the world. For both sides, then, acceptance of evolution postulated an explanation of all things, including the spiritual, in terms of an evolution from preexistent, quasi-eternal, ever-active matter. Seen this way, evolution was taken to necessarily exclude belief in the first article of the creed as the starting point of our theology. Such assumptions seemed necessarily to entail a pantheistic and/or atheistic mind-set in so far as it includes any attempt to account for the religious. Regardless of whether evolution touches upon the origin of the world, evolution does have deleterious consequences for our understanding of divine transcendence and the mystery of the Trinity. When this account touches upon the origin of Adam and Eve, it has particularly disastrous consequences for traditional Christology, soteriology and moral theology.

Some think the initial opposition to evolution on the part of Catholics in the nineteenth century was but an exaggerated reaction to the theories of Darwin. Opposition, so it is said, betrayed a lack of understanding of modern science, another version of the "Galileo case." Opposition to the theories of Darwin were taken to have stemmed from a failure to appreciate

---

14. The views of St. Thomas can be found in *ST* I, q. 91; and St. Bonaventure, *II Sent.* dd. 12–18, *Brev.* p. 2, and his *Hex.* It is false to assert, as does Galleni, "Evoluzione," 1:579, that with the exception of St. Augustine the Fathers and great scholastics were mostly interested in "reconciling the biblical Creator with the platonic demiurge rather than assessing the historical character of revelation and the importance of the history of creation for its own sake." That last is exactly what they, in fact, do, St. Bonaventure being an outstanding example, on a very sound metaphysical basis, and that is why their views about what actually happened, not what might or might not have happened, have normative value for understanding "origins," especially human. Their views do not become irrelevant, merely because they had never studied or commented upon a scientific hypothesis called evolution of the species.

the weaknesses and radically non-Catholic character of the Protestant "special creation" as the only alternative to the atheistic evolution of Darwin and his immediate disciples and supporters.

In reality not all Catholics who were opposed to atheistic evolution subscribed to the special creation hypothesis. Special creationism was first proposed in such terms by early (seventeenth century) Calvinist theologians and apologists. Special creation of this sort claimed that (virtually) every species or kind was immediately created by God out of nothing in a manner similar to the creation of Adam and Eve. This part of the theory is clearly contrary to Catholic doctrine on the formation of Adam and Eve out of preexistent matter, in the first case inorganic[15] and in the second case out of organic matter.[16] Special creation, as an alternative to evolution, both then and now, lends itself to a radical denial of created cooperation with the Creator in a procreative way, especially in the order of salvation, of a radical denial of Marian mediation based on the Immaculate Conception, and the real presence in the Eucharist, as well as sacramental efficacy *ex opere operato*.

Neither Special Creationism nor Evolutionism: A Third Way

Catholic creationists are not immune from such tendencies. While for some years I gave limited support to this theory after dropping an earlier support for theistic evolution, I intend with this study a) to reject that theory entirely and b) rework the theory of theistic evolution. I intend to argue for the radical coincidence of creation and evolution in conformity with the thought of John Paul II: one way in the created because in another way *eminenter* in the creative act of God according to the *signa voluntatis divinae*. This is the only basis for any possible supernatural order where the created can enter into the divine Trinitarian realm.

I will claim that in the primary sense this is manifested in Mary Immaculate via the order of the hypostatic union and in all others through her mediation. It is in theory and practice the reality of the Immaculate Conception, in God and in the Mother of God which explains how the creative makes possible the evolutionary and renders the evolutionary creative: the mediation of the Spirit and of the Virgin Mother. It is this term: Marian mediation based on the Immaculate Conception that I wish to introduce as accounting

---

15. Or possibly organic and so possibly active as secondary instrumental cause in the formation.

16. Passive, in sleep.

for the valid insights in each of the two other alternatives, while avoiding their weak points both notionally and linguistically.[17]

In order to make clear the fundamental differences of this third approach to the origin of the species from that of special creationism (although it is in fact a form of creationism), and from that of theistic evolution, despite its sharing some elements of the current formulation of the problematic and certain concerns of theistic evolutionists bearing on the starting point for any discussion of continuous creation (as outlined by John Paul II), yet with significant differences centering on the Kolbean insight into the mystery of the Immaculate Conception in the Spirit and in Mary, I shall call this more exactly not another version of theistic evolution, but an aspect of Marian mediation.

In this reworking of the problematic, origins are explained dynamically and so notionally as *progressive creation toward an end*, where the prime agency is the will which wills such an end to be and so is the source of all physical or efficient causality at each level (species or kind) of finalization. This, in effect, affirms with Scotus a relative, not absolute fixity in the created essence, whether in the mind, or in the extramental as common nature, providing grounds for introducing the concept of *macro*, as well as *micro* evolution in both orders. Change is not merely movement within a fixed, single species, invariable even by divine command, but it is also movement within the species, considered ever more perfect, to the degree it undergoes recapitulation within a higher form, a change in species, yet without loss of continuity, both in the order of reality and of thought. Change from the first moment of the created world is not merely motion within predetermined limits, nor mere casual succession without immanent teleological meaning and direction. Change includes also the progressive transformation of species as well as individuals via transfinalization and transignification based on an ordered efficiency located in will and person rather than in the physical, in the voluntary-spiritual rather than in the intellectual-natural. Change as the basis of time is not merely an accident of fixed natures exempt from any change in themselves, nor a mere succession independent of creative direction in the strict sense, both by secondary agents as well as the primary agent of movement towards a new term. It is the *a priori* of finite being and operation. Change, then, before it can be micro-development, is radically macro-development, or evolution in the proper sense, in one form or another, at every higher level of organization of the world. This hierarchical and hierarchizing order includes the recapitulations of the inorganic, organic, cultural,

---

17. In particular, the ambiguities entailed by current usage of *evolution* and of *special creation*.

religious, until it reaches the final term: the incarnation first and then the consummation of the kingdom-church. Such a concept of the temporal character of all finite existence and all spiritual activity understands there is both an "already" and a "transformation." The *already* is the principle of continuity-relative stability. The *transformation*, corresponding to the "not yet," refers to the graduated or ordered progressive recapitulation toward a higher mode of being and acting, based on a multiplicity of forms in finite species. According to such great theologians as Bonaventure and John Duns Scotus, we may indeed know the common essence (species) in each singular, making that singular what it is essentially (though not single, contra Ockham), but not absolutely *pro statu isto* (against the strict creationists).

The reason for this choice is not at all any concern to resolve purely scientific disputes over the question of the origin of specific differentiation, whether by a non-temporal act, or by a process involving dynamic, graduated succession. The reason, instead, is about the need for acknowledging that the roots of all efficient productivity at any level is found in the personal-dynamic final causality primary to all physical or efficient causality. This is first at the level of a strictly divine creative act,[18] and then in secondary causality at the level both of the image (personal agency in proper sense) and of the sub-personal (at level of vestige). The evolutionary-historical conditioning at each level constitutes the essentially precious character in the idea of creative evolution, so much misrepresented outside a fully Marianized context.

Immaculate Conception and Creative Evolution

This approach is adumbrated by St. Maximilian Kolbe in the famous final passage of his writings where he defines Mary, the Spouse of the Holy Spirit, as created Immaculate Conception and the Spirit uncreated Immaculate Conception. In this relationship between the uncreated and created Immaculate Conception, all the love of the Trinity (origin of all primary activity) meets all the love of creation (origin of all secondary activity), the vertex of love, divine and human, perfectly penetrating each other, without any confusion of persons or natures (principles of operations) yet so transubstantiating the being and operation of this singular creature as to be one activity, wholly spiritual. Mary, therefore, is made the unique icon of the Holy Spirit because she not only is conceived immaculately, but is the Immaculate Conception. This vertex of love underlies Kolbe's preoccupation

---

18. The origin of the ideas in God: primarily intellectual or voluntary, and if the latter, arbitrary non-rational (Thomas), or reasonable-ordered by fact of being willed (Scotus).

with the law of action-reaction as, not merely a law of science,[19] but as it undergirds his concept of development both in the cultural and in the spiritual orders, where true development in each represents higher states of the same substratum as specifically different.

This is why the creativity of the Spirit Creator terminates not at evolution in *originating* the world. However, in the Spirit's continuing work of creating and acting within creation, there is an evolutionary character, better termed *mediation*. This is also why activity *within* the world, because it is tied to the mediation of the Immaculate, *is* evolutionary. In one way or another, the mediation of the Immaculate conditions the entirety of creation, from its first origin, to successive origins of more perfect beings or states of being (spheres), wherever there is anything material or spiritually potential (Angelic) that constitutes a factor of continuity. This junction or vertex, at once *creative* and *created*, underlies the term *procreation* which in its absolutely final action terminates by the joint action of uncreated and created Immaculate Conception of the incarnation, viz., the total transignification and transfinalization of the flesh in divinizing it. The *mediation* here can rightly be described as *theistic* or *progressive evolution*, where the created agent's agency terminates in the Creator: Mary procreates God. It is *here* that the *valid core* of evolution as bearing on a being essentially greater than the effective agent is found. Mary truly is Mother of God in the proper sense, and her procreativity may be described as mediatory rather than evolutionary. All other forms of development more or less reflect and anticipate the vertex of creation from the divine and from the created point of view.

Addressing the Oversimplification of the History of the Controversy

The oversimplification of the history of the controversy in terms of a dilemma, then, is a caricature of the facts. The almost universal Catholic opposition to the theories of Darwin, whatever the linguistic excesses of a few over-zealous polemicists may have been, arose from a perception that the views of Darwin on evolution were not legitimate science nor added up to a legitimate scientific hypothesis. Critics in common saw three major problems with Darwin:

19. Radically evolutionary in its implications as the *a priori* of scientific understanding.

1. They accused Darwin's ideas of being a pseudo-scientific version of the evolutionary pantheism of Hegel (and many other proponents of materialistic ideologies in the century of materialism).

2. They took these ideas as entailing a denial of points of fact included in the revelation of how the world we know originated, including the direct formation and graduation of the species by the Creator, the special formation of Adam and that of Eve from Adam as a single couple, the fall, the punishment, the universal flood.

3. They understood Darwin and his proponents to be ascribing a purely mythical character to the creation account in Genesis, to the exclusion of any historical veracity.

This is perfectly clear from the decrees and canons of the First Vatican Council (1869–70) on creation and the early decrees of the Pontifical Biblical Commission, and from the encyclical of Pius XII, *Humani Generis* (1950) in which he permits within well defined limits the discussion of the possibility of a genuine scientific hypothesis of an evolutionary formation of the body of Adam (not Eve) and how it might be reconciled with the revealed accounts of the actual formation. Nonetheless this last permission would have been impossible, had that direct formation of the species man and implicitly all the other "kinds" (creative element) not out of nothing (except reductively to the initial origin of all), but out of preexisting matter, either inorganic or organic, conceived as radically active (as in the cosmology of Scotus), i.e., creative evolution of the higher species from their inclusion potentially in the *rationes seminales* of the identical substratum (the original matter so conceived) underlying each specific change in time. The permission of Pius XII, in effect serves to *correct* a *misreading of the problematic* in terms of a *simplistic dichotomy* between evolution or creation. Pius XII was pointing to the third possibility: not only their correct correlation, but their interpenetration in a truer definition of re-creation eventually emerging as procreation, in virginal form, touching God himself.

Bonaventure and the Medieval Roots
of the Formulation of the Problematic

The roots of this formulation of the problematic, though not expressly present till much later, are to be observed in medieval theology, as is clear from the commentaries of St. Bonaventure on the definitions of the Fourth Lateran Council (1215), especially in an earlier work, the *Itinerarium Mentis in Deum* and in his last work, the *Collationes in Hexaemeron*. The

Seraphic Doctor underscores the three crucial errors whose very nature is calculated to alienate from faith in Jesus Christ and membership in his church those adopting these errors:

1. the eternity of the world (viz., the world as self-explanatory);

2. the unicity of the agent intellect (viz., the deification of the human mind as one in all, or totalitarianism);

3. consequently the denial of personal freedom and of rewards and punishment in a future world.

In one word these are but the three key aspects of natural determinism so prominent a feature of intellectual systems accepting one or another form of atheistic evolution as a theory of origins.

But it is also clear from his insistence on the essentially historical character of the process of salvation and constitution of the economy of salvation once established by the salvific sacrifice of Jesus, that the continuation of creation in the work of the Spirit takes on a developmental or evolutionary character, that of graduated order entailing not merely action from above, but also from within, a kind of spiraling movement upward to the final point of "recapitulation."

Whence, the importance of the theory of seminal reasons, and of multiplicity of forms under the unity of a higher form in each more perfect species. This spiraling or hierarchizing is particularly evident in his explanation of the historical character of typology and prophecy. So too, in the *Itinerarium* he relates all the process of interiorization and elevation of chapters three through six to an earlier process of sensibilization reflecting both the unity and historicity of movement, extramental, but only formally existent as an intelligible and sensible one in the mind through a personal *dijudicatio*. He does not call this understanding of secondary action evolutionary, but it surely furnishes elements that are the basis of such a notion of time and history and religious life, and surely related to the prioritization of the critical problem, though without the conclusions of Kant.

Atheism or Occasionalism? Is Theistic Evolution the Third Option?

Is there only evolution (taken to be, by definition, atheistic) or special creation (occasionalist)? Or, is there a third option: Marian mediation of the Immaculate, viz., creative development of the created with the participation of the created means historically what creation *ex nihilo* means theologically in the eternal counsels?

Some will immediately say that any talk of a third option is a contradiction in terms metaphysically, scientifically is shown to be indemonstrable in fact (nature), and historically falsified by the testimony of Scripture. We may admit the plausibility of these points on the basis of what is called uncritical (non-scientific) perception of the natural (physis) as absolutely unchangeable in any state, and in terms of a *meta-physis*, or knowledge of the trans-physical as postulated by the primarily stable world order of Aristotle and a literal reading of Scripture concerning creation: of the world and of the species. The options are only two: evolutionism or special creationism.

Is this a genuine dilemma, or is there at least possible a third alternative, not the hybrid theistic evolution as this alternative is now sometimes presently and seemingly favored by the present pope, but Marian mediation? It should be noted that the church has condemned atheistic evolution, not evolution as such, as incompatible with the first article of the creed. Whether or not evolution as such is incompatible with belief in an omnipotent Creator who alone in any sense can create, or the notion of the Creator as exclusive to the uncreated or uncaused efficient cause, who alone can call out of nothing, can only be said to have been implicitly condemned (Lateran IV, Vatican I), if we maintain that Aristotelian concepts of science and metaphysics (and history) have been imposed as binding on all Catholics. There is no such imposition.

Aristotle, Kant, and Scotus: Evolution, Nature, and Science

Before the fourteenth century, at which time Catholics were generally permitted and encouraged to base their thinking on Aristotelian premises, the philosophy of Aristotle had been subjected for over a century to *monita* and even condemnations as false and dangerous to faith. Theistic evolution is contradictory in Aristotelian terms. It is not on Scotistic in terms, in the sense that, for Scotus as opposed to Aristotle, it is not a *fixed natural order*, but the *critical problem* that constitutes the point of departure, not only for science, but also for metaphysical reflection and theological belief. In so far as atheistic evolution appeals to Kant as the grounds for science, Kant becomes incompatible with faith. But the believer, e.g., the Catholic who calls himself a transcendental Thomist, can also appeal to Kant rather than Aristotle as grounds for a cosmology and cosmogony compatible with belief in the first article of faith, namely theistic evolution, just as the Averroistic appeal to Aristotle in favor of pantheism does not *per se* entail a condemnation of the Aristotelian point of departure in philosophy as grounds for a correct understanding of creation and the created. Contemporary special creationists who base their support for special creation of the species (and hence a "literal" reading of the six days) on the premises of Aristotelian naturalism explain the *ex nihilo* in the definition of creation, but fail to see that they do not account for the supremely volitive character of the creative act, whether in God or in its created term (*formaliter immanens, virtualiter transiens*) not natural but primarily free on both counts. Hence, the created before being nature is contingent, and thus with only a relative, not absolute intelligibility apart from the knowledge of the signs or reasons of the divine will rather than intellect (Scotus). In a word, these creationists fail to state fully why the starting point of the transcendental Thomists, postulating some form of theistic evolution, is *a priori* impossible, and, if impossible, how to account otherwise for what makes the theistic evolutionary approach seem plausible and attractive, philosophically speaking, even if not making any direct contribution to this or that scientific hypothesis.

This opens the door to a different reading of the data or content of science, not in terms of fixity, but of changeability, or "evolution." Such a reading is based on Kantian premises: that the noumenon or data of science can only be classified or understood as species and as beings by considering the real or extramental or extra-scientific object as singular, and the order among these as sequential, whereas the critical and discerning understanding of different species or beings as fixed classes and the critical interpretation of their temporal sequence (relativity) in terms of cause and effect is primarily notional and hypothetically true (subject to modification), rather than real and absolutely true (not subject to change and modification). The concept of evolution in itself is not a fact or a *datum*, but the *a priori* intellectual premise for any physics or science dealing with the extramental, a condition coloring any hypothesis. On these grounds the theistic evolutionist will also admit the distinction between macro and micro evolution, but unlike the creationist does not posit it absolutely or primarily in the extramental realm, but in the mental or notional or scientific, where it functions as an instrument for conceptualizing change in terms of cause and effect, where cause is understood to be the action or measurable movement of a singular or many singulars perceived as a prior phenomenon in relation to another perceived as following, to be verified or falsified always in terms of experiment or experience: following *propter* or only post. Extramental evolution is only micro, and is not natural but voluntary, the fruit of will, source of all real movement, hence never limited merely to the natural or specific as unchanging determinant of all micro evolution within the limits of a species. The present order of cause and effect tells us nothing about a possibly different earlier order, or what might be a future possible order where a present singular appears to have become a different species. Phenomena, which in the Aristotelian perspective appear to exclude any form of evolution in virtue of a realistic or physical interpretation of the key *a priori* of Aristotelian physics, viz., fixed species, within the Kantian appear to postulate some form of evolution to explain the appearances, even when mechanisms cannot be verified or falsified. Evolution, like ontology, gives no new knowledge, but is the indispensable context for understanding all data.

Person, Freedom, and Presence in the Creative Act

Further, while the creationist, like the atheist, argues in terms of efficient causality in dealing with the validity or non-validity of evolution as a concept, the theistic evolutionist replies to both by insisting that not efficient, but final causality, understood as personal, viz., finality determined not by nature or species, but by creative will[20] permits the construction of a concept which simultaneously asserts creation and evolution. A creative act is always a willed act. It is free and so contingent on choice, not necessity of nature as essence or species. Hence, essence is always present in the term of the creative will, but relative to the same voluntary determination, even as a divine idea. Where a creative act is fully will, as with the one omnipotent Creator, the term is fully *ex nihilo sui et subjecti*. In the primary sense of creation as an act of will, the term of creation is not a term as effect or sequence, as being or species or nature,[21] but as end. Creation *ex nihilo a parte rei* is an exercise of personal or exemplary influence—action as source of action, being as source of being—not in terms of efficient causality, but of final, therefore not in terms of nature, but of the voluntary or love: *volo ut sis*. Hence what any creature is as a kind is relative to what end is assigned creatures singly and collectively. Thus, the created *ex nihilo* effectively are the single existents being finalized, or evolving. In this sense created wills, acting scientifically or intelligently in respect to noumena critically perceived, can enjoy, not absolutely, but relatively, creative power in respect to the finalization of creation, which is progressive creation. In this way being and becoming can be simultaneous without contradiction within a univocal notion of creation as theistic.

---

20. In Hopkins' terms, *instress* rather than *inscape*.

21. These are valuable, but merely notional definitions of concepts after the fact and only relatively or hypothetically valid.

The implications of these considerations are far reaching. A metaphysics of the finite requires not only that evolution finalizing and so effecting be considered as the primary condition of finite being, whether macro or micro (understood as identical in singulars and in their essentially sequential order as world), it also requires that evolution as finalizing and effecting be understood as the very heart of being created each according to its kind and in relation to the others, and that the Creator himself in so creating chooses to be present to what he has created, viz., part of the process of creating as coming to be. Whence secular existence as distinct from divine, changeable existence as distinct from the unchanging, is by definition theistic evolution. And changeless being, once that being has chosen to create the essentially changeable or immanently developmental, himself enters the process in some paradoxical, antinomical, but not contradictory or impossible way, as every creative artist in some way *instresses* himself in his work without ceasing to be himself. This immanent presence is the inner dynamism of evolution, and so theistic, impossible to fully verify scientifically, but perfectly consistent with the meta-physical premises of all modern science and perfectly consistent with praxis understood primarily as finalizing will. Proof for the existence of a creator God rests not on the principle of cause and effect, never terminating at the notion of God as creator, but on the principle of sufficient reason. The data of science can only be explained sufficiently in terms of evolutionary finality, one reflecting evolution as a level more proximate to the Creator, that of moral experience in individuals,[22] and in terms of social relations between egos[23] and in terms of the relation of both singular and social to the Creator.[24]

Distinguishing "Evolutions": Magisterium, Metaphysics, and Revealed History

Historically, even at the time of the first publication of Darwin's work, some Catholic scholars, e.g., John Henry Newman, seemed open to the possibility of a different approach, at least for Catholics, one recognizing that the explanation of the work of the six days in Catholic tradition, both patristic and scholastic, did not coincide with the Protestant, or at least Calvinist theory of "special creation," viz., the creation of each species out of nothing in a time

22. E.g., psychological analysis of ego or personal experience of thought as proof of existence in relation to problems of guilt and super-ego.

23. The problem of hate and charity, eros and agape.

24. The problem of religion, of the natural and spiritual, of the literal and symbolic, in relation to the transcendent Other.

span of six twenty-four hour days, linked by nothing other than the creative
will of God, a kind of "scientific voluntarism-occasionalism" as opposed to
the "scientific nominalism" of atheistic evolution (denying any reality or at
least value to universals): pure Lutheran fideist literalism, versus pure ra-
tionalism-symbolism in exegesis. On the assumption that genuine scientific
grounds could be brought forth to support the validity of the "evolution" of
new and higher species of primates via the processes of reproduction and
growth of the less developed species, could not the possibility of such activity within the context of and limited to the context of the work of creation
accomplished during the "six days," whether literally or metaphorically (or
mythologically) such, be compatible with belief in the first article of the
creed? Whence a radically different approach: not creation or evolution, but
creation and evolution, viz., theistic evolution.

Obviously, the sticking point, as with special creation, would be a truly
evolutionary explanation of the origin of the human bodies of Adam and
Eve: not only evolutionary, but evolutionary in terms of certain theological knowledge of what actually did happen on the sixth day as the crowning touch of the entire work of creation. But the possibility of "Catholic
evolutionism" as a coherent hypothesis compatible with Catholic tradition,
indeed perhaps postulated by it, depends on the legitimacy of the separation
of the question of the origin of the species (including the bodies of Adam
and Eve) from the other two questions of origins: that of the spiritual in the
world and that of the world as a whole.

The initial declarations of the magisterium on evolutionary theory of
origins did not consider such a separation and envisioned evolution of the
species only in its atheistic form as entailing *eo ipso* a denial of the creation
of the world and of angels and souls.

Subsequently, from the pontificate of Pius XII, and especially during
the pontificate of John Paul II, the magisterium, without defining whether
"theistic evolution" is true because it happened, historically speaking,
nonetheless, has recognized the legitimacy of the disjunction of (a) the
question of the origin of the species from (b) those of the world and of the
spiritual, with the consequence that all forms of evolution, provided they
do not entail the denial of the origin of the world and of the spiritual in the
world by creation out of nothing, can be entertained by Catholics as a possible opinion compatible with Catholic belief. Indeed, it would seem that
over the past fifty years the vast, vast majority of theologians have come to
admit the possibility as more attractive than its contrary. And over the past
twenty-five years this possibility seems to be entering the general teaching (not only private opinion) of the pontifical magisterium and is at least
tolerated in the *Catechism of the Catholic Church*.

When we further consider the current favor shown Transcendental Thomism (St. Thomas based on Kant, not Aristotle) and the possibilities for attaining ecumenical union between Lutherans and Catholics via a dynamic equivalency, not formal equivalency, reading of each others dogmatic differences and apparently contradictory doctrinal formulae, based on mutual acceptance of Kantian premises, it becomes clear that the proponents of theistic evolution are correct in assuming theirs is not only a theory not condemned, or merely tolerated, but is one being positively encouraged as part of a general renewal of Catholic thought and a solution of the ecumenical problem as the primary practical objective in all apostolic efforts of the Catholic Church. If this is true, they are also correct in predicting the eventual rescinding of the early decrees of the Pontifical Biblical Commission seemingly contrary to theistic evolution as merely cautionary condemnations, not absolute (in this, similar to the magisterium's treatment of Aristotle), so permitting a purely allegorical interpretation of the Old Testament in favor of theistic evolution and against both atheistic evolution[25] and special creation.[26]

What Kind of Creationism?

Obviously, some version of creationism with respect to (a) the origin of the world and (b) of the spiritual within it is the *only* position open to Catholics. But what should be the position of Catholics regarding an alternative to theistic evolution of the species? And if this alternative is best described as creationist, is it identical with what in Protestant circles is known as "special creation" of each kind or type out of nothing? The latter has never been a part of Catholic tradition, whereas theistic evolutionists claim their theory can be defended as implicit in the Catholic tradition.[27]

25. In terms of efficient causality rather than final.

26. As excluding absolute liberty of the Creator as well as liberty of the creative creature, subordinating both to a prior truth of fixed essences and laws.

27. E.g., in St. Augustine's theory of seminal reasons, or in St. Bonaventure's criticism of the Thomistic notion of *intellectus agens* as a substitute for divine illumination, and of a natural order of species as substitute for the divine ideas; or in the Scotistic critique of being as analogical in favor of univocity and priority of the divine will as source of divine ideas; or in the insistence of Ockham on singulars only as existing extramentally, all positions never condemned by the church, and in one way or another capable of supporting a theory of theistic evolution as a possible understanding of the Creative act (voluntary, and as such determining to an end) and its term essentially in time, whether from eternity or with a beginning, because time is not an accident of finite being, but its essential measure as in flux toward a "not yet."

Catholic creationism as an expressly formulated alternative to theistic evolution is a very recent, mostly post-conciliar reaction to the relative success of theistic evolution in the wake of *Humani Generis* and the inability of scientific evolutionists to prove evolution of the species as a possibility, much less a fact of history. A reaction cannot be defined except in relation to the action to which it is a response, or to those "actions" between which it is located as the correct view. Hence, before further chronicling the history of Catholic evolutionism in view of which Catholic creationism is an alternative, both views competing for support as the "middle position" between extremes, a brief definition of terms and typology of middle positions between unacceptable extremes must be presented.

Terms and Typology of Mediating Positions

Terminology must first reach a certain level of clarity and consistency, without which no fruitful discussion between parties can occur. By *origin* of something *within* the world already existing and *out of* something already existing in the world is meant a beginning, before which something which previously did not exist in the real world (as distinct from the mental or noetic) began to exist as a result of a causal process changing something which previously existed into something else. This is contrasted with a strictly creative origin of the world *as a whole*, or of something in the world after it begins to exist *by God alone* as the active agent *out of nothing*, viz., where the productive action traverses an "infinite" distance between point of origin and term of the action, one therefore instantaneous rather than successive as in the case of formation. Creative origins always entail an absence of succession, viz., time; formative origins necessarily entail some type of succession, even if the Creator is the one forming, whence the basis of the active cooperation of creatures with the Creator, both in the natural and in the supernatural order. Protestantism generally denies the possibility; Catholicism generally affirms it. Whence misunderstanding of what the Catholic means by creation in the strict sense and formation: creative origins in the broad, and so in some true sense active creativity also out of nothing relatively, immanent to the creature, above all evident in the artistic experience.

Whence also the radical possibility of giving a genuinely proper sense to the complex term: creative evolution or progressive creation. Everything in the world was created by God, but not every subsistent being in the world takes its proximate origin from a strictly creative act out of nothing and with God alone as efficient cause. And since both experience and biblical revelation (the formation of the bodies of Adam and Eve) verify the truth of this distinction, indeed make its profession obligatory, one can reasonably speculate on the possibility that not only individuals, but in some way what are called species or types also came to be in some instances, not by direct creation, but by way of a natural, formative process with a *terminus a quo* and a *terminus ad quem* (whereas immediate creation *ex nihilo* has only a *terminus ad quem* and so is not a process or evolution), instrumentally, if not principally, cooperating with the Creator. Could this be called evolutionary, especially if the apparent fixity of the species or "common nature," verified in some ways by science, is also relative to change in the existent, viz., only fixed so long as no agent provokes a change in being, whether transubstantial or transformative (to use the Aristotelian language)?[28]

If so, theistic evolution could be a hypothetically consistent explanation for changes in the singular extramental noumena and so the subsequent observance of types which prior to the formative (not strictly, but broadly creative) action which brought them into existence were not perceived in the real, as distinct from the mental world. In this theory what is called species is primarily notional and corresponds directly to nothing in the world of singulars and their interaction. All that the church requires of Catholics supporting theistic evolution (and promoting it), then, is a recognition of:

a. the specific difference and real disjunction between spiritual and material[29];

b. that evolution is a theory, not a proven fact.[30]

Thus, before the fall and after, before the flood and after, before Moses and after, we observe both physical and moral orders, not totally artificial, but with the element of the voluntary prior to that of the natural. Here the

28. In order to understand the argument at this point, a helpful comparison of what's being argued here can be made to poetic experience as explained by Hopkins on the basis of Scotus: the poet's vision—*inscape*—is not identical with a notion of the essence perceived, and the *instress* in the poem composed gives that poem something more than a that of a mere replication of the nature on which it is based.

29. Each soul or ego must first be considered as an absolute singular as not subject to change as is the material, and only on this premise can theories of personality and social development validly be constructed. Thus, history as entailing change in personality and socio-moral order is not properly, but only by analogy of attribution evolutionary, not reflecting, but being the partial origin of theistic evolution after the formation of Adam and Eve.

30. This is the case even if as a theory evolution may be used to explain events which historically did not occur by way of theistic evolution (the beginning of time, and the existence of angels and souls) in terms of a universal temporal relativity underlying the order of the world, the basis of history and relative differentiation of both natural and personal history in periods or orders whose laws or principles of interaction among singulars differ and sometimes oppose one another.

Catholic evolutionist must distinguish between natural law in reference to the purely physical, subject to broad evolutionary change qua order, both on the part of the Creator and of the creature administrator (angels and men), from the natural law in reference to the moral order, whose changes are reserved to the Creator in view of the proximate stages and final consummation of creation (age of nature, of law, of grace, of glory) all different, but within bounds of continuity established by divine "fiat."

Evolution or development is not a synonym for change or transformation. The production of something initially out of nothing is not evolutionary because the element of succession is lacking between nothing and something. But neither is change or transformation (generation and corruption) in the inorganic world the equivalent of evolution or development. Change involving transient action only among non-living "types" is merely that: mechanical rather than organic. Multiplication of individuals, or change of form, whether these are explained in terms of Aristotelian hylomorphism or more modern theories of motion, is neither micro nor macro evolution: it is merely monotonous, circular repetition. At this level there is no real difference between organic and mechanical production.

Transient versus Immanent Action and Conceptions of Time

Properly speaking the problems involved in understanding the origin of the species cannot be grasped until the distinction between transient and immanent action is grasped. Development, or more narrowly evolution in terms of the origin of a typical or specific individual capable of immanent or vital activity, only occurs within that type or kind of being in the real world. Micro-evolution in the biological order (notionally) or better biosphere (realistically), admitted by all, connotes the multiplication of individuals within a pre-existent type and in virtue of a dynamic transient action (movement) from within a living individual of such species: therefore, not only acting because acted on, but also acting spontaneously, or at the level of corporal life organic activity as distinct from mechanical.

At the level of life transient action, or generation of another individual like unto the begetter, is first of all immanent and organic, either unisexually or bisexually. With this, mere change attains a formally temporal or sequential character, no longer merely sequential or repetitive, organic rather than mechanical, linear rather than circular. This means that efficient causality, more fully realized, is organic, rather than mechanical. But what the linear concept of time above all implies is a progression or progress from a less perfect (point of origin) to a more perfect (point of arrival or end), or microevolution of the full potential of the species or type found in the first individual.

Whence the natural question: is it possible that such progression might eventually entail a differentiation of type, or macroevolution? If this is possible, at least conceptually, what does it imply concerning the original difference between mechanical action at the level of the inanimate and organic action in the biosphere? Is it also possible that not only noetically (in the mind) vital action enjoys priority over non-vital and that the non-vital is dependent upon it for action (priority of intellectual-free agent over natural, of personal over physical causality), but also in the historical-extramental order? If so, then the emergence initially of inanimate action, relatively superior to the simple chaos or relative disorder of the initial creation (without any transient action, but solely as the term of the act of the creative divine will, totally immanent to God) is intrinsically (immanently) ordered to the emergence not only of individuals (microevolution), but of species (macroevolution) or differentiation of individuals according to type, in which the less perfect is first (cause) and the then the more perfect (effect), that is progressively. Thus, circular motion, an accident of unchanging substance as it appears in the purely natural, or non-living realm, is in the organic or sphere of living beings subordinated to linear motion, in which change is an essential mode of created being and where generation or immanent efficient causality implies not only multiplication of individuals (microevolution), but transformation of type (macroevolution). Macro-evolution to be verified must provide a basis in theory at least for explaining how the vital can evolve from the non-vital (spontaneous generation), where the secondary agents act only mechanically, not organically and spontaneously.

There are only two possible approaches. One is atheistic evolution. This position affirms that the merely material as such is the source of all living species. Another is theistic evolution, which holds that in the original cosmosphere besides secondary agencies there was immanent the vital force of the divine will and intelligence (not in itself, but as the term of creative conservation and concursus with secondary being and operation). Evolution as the *a priori* form of all activity in the organic order postulates a creative character deriving from this way of distinguishing the original act of creation and its continuation in the form of conservation (continuity of being) and concursus (in the form of progression or evolution of being). No change is involved in the origin of being as such out of nothing; change or evolution is involved in its conservation and operation. Theories of creation alone explain the first (contra atheistic evolution). Theories of creation alone do not explain the second (contra special creation). To what extent theories of theistic evolution do is an open question. But given the inadequacies of special creation they are admittedly plausible.

Theistic Evolution: Mechanism, Metaphysics, in Historical Development

The proponent of theistic evolution must also explain three other points:

1. Why progressive creation in the emergence of differentiated types, the latter more perfect than the former, is in the proper and univocal sense limited only to the biosphere?

2. Why change in the noosphere, particularly human in the areas of culture, ethics, personal and social, and religion is not strictly evolution, but appears to take the form of progressive or regressive development, viz., has an essentially and not merely accidentally temporal character?

3. Why the juncture of these radically diverse types of linear motion, vital action (spiritual and organic, divine and secular), meets in human consciousness, first disjunctively, then synthetically, whether consciousness be considered psychologically and sociologically, or whether religiously?

One need not agree at all with Teilhard de Chardin's pantheistic evolutionism in recognizing in his terminology a very clear indication of the locus where any proposed hypothesis must be verified or falsified.

For the moment it suffices to note: whatever organic evolution of the species may have occurred as the instrumentality of the Creator during the *Hexaemeron*, including the human body as initially male and female (Gen 1:27) when only Adam existed as a single human, viz., before the emergence of a second singular human in female form (the difference of male and female being accidental, not specific), it ended *de facto* with the formation of Adam from the slime of the earth.[31] In this sense God alone is operative during the *Hexaemeron*, not to the exclusion of secondary activity, but as the source of its creativity or capacity to arrive at a specifically higher level (sphere or world defined by relations of space and time), with a higher goal. In this concept six days literally or six million days figuratively is a merely incidental question, since the creative-temporal character which defines macroevolution is essentially a metaphysical, or

---

31. *Earth* may be understood here either statically as passive, inorganic matter (Thomas) acted upon from without, or dynamically as matter immanently active (Scotus) rather than potential.

better meta-scientific question, whereas the actual "mechanisms" of this is a scientific question. This kind of macroevolution, partly biological and partly theological, no longer occurs because with the emergence (formation) of Adam and Eve such evolution as the instrument of the Creator ceased, and so does not admit of direct scientific study, although possible reflections of it in other orders do. Hence, the affirmation of the thesis can serve to qualify the interpretation of all scientific theories of physical action and so in a sense be indirectly verified or falsified.

It is superseded by a different form of development, the noetic (of ideas) and moral and social and religious in which the progressive creativity of God is complemented by that of angels and men. Theistic macroevolution no longer is merely organic, but the organic which may have occurred is colored by and is a kind of symbolic anticipation of higher forms of development, originally prefigured by it and so serves as the basis of prophetic symbolism (allegorical sense of the *Hexaemeron*) both for the unfolding of the angelic mind in one day or moment, and for the rhythms of human history. In this sense the preference for theistic evolution over special creation is a postulate of the essentially historical character of all created spiritual experience within the world: an already, but also a not yet, continuity. This includes an openness to further specification, verbal, ritual and institutional, a kind of theorization (St. Bonaventure) matching type and anti-type according to successive ages before and after the realization of the end of time (the incarnation) within time.

In this context the apologetical problem (miracles and prophecies) and the analysis of faith (faith alone, or faith integrated with reasonable and responsible motivation) and the development of dogma and theological systems take on widely different interpretations. The resolution of these questions determines how or how not the primary problem of the church today, the ecumenical question, is to be formulated and resolved in practice.

In the light of the foregoing, then, for the verification or falsification of evolution as a basis for explaining origin and development, theories of motion and action become crucial in validating the correctness of the very notion of evolution of the species. The Aristotelian: *omne motum ab alio movetur*, presumes a circular notion of motion based on the extramental distinction between the specific form (substance as static, not moving, or material substratum of motion) and the accidental (the locus of change of form as part of the individual). For Aristotle movement is in an eternally existing circle, within which the unmoved mover naturally and necessarily guarantees the unending generation and corruption of those substances which are the subject of scientific study. Without modifying the physics St. Thomas radically redefines the "unmoved mover" as first cause *outside* the

circle, or extramental world, finite in essence, potentially infinite in extension, both spatially and temporally. Duration pertains not to the essence,
but to the accidents of finite being composed of essence and existence really
distinct as act (existence) and potency (essence). Only the creator can make
created essences as being exist, whereas secondary causes can only multiply
individuals within existing species. Whence, all evolution is by definition impossible. In this perspective how the species were first produced and when is
mostly a mystery: by creation in the strict or in the broad sense (preexistent
matter as in the case of Adam and Eve) is much disputed. Those Thomists
who retain the physics of Aristotle reject all forms of evolution.

Evolution or Fixity? Linear Versus Circular Motion and Time

Transcendental Thomists who interpret the theology and metaphysics of
Thomas along Kantian lines (e.g., Marechal, Rahner, Lonergan, Coreth)
accept a modern linear idea of motion and unanimously subscribe to
some version of theistic evolution. Evolution is the preferred explanation
for the origin and differentiation of the species as notions or categories of
the mind for organizing the relations between singular corporal existents
in change or motion. Microevolution is considered in terms of singulars
alone, or macroevolution is accepted in so far as the singulars are scientifically classed as species so as to relate to one another. Microevolution
then entails macroevolution as radical scientific paradigms change and the
quantitative extramental of change appears and functions in a specifically
different way in the more advanced hypothesis.[32]

Bonaventure, in critiquing the excessive accent on necessity of nature
(fixity in modern creationism) in view of the freedom of God, but above all
of the relation of created essences to the divine ideas, substitutes a notion of
motion and change intrinsic to the finite substance. His notion is of a spiral
rather than circular or merely linear motion by which all progression after
the initial creation, ending on the sixth day (literal or metaphorical), tends
toward a progressive hierarchization or recapitulation of the lower grades
(species) of being according to the initial pattern of the *Hexaemeron* (the
spiritual or allegorical sense reflecting the divine ideas and their order in the
mind of God). Once again, the created agent cannot be the efficient cause,
either of the hierarchization in the original type, or of the progressive elevation to a higher order. To what extent during the *Hexaemeron* the ordinary
activity of secondary causes contributes instrumentally to this and to the

32. E.g., Aristotle, Galileo, Newton, Einstein. Cf. Kuhn, *Structure of Scientific
Revolutions*.

successive progression is not clear. Creation and elevation are primarily works of God, not however absolutely excluding instrumental cooperation in the case of the formation of the species out of preexistent matter, nor in the work of salvation of cooperation as primary or secondary moral agents. The concept or possibility of theistic evolution is neither clearly affirmed or denied. The context seems to exclude it. Nonetheless, the stress on moral causality as a higher form of cooperation in completing the work of creation and the view of motion, not as a monotonous circular motion at one level, but rather as a progressive but spiraling recirculation of types in anti-types toward a single end identical with its origin (alpha and omega via the medium) partially redefines the concept of motion as circular so as to include something basic to the modern idea of motion in the world as solely linear between an absolute beginning and end, first clearly introduced by Scotus. The spiraling concept of world history (natural and cultural and religious) as it appears in Vico and Hegel clearly does involve evolution incompatible with Catholic belief, but that is because the difference between uncreated and created action, natural and supernatural, is radically suppressed.

With Scotus we come to a genuinely linear concept of motion, in which all that moves is not moved by another physical cause, but primarily by a will which moves itself. Whence in the notion of creation a priority of will and liberty, not only in bringing to be, over physical or efficient causality, but also in determining possibles in the mind of God. The divine ideas of natural things are not primarily determined by a necessary essence prior to any choice on God's part and so in a certain sense a finite reality independent of God's will, but according to a certain order (*signa voluntatis divinae*), even if never executed. Not natural necessity, but the fittingness of divine choice (*rationes voluntatis* rather than *intellectus*) or the *decuit* stands behind the ordered choices of whatever God does. His absolute power by definition will always be an ordered power in whatever he wills to be out of nothing and how he wills it to be. Will is neither an efficient cause operating physically or by natural necessity (original sense of efficient causality in Aristotle) nor one operating arbitrarily, but the sufficient reason for all existence. Hence the Scotistic preference for Anselm's metaphysical proof from the idea of perfect being, understood as radically ecstatic, developed along the lines of univocity of being including its intrinsic modes rather than analogy of proper proportionality in place of the physical proofs based on the operation of cause and effect in the extramental order.

As to theistic evolution Scotus says nothing explicitly. However, it is clear that theoretically speaking there is nothing to show that it is intrinsically impossible, once we understand what Scotus means by an accidental series of "causes" and "effects"[33] which by itself cannot be shown naturally to have an absolute first which is not the effect of something else. The eternity of the world *a parte ante* cannot be demonstrated to be impossible. Hence, the validity of the so called five cosmological arguments for God's existence and for the notion of creation ultimately are inconclusive, unless made to depend on a metaphysical analysis of an essential order of causes[34] which does conclude to the existence of an absolutely first on whose *liberty* depends both essence (nature) and existence (singularity, *haecceitas*) of all else. Whence the importance of sufficient reason for what is directly perceived, and the intrinsic relativity of all existents and all orders of existence.

Kantian and Scotistic Notions of Reason Applied the Question of Evolution

Up to this point in the formulation of the problem of theism there is a convergence of Scotus and Kant in stressing the priority of the argument based on an idea rather than an extramental event (Thomas). The difference is that Kant stresses merely sufficient reason and rejects the ontological argument as invalid, substituting for it an argument based on desire or on conscience. Whereas Scotus at the ontological level sub-ordinates sufficient reason to the mystical in the initial judgment on being as a univocal idea. For Scotus this is a judgment in obedience and contemplation of the unknown God, whereas Kant excludes this.[35]

In this scenario theistic evolution as a divinely willed mode of moving from a less perfect to a more perfect order, whether this involves essence or existence, cannot be excluded absolutely as contrary to the notion of creation. But it may well be excluded by the concept of the Creator's ordered power.

---

33. Linear motion, where one will effectively initiate motion and imposes basic finality on natures, thus initiating motion.

34. Based on the *effectivum* and *effectabile*, the *finitivum* and *finibile* relations included in the univocal notion of being, the mystical and metaphysical before notional and epistemological, intuited before abstracted.

35. Luther with his faith alone retains the mystical part of this original spiritual experience of consciousness—*cogito, ergo sum*—but eliminates the obedience or humility in favor of interpreting the sola as autonomy. Whence there arises radically divergent conceptions of the critical question, viz., the problematic of personal judgment at the origin of all noetic and ethical and political development, prioritizing liberty over natural order and law, and so permitting the possibility of changes in the natural law: in age of nature, of law, of grace, of glory.

No doubt there are certain affinities between the Scotistic use of the ontological argument and the abovementioned possibilities underlying theistic evolution expressly affirmed in most modern thought based on the theory of science at key points dependent, rightly so, on the contributions of Kant while rejecting his rationalism and speculative agnosticism (though not practical) about the existence of God. Nonetheless, the differences are great: the validity of the ontological proof denied by Kant, and the affirmation of the primacy of Jesus and Mary and their mediation as the ultimate ratio of the divine will, even if not executed. Mediation and evolution in any form are mutually exclusive in ordered willing as conceived by Scotus.

Whence, it is clear that the notion of development or evolution *per se* is not false. It is rejected by some Thomists on scientific grounds (order of nature), not because scientifically impossible, as is the evolution of Hegel, or on grounds of unfittingness (Scotus and Bonaventure) in some contexts in terms of the divine ideas or the signs of the divine will. Growth at the vegetative level of the biosphere, fulfillment at the sensitive, and in so far as the organic is incorporated into the human world or the noosphere progresses, all reflect, not merely its possibility, but its existence extramentally. No one disputes this. And in so far as evolution is referred to living individuals of any kind, human included, in the biosphere, we may speak of microevolution.

May we also speak of a kind of macroevolution in reference to the species, or first individual[36] of any type reproduced in the multiplication of individuals from that material organism, not via a simple transient action from without the type, but via begetting (unisexual or bisexual) from within, a kind of causal action not only transient, but immanent, linking the offspring to the parent *in similitudinem naturae*? Minerals may be multiplied and changed, but they do not share the same nature, only the same matter. Instead, living beings share the same nature or species. Could an organism of one kind not be changed, but via a process of evolution or immanent development cease in the process of reproduction and multiplication to be what it once was and begin to be something hitherto not existing, to reproduce *in dissimilitudinem naturae*? The fact that at the moment this no longer occurs or science cannot verify how such might occur now does not resolve the question whether it may have occurred or might occur again, unless science is assumed to be omnicompetent in the matter. That the order of nature is relatively, but not absolutely stable, explains why scientists are

---

36. Only individuals, not universals, or singulars, not species, exist in the extramental world. Theories of a common nature in existents subject to generation and corruption as such outside the mind, on which theories of special creation depend, are only theories.

unable to verify or falsify evolutionary hypotheses in the biological order. That bears on a fact, but not on the intrinsic possibility of theistic evolution, or appropriateness of such from a finalistic point of view.

For the atheist the fact of evolution overturns the first article of the creed, because science is believed to be final. For the theist that does not follow, but is also leaves (a point little noted by creationists) the possibility of a limited evolutionism in the sphere of immanent activity, in one way in the natural order (*infra* human), in another way analogically in the personal (psychological), noetic (meta-physical, meta-scientific and meta-historical), moral (ethical, economic-social, and political[37]), and religious (theological). This grounds objectively the possibility of macroevolution so-called of the organic species, a possibility linked to the fact of doctrinal and cultural development in the noosphere and in the hagiosphere,[38] that exists wherever immanent activity of any kind with a material substratum is involved. All this further suggests the possibility that the Kantian insistence on the priority of the critical question, with its subordination of the notional to the real world of singulars or others and the experience of disjunction or dichotomies at every level of development between what is and the ideal,[39] must be taken seriously at every level of thought.[40]

37. With a bearing on property and common rights, e.g., between capitalism and socialism.

38. That of growth in holiness, even of the Word Incarnate.

39. Or in Antonio Rosmini's terms *Ideal being* where being or real coincides with infinite Thought.

40. This is confirmed by the encyclical *Fides et ratio*, where Rosmini and Newman are both praised as examples of Catholic philosophizing appropriate to a contemporary Christian metaphysics. Rosmini formulated the tradition about truth and faith in Kantian terms to refute the errors of Kant, but not to reject his starting point. Newman went further. In his two best known speculative works, the *Development of Doctrine* and the *Grammar of Assent* he quite obviously uses not only Kantian terminology (becoming quasi-universal), but in a Kantian way. Doctrinal development and change are not unlimited, but it is true change of formulation (verbal species) within the limits of dynamic equivalency. This opens not necessarily on modernism, but certainly on possibilities of ecumenical union of the baptized short of formal equivalency, but not without dynamic. A recent example this effort is the Lutheran-Catholic accord, accepting both good works and the *simul justus et peccator* based on the *sola fides*. The *formulae* are specifically different, yet subject of specific change in meaning, in ceasing to be mutually exclusive, to being mutually inclusive. Newman himself in his *Lectures on Justification* suggest the dynamically inclusive formula synthesizing both points as equally true, thus: we are justified by God's grace, impetrated by faith alone, effected by the sacraments (word and rite) alone, manifested by good works alone. In the *Grammar* the Kantian (and implicitly evolutionary) context is still more clear in the acceptance of a disjunction between notional and real apprehension, between notional and real assent and the need to posit a methodological doubt if any sense is to be made of interior reflection as well as a personal illative sense supplementing

The Meaning of *Species*: Augustine,
Bonaventure, and Scotus

What then is meant by species or common nature or *ratio seminalis* to use an ancient term dear to the Augustinian tradition and claimed to support the position of theistic evolutionists? Individuals are classified in types and to this extent the type or species is in some way "unspecified" or indistinctly real or extramental. But as distinct the species or type only is found "formally or objectively distinct" (distinction of reason with a foundation in the extramental) in the mind. As a fixed or universal form (the same or univocal in many individuals) does it correspond formally to anything in the singulars of the real world? If the *ratio seminalis* corresponds to something in the real world, then the *Hexaemeron* or days of the creative work of God must be reduced to the first moment of time. All the rest is development involving secondary agents as well and so in a sense macro as well as microevolution. The church has never condemned this antinomy of a Platonically inspired reading of Genesis, even if few have followed Augustine literally. St. Bonaventure combines an extended *Hexaemeron* with the unified one of Augustine in referring the first to the literal, the second to the spiritual. But this does not change the fact that this curious paradox in Augustine leaves open the possibility of theistic evolution as an explanation for the emergence of the species in succession under the operation of secondary causes. But this is not expressly affirmed by Augustine or any other Father. The question of the nature of the *rationes seminales* is not the same as that concerning the possibility and fact of an evolutionary origin of the species in the real world, but it is surely inseparable from it. And it is a question long at the heart of philosophy as well as science.

Anyone who affirms either the extramental fixity of the species (creationist position) or their relative developmental character in a single subject capable of immanent activity, either necessary or free, natural-physical or artificial-aesthetic, determined or spontaneous (evolutionist position), must also deal with the questions touching the realism of concepts or universals which in an evolutionary perspective are not absolutes, but means to an end, viz., the convergence or merging of the temporal-historical finite with the eternal end, the already totally life hence totally good, viz., transcending the limits respectively of biosphere, noosphere, nomosphere, in being without a not yet.

---

both formal logic and notional assent in order to arrive at the certitude of truth, both natural and supernatural, thus correcting not only the sensism of Locke, but the rationalism of Kant, on Lockean and Kantian premises.

The problem of atheistic evolutionism is that of ignoring the question in the name of an autonomous science, thus condemning *a priori* science itself (as Kant saw) to the irrationalism of Hume. The problem of creationism as an explanation of the origin of the species is to show that such an explanation is not simply another form of the exaggerated realism of Roscelin and later of the fideists (Henry of Ghent) who imagined that the species corresponded "literally" to something in the individual, so excluding not only change in species, but any kind of true causality above the level of occasionalism or of the "God alone" of the Protestant anti-Marian fideism-pietism. In both cases, but in opposite directions, the major defect is the failure of constructing a psychology of human experience only in terms of a body-soul relation in which soul and spirit, and hence heart and spirit are identical. The creationists insist on merely talking about soul as informing a body without any independent relation to the divine. The evolutionists talk about soul and body as a coincidence of opposites firing from within the dialectical process of thesis, antithesis and synthesis (Hegel). Both omit St. Paul's insistence of the transcendent element, viz., spirit in the primary experience of being: not the product of my soul in becoming conscious, but the sign of a transcendent spirit not produced by me or becoming me, but present and acting personally in me, who becomes apparent to me in the spiritual experience of Marian mediation, or, more metaphysically, of the Immaculate Conception in total consecration.[41]

The problem of the theistic evolutionist is to show how the admission of a possible evolution of the species in the real world does not in the noosphere constitute an acceptance of Ockham's nominalism-conceptualism-voluntarism, viz., that species qua universals exist only in the mind as general categories for classifying real existents, that in the real world one finds only the singular existent, acting freely or determinedly, whereas the essential or fixed and naturally necessary, is only found in the mental world. The objective concept does not correspond exactly to anything real, as it is a product of an acting subject. The same problem analogously

---

41. On this cf. the Kolbean thesis of created and uncreated Immaculate Conception for the definitive paradigm of the metaphysical experience, the *a priori* both of the notional and of the practical as desire and as agape. Also, the concept of heart as biological (organic), psychological (soul or mind as seat of intelligent desire and affection), and personal (synonym for person and personality) with subsequent qualification of memory, understanding and will as manifestations of heart and person; also, personality as experience or consciousness of person-heart, as pure heart, simple heart, obedient heart, each contrasting with disobedient or autonomous heart, the ultimate solitude. In this perspective personality development as well as spiritual growth can be most effectively conceived or objectified as the form taken by theistic evolution in the noosphere, without the pantheism of Hegel and Teilhard.

is found in the verbal order, whence the impossibility of the literal truth of Genesis on origins. The problem of theistic evolution as an alternative both to atheistic evolution and special creation as an explanation of the origin of the species is that of finding a solution to the question of species as universal and also realistic, viz., corresponding to something also in the real world, stable and fixed as a point of reference for a taxonomy purely notional, and which also avoids the radical voluntaristic determinism of the old Protestants, also the heritage of Ockham and the deterministic naturalism and rationalism of the Aristotelian Averroists.

I believe that can be found in the essentialism-exemplarism-personalism of Bonaventure and Scotus rather than in the nominalist, naturalistic existentialism of Ockham and Kant. As a valid alternative, avoiding the objectionable features of a theistic evolution based on the premises of Ockham as developed by Kant to form the theoretical basis of all science, natural and cultural (the humanities as speculatively expounded in modern psychology, ethics and sociology-politics-economy), yet as affirming the contingent rather than the necessary at the heart of all development, and thus the emergence of the phenomenologically and specifically different, the Catholic alternative to Kant and the transcendentalists not identical with special creation, this alternative may also be called theistic evolution or progressive creationism. This conception of evolution can be seen as the core of natural change, development of doctrine as the core of learning, attaining maturity as the core of psychological growth, spiritual progress at the core of the process of justification.

To grasp what follows in tracing the origin of the modern theory of theistic evolution in Catholic circles, with Catholic origins and terminology, but with anti-Catholic content (and understanding how to refute it at its weak points without falling into the trap of special creation) one must keep in mind the Teilhardian distinction between biosphere, noosphere, hagiosphere, how the immanent activity in all three is connected, how evolution in so far as a possible theory situates these not in a circular image of space and time (Thomas and to an extent Bonaventure), but a linear or univocal concept of time and duration, including God (Scotus).

With the insight of Scotus theistic evolution as an explanation for organic change at the biological level can be pursued in two quite opposite manners:

1. As an initial account of a univocal concept of being as applied to the finite as radically *in fieri*, as a concept radically non-conceptual (traditional Catholic as articulated by Scotus) and so a conceptual postulate of the finite mode intrinsic to univocal being as contingent

rather than necessary, at the noetic, aesthetic, ethical level where what progressive creation as theistic evolution means properly ascribed both to the divine and created will as principal agent in the full sense, is most clearly seen in Hopkins aesthetic theory based on Scotus (inscape and instress);

2. Or it may be approached as a concept linked primarily not to being but to thought, the *cogito, ergo sum,* as explained by Kant, with being as a necessary postulate of thought.

It is at the intellectual or epistemological-grammatical-logical-rhetorical level of culture an aspect of transcendental Thomism (baptism of Kant) and at the level of religion an aspect of historicized theology (process or neo-Hegelian theology via Karl Rahner—existential; via Maurice Blondel—action; via Bruno Forte—mutual relations between Creator and creature in terms of Trinity).

Catholic Authors on Theistic Evolution

It is hardly surprising that, even before the legitimation of Catholic efforts to disjoin discussion of an evolutionary origin of the species from belief in the creation of the world and of the finite spirits, the first Catholic voices in support of an alliance between creation and evolution[42] should have been heard in the English speaking world: St. George Mivart,[43] J. A.

---

42. What today goes under the heading of theistic evolution, viz., that evolution *per se* is not opposed to Catholic belief, but only its atheistic version *a la* Darwin, Huxley, Haeckel, et al.

43. *On the Genesis of the Species* (1871). Galleni, "Evoluzione," 583, points out the importance of St. George Mivart (1827–1900) who insisted on the fact of evolution, not the mechanics of the theory, as fundamental for the resolution of the question of theistic evolution. Mivart thought the fact was beyond question, therefore biblical exegesis of the entire Bible, and the whole of theology should be revolutionized on an evolutionary, historicist basis. But this is evidently a gross *petitio principii,* no doubt one of the reasons for his troubles with the Holy Office. He failed to see that evolution as such is not a fact of science, but a postulate of a meta-science, rationalizing the possibility of science. It is as postulate, not as fact, that the present Holy Father ascribes a very high degree of probability to evolution as opposed to creationism. Thus affirming the possibility of explaining the origin of the species prior to the appearance of Adam as first man, and of his subsequent development does not *per se* contradict the cautions of Pius XII or the decrees of the biblical commission about the historical sense of Genesis, even in the first eleven chapters, nor eventually lifting cautionary prohibitions about the dangers of affirming acceptance of theistic evolution, if it is clear a Catholic version obviously avoids the pitfalls, as with the initial condemnations of Aristotle replaced with approval.

Zahm, CSC,[44] etc., in the latter half of the nineteenth and early twentieth centuries, where evolutionary thought had become "politically correct" under the name of social Darwinism.

At the same time in various Catholic centers of biblical study purely symbolic or mythical interpretations of the first eleven chapters of Genesis began to be proposed as compatible with Catholic tradition. Whatever the motivation of these proposals, in each instance there is no doubt that without such an interpretation it was next to impossible to reconcile evolutionary theory in any form with belief in creation as it actually or historically occurred. It is useful to recall these, if only to show the problems a coherent Catholic theory of theistic evolution must meet to be considered not only a speculative hypothesis, but reasonably probable (on which the evidence from all sides tends to converge). Is it possible to affirm the doctrinal and historical truths revealed in Genesis while interpreting the literal sense in the direction of theistic evolution rather than special creation? I think it is, provided the key to metaphysics is recognized as the Immaculate Conception, at once a singular who is universal (mediatress) and a universal (abstract) who is totally real and singular. In the essence of the Immaculate Conception, the necessary and contingent are perfectly blended, as the basis both for nature and for history to serve as prime cyphers of the finite and for the literal sense of Genesis (theistic evolution) and allegorical (spiritual or doctrinal) to be harmonized in fidelity to the truth.

But these first attempts to promote a kind of marriage between creationist and evolutionary thought initially went no place. Indeed, in the Catholic theological world of that day these attempts sparked official condemnation as being at least highly dangerous, scandalous and temerarious. In consequence, promotion of such harmonizing was silenced as conducive to modernism. Nonetheless, the condemnations did not directly address the theoretical question: is every theory of evolution intrinsically atheistic in thrust? or is it possible to construct a theory of "theistic evolution" not necessarily opposed to Catholic belief and tradition? The condemnations merely asserted that in fact the authors in question had not succeeded in this and hence their works included speculation inimical to belief in the first article of the Creed. Nor was any explicit attention given to one of the legitimate concerns of these first proponents of theistic evolution: the dangers of "special creation" or formation of each and every species directly out of nothing, as a subtle form of the Protestant "solus Deus," utterly subversive of the Catholic tradition. Thus, despite the condemnations of the initial

44. *Evolution and Dogma*. Fr. Zahm was an early professor at Notre Dame University, USA. An early proponent of similar ideas in France was Leroy, *Ľevolution*.

presentations, support for some form of theistic evolution among Catholic philosophers and theologians increased as it came to be seen as the only sane middle position between the extremes of Darwinian (atheistic) evolution[45] and special creation,[46] without which the rest of Catholic doctrine and practice would tend more and more to fossilize in contrast with the stimulating and attractive aspects of modern thought and practice. Especially important aspects of modern thought and practice were those occasioned by the new and seemingly irreversible contributions of modern science to a concept of motion, act and actuality, more realistic, profounder and truer than that grounded in the ancient hylomorphism. This development posed a contrast between a static, extrinsic concept of efficient causality and motion (on which creationist theories of origin had been based) and a new and more valid concept of motion as immanently dynamic.

The atheist claimed this starting point excluded *a priori* creationism as such and so of the first article of the creed, on which Catholic religion and theology absolutely depends. According to the theistic creationist, however, evolution as such not merely does not exclude creation, but affirms it in a truer and more vibrant manner under a new form as St. Maximilian would say of progress in spirituality and theology recognized as essentially Marian. The content is the same, but is now in a specifically new format or manifestation, one calculated to deepen rather than change the church's understanding of revelation and of herself and so more appropriate (*decuit*) in guiding her closer to the realization of the kingdom.

Between the two world wars another attempt was made to alter the traditional Catholic perception of the doctrines of creation and evolution as natural enemies, not merely as a way to resolve a problem of apologetics, viz., there exists no necessary opposition between science and faith conceived as an assent radically independent of reason and good works and ascribable only to gift of Spirit (analysis *fidei*), should evolution of the species be demonstrated to have occurred. Rather, it is a way to realize, in a Catholic context, elements presupposed by salvific revelation hitherto only explicitly recognized outside the church in twisted form. Thus, in addition to the scientific and philosophical elements a strictly theological consideration was introduced as an argument in favor of theistic evolution of the species, or as it was then more commonly known "mitigated transformism." And it was this: there is first no inherent contradiction in affirming both the creation of the world by a divine agent outside it,

45. Simple denial of any creation by a supernatural agency and the reduction of reality to an eternal matter.

46. Denial of any active role to creatures in the continuing work of creation after the initial creative act of God.

and the structuring and graduation of the species within the world not only by the Creator from without, but in conjunction with natural agencies implanted within the world by the Creator and capable of generating singulars like themselves, but specifically different and specifically more perfect in being. Second, and more importantly, this is nothing less than the Catholic tradition itself, witness St. Gregory of Nyssa and St. Augustine in particular with his theory of *rationes seminales*.[47] Indeed, according to the supporters of this reconciliation, while considerations of efficient causality showed how such a solution might well be possible, though not whether in fact the Creator so created, teleological considerations of the world actually existing tended more and more to postulate a theory of theistic evolution as the only coherent explanation of cosmic finality. No less a respected scholar than E. Gilson seems to have subscribed to this in one of his last works: *D'Aristote à Darwin et retour: essai sur quelques constantes de la biophilosophie*.[48] He rightly rejects the scientific bloopers of Darwin

47. The initial proposal of this novel interpretation of St. Augustine and St. Gregory concerning the fixity of the species and the priority of immutability over change unanimously witnessed by all the Fathers and clearly attested by St. James (1:17) gave rise between 1920 and 1960 to considerable bibliography on the subject. The vast majority of scholars concluded that such interpretations represented a complete misunderstanding of Augustine's mind on the *rationes seminales* and directly contradicted his repeated affirmations of the immediate formation of the bodies of Adam and Eve by the Creator. Cf. Sagüés, *Deo creante et elevante*, 2:680–61 for bibliographical details. In note 61 of page 681, Sagüés rightly observes that a correct understanding of Augustine's *rationes seminales* is to be found in the commentaries of St. Bonaventure, *II Sent.*, d. 7, p. 2, a. 2, q. 1, and d. 18, a. 1, qq. 2–3 and the *Scholia* of the editors of the critical edition (2:199–200, 438, 443). Despite the recent flurry in favor of Augustine as an evolutionist, as in the work of Jaki, *Genesis 1*, the scholarly consensus that Augustine is not a theistic evolutionist still stands. Jaki's total misunderstanding and indeed caricature of St. Bonaventure (*Genesis*, 133–36) is a good example of how the proponents of such an interpretation of Augustine fail to grasp his metaphysics. The article of Reale, "Agostino di Ippona," 2:1533–50, despite many interesting observations and an up-to-date (but somewhat one-sided) bibliography, suffers from the same lack of appreciation for the Augustinian-Bonaventurian notion of *ratio* and its reappearance in Scotus as *natura communis*.

48. First published in Paris in 1971, an English translation appeared under the title *From Aristotle to Darwin and Back Again*, Gilson rightly points out the importance of the distinction between the "extrinsic teleology" characteristic of the machine or human artifact and that "intrinsic teleological character" especially noticeable in the world of organic nature, a distinction often overlooked by creationists in discussing the argument against evolution from intelligent design. But that "intrinsic teleology," far from providing an evident opening on a possible evolution of the species, tends to confirm the concept of a stable, unchanging species at the heart of and delimiting all change (microevolution), as precisely the intrinsic finality or intelligibility governing that change. This is the view of Thompson, *The Work of Jean Henri Fabre*, 62–70, where he notes in particular the importance of animal instinct in this regard and a number of

and company, yet insists that these bloopers are but the misperception of a valid insight: evolutionary teleology and the postulation of some form of theistic evolution of the species.

Among the now forgotten names in favor of this view between the two world wars are the Belgian Canon H. de Dorlodot[49] and his English counterpart Canon E. Messenger.[50] Though with little immediate impact on the common theological view before Vatican II, viz., that evolutionary theory in any form is incompatible with revealed truth about origins,[51] in Catholic academic circles and in many textbooks of neo-Thomistic philosophy, in the French and English speaking world, e.g., in the writings of A.D. Sertillanges, O.P., and the textbooks of C. Bittle, OFMCap. and H. Grenier, widely used in seminaries during the mid-twentieth century, the possibility of theistic evolution as an explanation for the origin of the human body, was presented in very favorable terms.

---

insights of Bergson which support his approach (against theistic evolution).

49. *Le darwinisme.*

50. The two works by Messenger with considerable circulation: *Evolution and Theology* (1931), and its sequel, *Theology and Evolution* (1949).

51. A very detailed and accurate assessment of evolution from a theological vantage point published shortly after *Humani Generis* is that of Sagüés, *De Deo Creante et Elevante*, 2:661–81. His exposition (in the four volume manual of theology authored by a group of Spanish Jesuits at the request of Pius XII, surely one of the best, if not the best work of its kind published in the twentieth century) of the traditional doctrine on the origin of the human body, both male and female, in the light of the recently issued Encyclical *Humani Generis* is set forth as a demonstration of the following thesis: *Protoparentes conditi sunt quoad corpus a Deo immediate* (The bodies of our first parents were formed immediately by God). After carefully explaining the terminology and precisely identifying adversaries of the thesis, viz., not only the "rigid transformists" who affirm an evolutionary origin of soul as well as body, but also the "mitigated transformists" who defend a natural evolutionary origin of the bodies of Adam and Eve as term of a natural process of generation by a brute without allowance for a miraculous or supernatural action as principal cause and carefully showing that his position exactly states the mind of Pius XII, he states that his thesis taken as the obvious meaning of Scripture and Tradition dealing with the point is simply *De Fide*. Making allowance for the very limited permission to discuss the scientific probabilities of evolution (not very high, he claims even in the estimate of many scientists of the time) he says that it is absolutely certain theologically speaking that no form of evolution had anything to do with the formation of Eve's body, that it is equally certain a purely natural evolution (such as that proposed by Teilhard) had nothing to do with the formation of Adam's body and probably not even that allowing for a supernatural agency as principal cause of the formation of Adam's body from pre-existent organic matter, indeed that the majority of respected Catholic theologians *circa* 1955, such as Ruffini, Ternus, Boyer, Daffara, Baisi, held the same position. Given the difficulties of reconciling any version of evolutionary theory with the metaphysical-historical facts narrated in the first chapters of Genesis it is next to impossible for evolution to be true.

Whatever one's final assessment of theistic evolution, it is important to keep in mind not only the influence of certain aspects of contemporary philosophy, but also the manner in which these theories of "theistic evolution" were initially related to and expressed by way of scholastic-Aristotelian terminology. All of them insist first on the initial creation of all matter before the "first" day, that is before the appearance of any recognizable order; that no subsequent matter has in fact ever been created, whence the assumption that all subsequent development, whether brief or lengthy (young or old world scenarios), is not out of nothing, but out of (*ex*) preexisting matter, relatively unformed, but capable of being formed, "educing" from the potentiality of matter the latent forms (essences, kinds, species), each more perfect type of being a more developed form of matter, until the appearance of the most sophisticated form of organic life, the human body, male and female.

Evolution and Catholic Understandings of Nature-Essence

Neo-Scholasticism and Catholic Evolutionists: Changing Paradigms

First, to the theological fact of the same matter forming the original substratum of subsequent development and the Aristotelian theory of hylomorphism as the most sensible point of departure for explaining how the world arrived at a relatively finished and highly sophisticated state, these first Catholic proponents of theistic evolution introduced a crucial novelty. Not only are all the subsequent types of things, organic and inorganic, "out of" preexisting matter, unformed or only imperfectly formed, but the higher types or species arise "through" the specific activity of the lower species, until at the higher levels of organic life (the primates) the generative power of sexual intercourse terminates not at the birth of an individual of the same kind (ontic), but at the birth of the first human couple[52] of a different and higher species (phylon), the *homo sapiens*. This is taken as the achievement of the hominization of matter and the inception of a new and higher form of continuing creation (evolution), the gradual appearance of the cultural, or inculturation of mind (noosphere), of the personal (ethosphere or deontological) of society

---

52. A first individual qua twin, male and female united before birth, but after whose birth divided into two individuals to form a single couple.

(polisphere[53]) and of religion (hagiosphere[54]). The subject out of which the higher species evolves is, then, not only the material, but also in some way the efficient cause of the new species, and so is not merely passive in the hands of the Creator, but actively contributing to the origin of a new species. This is true not only of the species or types of life before the appearance of *homo sapiens* or Adam, but of all subsequent and more highly developed stages of hominization (culture; personality; socialization) culminating in the kingdom: fully holy and fully secular or macro-cosmic.

To this is added a second element, also familiar to students of scholastic theology and philosophy. It is that of the obediential potentiality of all creatures to be elevated to a higher order of existence, or to act fruitfully at a level of existence transcending the limits of their nature, e.g., as instruments of the Creator in performing a miracle. Thus, in its original, unachieved state the matter created by God is potentially all things which the Creator made it to be, not only passively, but actively, a potentiality, however, only achievable to the degree the innate tendency or dynamism to develop, viz., evolve, is subsumed instrumentally by a supernatural agency and so guided teleologically. The point is crucial in recognizing how theistic evolution differs from atheistic evolution wherein motion or efficient activity at the higher stages of duration,[55] such as the organic, the humanistic, the cultural, personal, social and religious, is reduced to purely mechanistic or materialistic terminology of the inorganic or "molecular" sphere, without any reference to the teleological.

But it is also crucial in appreciating why theistic evolutionists reject the special creation alternative (dubbed watchmaker physics) which, insisting on the exclusive role of a Creator (or *agens intellectuale*) outside and above the created cosmos or outside and above the material both molecular and organic, fails to account for the immanent and autonomous dynamism of the created in terms of its goal to be achieved. From the standpoint of the theistic evolutionist, the creationist who believes in the extramental character of the species as fixed and unchangeable will tend to say science disproves evolution, therefore the species were created one by one from nothing. At the opposite extreme the Darwinian will hold that science proves evolution to be possible and to have occurred; therefore, the creationist account of the origin of the species is false. The Catholic theistic evolutionist will say science can neither prove or disprove theories about the origin of the

53. Total socialization of the individual in a single communion, or world as fully secular, fully evolved.

54. The incarnation of the uncreated and sanctification of the secular or finite fully secularized.

55. Or cosmos as *saeculum*, age, viz., temporal.

species, but can only suggest hypotheses to be evaluated in the light of what is the most general condition of all created existence: duration or evolution. Motion or the temporal is the intrinsic constituent of all reality or realities subject to change, not a fixed essence called species.

Hence motion, in so far as it is what science studies, will tend to suggest not an atheistic explanation for the existence of extramental cause-effect activity of created agents, but a theistic. This will be precisely to the degree a first creationary origin affirmed on theological grounds because exclusively divine,[56] is prolonged in the form of evolution systematically guided toward a final goal. In effect sound science tends to explain coherently the origin of a world system not primarily in terms of an efficient and final causality extrinsic to the effect (differentiated world system) reflected in the watchmaker model consequent on the origin of the species, but in terms of the teleology immanent to natural organisms prior to their development. In such a scenario, originating activity governing descent of the species from the original matter is at once supernatural[57] and natural.[58] From within, not without the original matter in the course of ever more sophisticated organization, the actively creative presence of the divine influence is manifested in the progressive emergence of the species, each successive one enjoying an ever more perfect capacity to actively cooperate in the process. Creative evolution (Bergson) is another name for what is meant by theistic evolution. The temporal process, object of scientific study, in fact is principally a theological reality, viz., the creative in visible form. Hence it must be primarily validated on theological and metaphysical grounds, which means that if validated as true theologically, it must at least be possible scientifically or at least not philosophically demonstrable as a contradiction in terms as a basis for meaningful science.

The atheist will say: evolution is a scientific theory which if true renders Christian faith obsolete. The theistic evolutionist will reply that evolution is precisely the process which the Creator used to fashion the world as we have come to know it since the emergence of Adam, a "religious" reality which if no longer occurring in the "biosphere" nonetheless conditions its structure and hence the cultural history (both in its personal and social aspects) or "hominization" subsequent on natural history. And while

56. Omnipotent, or absolute Power of the Father expressed solely in the Fiat of the Word.

57. Creative dynamism, or ordered power of the Creator Spirit now immanent to the process of development or evolution, unfolding intelligibly the potentiality of undifferentiated matter.

58. Initially passivity or the original created, viz., matter, not nothing, out of which now all development proceeds.

these two aspects of history or time are quite distinct, the underlying priority and continuity of their material substratum as an active obediential potency constitutes the basis of a "continuing creation," spiraling in linear, yet ever more sophisticated levels and types of existence terminating finally at the incarnational sphere[59] wherein the Creator Spirit is fully embodied, hominized, enculturated, personalized and secularized, and matter sanctified, immortalized, divinized and communized. For many of its proponents the Incarnation marks the last and highest point of evolutionary development when a divine person becomes part of the very process of continuing creation resting on the evolutionary character of matter, so heralding the proximity of the eschaton or kingdom. Whence the importance of inculturation and continuous adaptation of unchanging ideals and principles to ever-developing and evolving cultural and religious forms, precisely under the impact of the divine energy now incarnate in history. Whence, evolution correctly expounded as a sign of the initially creative starting point of all secondary activity in the transcendent creative act at the beginning of the world, gives an even surer demonstration of God as Creator than the traditional five ways expounded on a creationist basis, against the purely pantheistic and materialistic interpretation and misrepresentation of evolution as independent of the supernatural.

This brings us to the third and perhaps most appealing innovation introduced into neo-scholastic philosophy by theistic evolutionists. This is the existential, viz., the concept of authentic action as a concrete realization of the spiritual energizing the creative or originating aspect of dynamic matter over the conservative aspect.[60] The act of existence, fundamental to Thomistic metaphysics, no longer is understood merely in a static, hylomorphic sense, but in a dynamic sense as the supernatural or uncreated power inserted by the Creator in the finite or material before the first day. Whence the view of the creation of the spiritual world with the material. These are the *rationes seminales* or intelligences of Augustine viewed dynamically, or the ideas of Plato, no longer extrinsic, but concretized within the active potential of matter to actively and successively generate higher and higher visible manifestations of the real: mineralsphere, biosphere, noosphere, christosphere. Each stage or age or *saeculum* (constituting the secular) entails not only an action of the finite, but of the Creator in infusing an ever more perfect form of spirit to account for the progressive spiraling, otherwise incomprehensible leaps, like the "big bang," the appearance of man, of culture, of

---

59. Christogenesis or appearance of God the Creator as Jesus, procreated by the Virgin Mother.

60. Generation or corruption in inorganic, reproductive in organic sphere, with analogous interpretations of the Creator's role.

the subjective-personal, of the communal free, of the holy, with not merely a powerful influence of the Spirit, but of the Spirit himself, the unity of Father and Son. This divine presence within the finite-material is what is meant by existential or action (Blondel), an existential guided by the Creator before the appearance of man, an existential thereafter guided by *homo sapiens* in cooperation with the Creator. Here the theistic evolutionist points out the superiority of the Catholic notion of evolution over Protestant creationism. To borrow from Teilhard, matter hominized no longer evolves, but is capable of guiding evolution or continuing creation to its end.

With this any essential difference between creation and return of creation to God in terms of hierarchization (mediation) or elevation from a lower grade of existence to a higher by way of action of a higher personal agency outside the subject elevated or recapitulated is rejected. Whereas atheistic evolution simply rejects the Christian notion of creation, theistic evolution does not.[61] Rather, the major difference between Catholic creationism and theistic continuing creation (evolution) lies in the denial of any real distinction between *exitus* and *reditus*. Theistic evolution (continuing creation) conceives the duration of the created not as radically circular, and predicamental, but as radically linear (spatial) and spiraling (temporal). It is transcendental and effectively in continuity with eternity at both terms (beginning and end), so permitting a dynamic, mutual relation (even if unequal) between eternal and temporal. This understanding permits the eternal to enter time (order of evolution) and time (evolution) to be eternalized (immortalized), or the divine without ceasing to be divine to be part of continuing creation (created actuation by uncreated act personally) and the created-human without ceasing to be human and evolutionary qua person to be also divine and holy. Thus, both the absolute (radical immutability) as basis of existence and the evolutionary (radical change) as basis of existence (Marechal) are fundamental conditions of all being, points of departure for any metaphysics and any history.

Teilhard de Chardin: Insights, *Monita,* and Disciples: Some Distinctions

Without doubt even before the publication of his writings the thought of Teilhard and other Jesuits sympathetic to him influenced the first formulations of theistic evolution. The *monita* and condemnations of Teilhard were well known to those supporting theistic evolution, not merely as a

---

61. Even though modifying the traditional concept of creation as entailing a non-mutual relation between Creator and created.

scientific hypothesis, but as a universal condition of all existence (ontological) and all thought (hermeneutical) and all action (deontological) and indeed all theology (inculturation of the holy via doctrine, disciple, liturgy and ecclesial communion). Evolutionists and anti-evolutionists among Catholics accepted the *monita*, and the fact of serious doctrinal error in his writings. But since none of the *monita* touched the scientific value or better the interpretive value of Teilhard of modern science, supporters felt at liberty (nor were they ever formally reprehended) to point out[62] that these errors were merely incidental to the core insights of Teilhard concerning the radically evolutionary character of all finite existence. For supporters of Teilhard, this was an insight signaled by the irreversibly new notion of motion and nature as dynamic rather than static, or natural, nature and species (whether extramental or mental) as subject to development rather than fixed, immobile. This was a crucial point the critics of theistic evolution generally failed to deal with in their insistence on a static concept of nature in order to define the gratuity of supernatural grace, a position making it impossible to deal with the immanent and personal in the psychic, social and spiritual orders.

In order to see more clearly the nub of the controversy, and how theistic evolutionists distinguish their position not only from Darwin, but also from Hegel, attention must be given to a more exact formulation of the problematic of the origin of species and how this relates to parallel problems such as the critical problem or question in epistemology and metaphysics.

The difficulties being such, it is obvious other non-Catholic sources, such as the notion of "creative evolution" and the mystical "*elan vital*" driving it of H. Bergson (1859–1941),[63] would have and did have considerable bearing also on the formation of the present theory of theistic evolution as a basis for reconciling the apparently opposed concepts of creation and evolution. But far more important for the popularization of these ideas among Catholics, in particular Catholic clergy and theologians, was the wide circulation after 1955 in all major languages of the once and still forbidden[64] works of the Jesuit Teilhard de Chardin (1881–1955). Teilhard was an evolutionist

---

62. E.g., De Lubac, to his death, was a major defender of Teilhard.

63. Cf. Vanzago, "Bergson, Henri," 2:1584–95. On the dependence of Teilhard on Bergson cf. Vanzago, "Bergson, Henri," 1594.

64. In the midst of all the praise showered on Teilhard on the centenary of his birth in 1981, the *monitum* of 1962 was publicly renewed on July 11, 1981 (signed by Cardinal Seper of the Congregation for the Faith and Cardinal Casaroli, Secretary of State despite having two months earlier sent a letter to the then Msgr. Poupard, Rector of the Institut Catholique of Paris, commending Teilhard for his contributions to the church).

from his youth and is thought to have been involved in the cases of the Pilt-down and Peking man frauds. His goal in life was to remake from within not only Catholic thought, but the Catholic Church on an evolutionary basis, this without benefit of St. Augustine. Not only Catholic critics, but scholars sympathetic to this Jesuit considered his opinions to be pseudo-science and pseudo-theology.[65] In a word he was a pseudo-mystic capable of consider-able influence over the minds of those who had no firm mastery either of science or of theology (whose numbers are legion today) by providing what appeared to be a highly sensible system for making sense of the world and religion at its current stage of development. Teilhard was providing an attrac-tive, unified vision of existence. It is the existential, or "mystical" appeal of "creative evolution" which is its distinctive feature vis-à-vis the idealistic evo-lutionism of Hegel and accounts in great part for its successful propagation, why it may be likened to a Trojan horse in the City of God[66]: not because it is scientific, but because it is pseudo-mysticism.[67]

The first principle of Teilhard's system is "theistic evolution" in its most radical form: evolution is the fundamental principle of creation in all its aspects. Far from being blind chance, evolution *per se* is the heart of intel-ligibility and so finality.[68] Cosmogenesis, Noogenesis, Christogenesis are the three words Teilhard coined to cover what is nothing but a crude adaptation of Hegel to make the Creator himself a part of and the final outcome of the *self-explanatory* process of becoming.[69] That is why in the English speaking

65. Cf. the review of his work by Simpson in the *Scientific American* for 1960. In his introduction to the English version of *Phenomenon of Man*, J. Huxley insinuates the same.

66. The analogy is borrowed from the book of Hildebrand, *Trojan Horse.*

67. This is reflected in an assessment of Teilhard by Arupe in 1981: the achievement of Teilhard is to have fused in a single profounder vision the ancient affirmation of the spiritual, based on the fixism that seemed to exclude evolution, with the evolution of the species, now seen not to exclude, but conclude in the spiritual. Letter of the General of the Jesuits to the Jesuit Provincial of France for the centenary, in *Il futuro dell'Uomo*, 4–5.

68. In the language of an earlier generation not *being*, but *becoming* is the root of intelligibility Nonetheless, even today theistic evolutionists are not sure evolution does not include some element of chance, perhaps "intelligent" chance, which is what "be-coming" instead of "being" as the fundamental aspect of reality really means. Thus, they do not care much for the medieval use of the word "necessary" in respect to divine Providence. Cf. Galleni, "Evoluzione," 584, where he criticizes the medieval scholastics and Bishop Tempier of Paris in particular for a "fixism" making all development near to impossible. In fact, all that the medievals wished to do was to assert the fact that chance and change are only relatively such, and fall within limits defined beforehand by divine Providence. On the various senses of necessity as understood by the medieval scholastics, cf. Bonaventure, *Myst. Trin.*, q. 7, a. 1.

69. His basic views are summarized in one of his best-known works, *The Phenom-enon of Man*. On the continued influence of Teilhard, particularly his "global view of

world this mind-set is known as "process theology" and is associated with the names of Alfred N. Whitehead and Charles Hartshorne, the first of whom was deeply influenced by Bergson's notion of "creative evolution."[70]

The works of Teilhard are still the object of an official *monitum*[71] of the Catholic Church as pervaded by errors directly subversive of faith and morals. That notwithstanding, the errors in question in one form or another have been widely professed by persons claiming to be Catholic and Catholic theologians. Whether this came about through their study of Teilhard is not my concern at the moment. Rather the widespread circulation of his views after 1955 and at the time of Vatican II (1962–5) and during its immediate aftermath had not a little to do with the rapid rise in the fortunes of theistic evolution in Catholic theological circles between 1960 and 1970. From being a theory mostly frowned upon in the immediate aftermath of *Humani Generis* (1950), by 1970 it had come to be regarded as the basis of the Catholic explanation (with or without all the aberrations of Teilhard) of the origin and end of creation, indeed the only premise on which the results of modern science can be interpreted intelligently. Evolution far from being anti-creation and atheistic in itself, is theistic and creationist, once purified of the gross misperceptions of Darwin. All this occurred precisely in the face of growing and strong opposition to the theory of evolution from scientific quarters, not only to the absence of any scientific proof for evolution, but to its very scientific character. And so, with the rise in fortunes of theistic evolution a little remarked, but important change in the problematic occurred: no longer was science imposing evolution on theology; theology now seemed to be imposing evolution on science.

Humani Generis, Scholarly Reactions, and Subsequent Magisterial Teaching

Voices, both sympathetic and opposed to evolution, with proverbial hindsight, have sought to find in *Humani Generis* the cause of this exceptional shift in opinion. Those antipathetic often claim the pope should have

---

evolution" as an all-embracing perspective based on the priority of change rather than of the unchangeable: *id verius quod posterius*, not *id verius quod prius*, in ecclesiastical and theological circles as well as lay, cf. Galleni, "Evoluzione," 1:588–90, and in the same reference work (organized on the premise that the evolutionary perspective is certain and the creationist false) by the same author "Teilhard," 2:2111–24.

70. Cf. Vanzago, "Bergson, Henri," 2:1593. Other important contemporary thinkers supporting one or another version of theistic evolution and influenced by Bergson are E. Le Roy (1870–1954), M. Scherer (1874–1928) and M. Heidegger (1889–1976).

71. Since 1926 often repeated and renewed as late as July 11, 1981.

condemned outright scientific theories of evolution along with his condemnation of philosophic evolutionism (historicism), of which Teilhard
was the then best-known exponent. Without that condemnation, they
claim, the next step to a positive approval of evolution in some form as
fact is inevitable. And the sympathetic agree: *Humani Generis* is the cause
of the shift, and was a prelude to an official adoption of theistic evolution
as the Catholic understanding of the graduated structuring of the world,
already evident, it is claimed, in the 1996 address of Pope John Paul II to
the Pontifical Academy of Science.[72]

Such an interpretation of the encyclical and subsequent events is highly suspect, above all because it substantially misrepresents a simple instance
of an ancient church policy as if it were a startling innovation. The church
has never claimed any direct authority to adjudicate hypotheses of a purely
scientific character. This was evident even in the Galileo case. Rather the
pope simply gave permission to examine and assess scientific hypotheses
that appear to have some relation to revealed truth.

First, what the pope did not do. He did not reverse the strictures on
evolution of earlier declarations, viz., that, on the face of it, theories of evolution appear to contradict what is known of origins and human origins
in particular, both body as well as soul, both Adam as well as Eve, and for
those not well trained in theology and science are dangerous to faith and
conducive of naturalism.

The pope, however, did not merely indicate the need of prudence in the
study of such hypotheses. He also defined more exactly the limits of any discussion: the *possibility* alone of evolution as a legitimate scientific hypothesis,
not the certainty of its having occurred. Therefore, the pontiff is saying that
we are not in a position to make the fact of human origins the direct object of
scientific observation. This has become a matter of history whose knowledge

72. Cf. in the appendix to vol. II of *Dizionario Interdisciplinari di Scienza e Fede*
the arrangement of Papal documents of all kinds, including the 1996 address of the
present pope to the Pontifical Academy of Science, from Pius XII (1939) to 1998,
and of excerpts from *Dei Filius* of Vatican I and *Gaudium et Spes* of Vatican II, to
suggest just this gradual shift from total opposition to evolution of the species to full
acceptance of a global evolutionary perspective a la Teilhard de Chardin. That those
subscribing to such a view are in some way aware that this is a tendentious reading not
proven from the actual content of the documents cited is obvious from the surprise
of one of the editors, Galleni, "Teilhard," 2:2122, that so shortly after all the praise
from the Vatican showered on Teilhard in May, 1981, the *monitum* of 1962 should
be confirmed without modification. Whatever the basis for the praise, the renewal
of the *monitum* is a blunt reminder that the "global" approach to evolution is not the
teaching of the church, whatever its popularity in some ecclesiastical and theological
quarters, nor is it part of a trend signaled by permission to discuss the relative merits
or demerits of a truly scientific hypothesis of evolution.

is dependent on what the Creator himself has told us, and to which science can contribute only indirectly and at best by way of probable deduction. Such can never be a sufficient basis in itself for rejecting or radically recasting the only available historical testimony, that of revelation.

Implicit in this is another point over why evolution could not be immediately interpolated as a possible explanation for the work of the six days. Its recognition makes it fairly easy to understand why Pius XII was unwilling, even if a scientific theory of evolution were shown to be possible and probable on the basis of what is currently observable, to recommend evolution. There exists a qualitative difference between the activities of creatures before and after the completion of the work of creation on the sixth day.

St. Bonaventure has provided[73] one of the best and clearest statements of this point in his discussion of the seventh day or that of the divine rest: not from activity, but from the activity involved in the formation of distinct creatures in terms of their full capacity to act as principal agents in achieving the purpose of creation and in terms of the full number of distinct natures. This he calls the first perfection of the universe, its *esse permanens*, which when completed the Creator ceases to bring forth new "species" capable of contributing to what he calls the second perfection of the universe, the *esse decurrens*, by which the distinct creatures in acting and reproducing faithfully according to their natures and coordination contribute to the harmony and beauty of the Creator's achievement.

Stability, therefore, is the basis and context of change. Without "fixity" there can be no development. But that also means no macroevolution. The so-called "re-creation" based on the incarnation is not to be understood as a repetition of the original work of creation or as the production of a new species and so an exception, but as a new and different kind of process by which the human is elevated to the level of the divine and a most perfect goal of the universe is made possible, the maximum glory of the new-Adam and his Virgin Mother Mary, the anti-type of the "virgin earth," not only from whom but by whom his body is formed.

The two periods are quite different: in terms of principal agents and in terms of created starting points and goals of the respective processes. In the work of the six days God alone is agent and the distinction and coordination

---

73. *II Sent.*, d. 15, a. 2, q. 3. St. Thomas agrees: cf. *ST* I, q. 73, a. 1, ad. 2. So too Suarez, *De opere sex dierum*, 2, 11, n. 2.6. Although God might create or form new species after the sixth day, in fact with the exception of human souls, nothing new has been created, nor are there any grounds for thinking something new might be created. The conservation of creatures and administration of the world pertains not to the creative work completed on the sixth day, but to what follows. Whence it can be described as a "continuing creation" only improperly. Before the recent appearance of the theory of "theistic evolution" no sound Catholic theologian thought otherwise.

of creatures the end. In the second God only enters as a principal agent at the incarnation; otherwise constituted species are the coordinated principal agents, the goal being not the constitution of new species, but faithful acting according to nature so as to attain the return of all things to the Creator.

With this in mind it is not too difficult to grasp the basis for the limits Pius XII places on discussion of evolution and origins. These limits are what we already know from the sure teaching of the church about origins, more exactly that period of time or duration running from the beginning of creation to the completion of the work of the Creator on the sixth day. Even in the event that evolution should be demonstrated to be a genuine, viable scientific hypothesis (and not a mere disguise for a modern form of pantheism and naturalism), it would have to be so formulated as to respect the following theological certitudes:

- the direct and immediate creation *ex nihilo* by God of every human soul at the moment of conception,

- the immediate formation of Eve directly from Adam by the Creator and

- the immediate formation of Adam from antecedent matter by the Creator.

Whether that matter was inorganic, or already living in some way the encyclical did not decide. Evidently, however, on the hypothesis that some kind of evolution was involved, where the starting point of the formation was already living matter (rather than the slime of the earth), the evolutionary aspect of the process could not be merely natural. This is because as the pope remarks that would make a brute a progenitor or father of Adam in the formal sense, something contrary to the revealed account. Hence, such a process would have to involve some miraculous intervention of the Creator, in which case the natural process is a mere instrument, incapable of itself of begetting in such wise as to justify calling the beast the progenitor or father of Adam.

What was realized by most theologians in 1951, with the limits of the discussion so tightly drawn and with the introduction of the supernatural, one could hardly describe this as a scientific theory to be evaluated principally on scientific grounds. Rather it is a theological one for which there are no known theological grounds.

What was relatively seldom noted was the lapse in logic in employing a term characteristic of *esse decurrens*, evolution or development of a species within limits initially set by that species (microevolution), to the quite different activity entailed in bringing that species to be initially, viz., in originating its *esse permanens* (macroevolution). Conversely, the application of the term "continuing creation," while appropriate to describe the activity involved in the completion of the initial creation within the *Hexaemeron*, is hardly used with exactitude to describe the quite different developmental activity of natural agents following on the completion of the creative work.[74]

In one way, however, Pius XII did not only permit, but in a certain sense encouraged the scientific study of a scientific hypothesis to resolve the question: does such an hypothesis enjoy any scientific certainty, and are there any grounds for indicating how such a certainty, if proven, might be reconciled with revealed fact, or whether any such reconciliation were needed in the event science disproved evolution. The encouragement was genuine, but it hardly predicted an outcome in favor of theistic evolution. Careful assessment of subsequent scientific study shows the absence of any scientific proof for the hypothesis of macroevolution, and indeed serious doubt about the scientific character of a hypothesis incapable of scientific verification or falsification. Indeed, according to creationist scientists, microevolution tends to suggest something quite different and not rightly termed evolution.

Humani Generis and Patristic-Scholastic Terminology: Bonaventure and Scotus

What this means in more traditional patristic-scholastic terminology might be formulated thus: all change and/or development in the world as we know it since the completion of the Creator's work on the sixth day presupposes the fixity, or better stability of the species as a point of departure for all natural processes and defines the limits within which such change and development (read evolution if it so pleases) occurs. The "within" equals "micro." Differentiation of species, or origin of species—note well: not change of one species into another—equals "macro." Of such "change" there is not a shred of scientific evidence to be had from those natural processes which are the direct object of scientific reflection. And since, as we have already remarked, there exists no basis for a simple extrapolation of laws governing change after the "sixth" day onto whatever processes might have been involved in the differentiation of the species, there are insufficient grounds for employing theories of evolution, whatever their

---

74. One may use the term creative in a broad sense to describe the original (or originating) character of the activity of creatures capable of artistic or intellectual or voluntary agency, but such activity is not evolutionary in the natural sense.

possibility and probability, to explain the origin of the species, where the species is not the principle, but the term of a process.

Ratio Seminalis *and* Natura Communis

The full differentiation of the species, according to St. Bonaventure, is the term of the process. But the same species, called by the Saint at its initiation a *ratio seminalis,* is its point of departure, not a less perfect species out of which and/or by which full differentiation originates. The theistic evolutionist holds the more perfect species somehow comes to be, not only out of, but by means of the activity of a less perfect and different species. Bonaventure on the contrary holds that all the species in their initial *esse permanens* qua *rationes seminales* were "concreated" with matter in the beginning before the first day, and afterwards by the Creator alone as efficient cause, brought in orderly sequence to their full perfection in *esse permanens* qua *species,* so as to enjoy within the cosmos in fact as well as potentially an *esse decurrens:* full distinction as autonomous species, not a change or transformation.[75] Indeed, from what the Seraphic Doctor tells us about the meaning of the term species, it seems probable he would reserve the term species to the *rationes seminales,* not as initially "concreated," but as fully and autonomously distinguished one from another.[76] By origin *materialiter* Bonaventure means, then, the reproduction or simple eduction of an individual form from the potentiality of matter fully constituted by the Creator as a species in *esse permanens,* whereas by origin *seminaliter* he intends the origin of universal form or *ratio seminalis,* the *natura communis* of Scotus.[77]

But neither is this by itself a basis for subscribing to a theory of "special creation" (a term popular with Protestant creationists) to explain the differentiation of the species in which each distinct species is produced immediately by an act of creation *ex nihilo.* St. Bonaventure, one of the best exponents of tradition on the work of the six days (the *Hexaemeron*),

---

75. *II Sent.,* d. 15, a. 1, q. 1, ad 1.

76. *I Sent.,* d. 31, p. 2, a. 1, q. 3. The term "species," he tells us, has a threefold connotation: 1) a certain likeness or form in sensible beings capable of being reproduced, both in new individuals and in the organs of perception of living beings capable of sensation (there the *species impressa*); 2) the property and root of intelligibility of such a being qua specifically distinct (the "specific difference" of logic) or its "specificity," or its proportional (numerical) character qua form; and 3) that "specificity" qua harmonious proportion, or beauty, attractiveness. In this perspective the more recent and somewhat more restricted sense of the term species in modern science, in particular taxonomy, derives from and depends on this philosophical analysis.

77. *II Sent.,* d. 18, a. 1, q. 3.

describes[78] such a theory in its various forms[79] as making little sense, neither in terms of the revealed account (for the first) nor in terms of metaphysics and physics (for the second). The work of the Creator indeed involves a process terminating at the distinction of the animal species. It is a process he describes as *seminaliter*, one to be carefully distinguished from that which he designates as *naturaliter*.[80] Both involve the species or *ratio* or essence or nature of a particular living creature, but in a different way. The first refers to the process by which in fact the Creator, as the only principal agent, brings the different species to full status or actuality as principal agents of reproduction. The second is the process of reproduction of the species once constituted. The processes are not identical and only to a point comparable. The second does not admit of "macroevolution." Should the first (in modern terms) be called macro or theistic evolution? Bonaventure would hardly be inclined in that direction, since the terminology seems to imply the similarity rather than dissimilarity is greater, when in fact the contrary is the case: whatever process, a miraculous event, one in which God is the sole principal agent, is always more unlike than like the "natural" process in which the sole principal agent is the creature.

But neither is Bonaventure willing to call this process of formation from some preexistent matter (and so not immediately from nothing) creation. Indeed, the "species," or *rationes seminales*, viz., creatures with the power of reproducing their species faithfully in a natural way (as principal agent), not changing it, were first concreated with matter before the first day, like the four basic elements, their presence in the unformed or chaotic matter making that initial finite reality called out of nothing a kind of *seminarium* out of which, but not by which, the entire work was brought to perfection over a duration designated the six days, after which comes the seventh day (of God, not of the world, which is evidently more than twenty-four hours). This seminal formation embraces two steps, the first creation in the strict sense, the second formation by God alone.[81] The

78. *II Sent.*, d. 15, a. 1, q. 1, dealing with the origin of animal souls.

79. He refers to them as the origin of the species *ex nihilo* or *materialiter et seminaliter*.

80. *II Sent.*, d. 18, a. 1, q. 2.

81. In the example of the Egyptian magicians who turned their wands into serpents and serpents who beget naturally offspring, given by St. Bonaventure to illustrate the difference between seminal and natural production (cf. *II Sent.*, d. 18, a. 1, q. 2), he assumes that in the preternatural prodigy of the magicians we have an example of a seminal production, not of a new species, but of one already latent in matter. Whereas in begetting offspring the serpent species reproduces not seminally, but naturally. No new species could be produced unless the Creator created additional species as in the beginning. Seminal production, it should be noted, in Bonaventure does not correspond to

obvious and literal reading of Genesis, then, is one which is also includes considerable subtlety without the adjustments of latter-day hermeneutics to get beyond a claimed simplistic myth.

Essentialist Versus Existentialist Metaphysics and Development

Although at first glance St. Bonaventure's exegesis may seem to the modern reader no longer accustomed to Christian metaphysics in an essentialist rather than existentialist key as one bordering on the incomprehensible, a brief comparison of the term "seminary" or *seminarium* employed by him to define more precisely the "chaos" can be helpful. This *seminarium* is not chaotic, but refers to the relatively incomplete condition of the initial material creation. This is similar to another ancient usage of that word to denote a school or place of development of the innate capacity of the human mind to know. The light of reason or capacity to know being is the capacity to know all that is in any way being. But without some "development"—or if you will "evolution"—of that capacity one can hardly say the human mind is fully enlightened, or that barring a miracle education can be completed instantaneously. But neither can one say that this development is at all the same as organic evolution in any form. Should mental development be called evolution, perhaps implying one can know something that is not being? Or rather is it not much clearer to call the process of learning under the guidance of the "seminary" master formation of what already is?

Adam and Eve: Distinction Between Formation and Creation

St. Bonaventure in any case does prefer the word formation, which is that of the inspired account for the origin of the bodies of Adam and Eve. Here he makes clear another capital point: the formative work of the Creator by which the "creative work begun in the beginning is brought to completion on the sixth day" (*operis inchoati completio*) is to be further distinguished. First, that bearing on the formation of heavenly and earthly bodies (the inorganic world). Second, that bearing on the formation of the living species

---

modern usage of that word as a synonym for natural. Further it presumes familiarity with the metaphysical concept of essence *a parte rei*. Implicit in this choice of the word *seminarium* is a clear allusion to Our Lord's parable of the Sower (Himself) and the seed, the earth or material element being the seminary, the place of the seeds. The parable is about human moral life and grace, but the prefigurement is in the distinctive process by which the species originate: neither immediate creation, nor evolution, but seminal or sowed formation. Cf. Matt 13:24–43.

(the organic world, especially of beasts) and that bearing on the formation of Adam and Eve. Only the second is a process which is properly called "seminal," viz., from preexistent *rationes seminales* by the further formative action of the Creator.[82]

The body of Adam, according to the Seraphic Doctor was formed immediately by the Creator alone from the "slime of the earth" or "virgin earth," among other reasons to stress the dignity and radical difference between the human body and that of the brute and to underscore the true origin and "paternity" of Adam in relation to the Creator. Whereas with seminal origination in the case of the animals there is a radical likeness between starting point and term of the process.[83] The formation of Eve's body immediately from Adam cannot be described as a "seminal process," because her nature is not distinct from, but identical with that of Adam, as his is not identical with that of the earth.[84] Whereas Bonaventure might grudgingly consent to calling seminal formation a kind of development or "evolution" managed by God—a terminology verging on equivocation, he would never consent to such a name in the case of human origins, so different is the process of formation of our first parents from the process of reproduction of the beast.

Rather the process, whereby the species concreated in the beginning without that full and orderly distinction necessary for autonomous functioning were brought to a state of full distinction, can be compared (up to a point) only with the process of human generation, often called for this reason not breeding, but procreation. The relation between the first moment of conception of a person who simply did not exist previously and the human being existing in the maternal womb on the day of birth, with a body sufficiently developed and distinct from that of its mother to be able to enjoy independent existence, is similar to that of the species indistinctly concreated in the beginning and distinctly formed (and so distinctly perceptible) at a later moment during the *Hexaemeron*. Both at the beginning

---

82. This introduces the question of the intrinsic activity of prime matter—Scotus and the problem of singular non-personal and personal in defining formation—related to the problem of common nature: absolute or relative, viz., relation to the/an exemplar. Exemplar cannot change, but individual existing can under divine creative influence, the *exemplatum* being not only passive, but dynamic qua *exemplatum*, thus cooperating at least figuratively in the process. This might be called "macroevolution" culminating in Adam: from both Creator and creation (virgin-earth, figuratively the Immaculate), thus male and female. This implies the distinction of man and woman and the multiplication of Adams. Key questions at this point are: is there a process with two terms? and is the subject or individual undergoing change by the Creator actively cooperating? If so, then some kind of genuine evolution is involved.

83. *II Sent.*, d. 17, a. 2, qq. 1–3.

84. *II Sent.*, d. 18, a. 1, qq. 1–2.

and end of the process of gestation, person and nature, body and soul, are the same person and nature, body and soul. The person born did not evolve out of something not a person; the human body did not evolve out of a body not human nor even out of the mother: it was procreated by mother and father and attained mature distinction by a process not identical with natural reproduction of the beast.

Does this creative process of formation in its three different forms involve a duration, a time span, or are they instantaneous and simultaneous as St. Augustine and a few other fathers, and perhaps St. Thomas thought? The church has never condemned that position, as it has not condemned the position of those who interpret the six days as periods of time longer than twenty-four hours, as the seventh day obviously is. St. Bonaventure recognizes[85] that on this question we cannot offer more than probable opinions—well founded in many instances, yet hardly the last word (which we may only discover in heaven). But what he has to say, with all due respect to Fr. Jaki,[86] is extraordinarily enlightening. The initial, unformed creation before the first day, may have had a duration, but it is measureless, first because there was in it no *esse decurrens*, involving succession to be measured, and second, because the Creator had not yet defined the measure of the various durations other than the aeviternity of the angels. Thus, it is impossible for us to say whether this period of the existence of the *seminarium* was a day, a year, a millennium, a million eons. In regard to this beginning St. Bonaventure agrees with St. Augustine: there is involved a certain simultaneity and instantaneity (absence of duration in coming to be). But in regard to the completion of the work of creation so that it might function for the end willed by the Creator, St. Bonaventure posits a succession of steps involving formative rather than creative acts of God, perhaps involving a duration longer or shorter, or not at all.[87] The obvious literal sense of day (of the first six days) is that of twenty-four hours, a view to which Bonaventure is inclined, but unwilling to give the status of absolute certainty. What is more important is his insistence that the duration of each creature within that of the universe is qualitatively different: time, history, aeveternity, and, finally, transcending all these the divine eternity. Clearly it is not possible to conceive of the world's duration as a single, univocal line, the knowledge of one part of which enables us to understand and apply the same laws to some other part. Since during the *Hexaemeron* neither the

85. *II Sent.*, d. 12, a. 1, q. 2, conc.

86. Jaki, *Genesis 1*, 133–36, where the noted author confesses that he has little esteem for the theology of the Seraphic Doctor on the question of origins.

87. Cf. Lombard, *II Sent.*, d. 17, c. 3, where he says Adam was formed instantaneously by God as a mature adult.

natural agency of the creatures already formed, nor their duration define the character of the processes terminating in the full constitution of the species as we know them, but only the will of the Almighty, there is but one way of knowing what was done and how it was done factually: revelation of that will. From that knowledge we can also afterwards gain profounder insights into the *esse decurrens* of the universe.

John Paul II and *Humani Generis*
on the Question of Origins

With this in mind one can also place the 1996 address of Pope John Paul II in better perspective. Obviously, he is personally inclined to favor theistic evolution, but hardly in a simplistic way. He would prefer for that process involving the Creator as principal agent before the seventh day the term "continuing creation," as an explanation of what is meant by theistic evolution. Whatever his personal opinions concerning the probability of some process which can somehow be called evolutionary in a technical sense (and not merely as a synonym for change), he is hardly imposing this on the church or in any way, even conditional, obliging any Catholic to assent to this. He clearly recognizes that the gaps to be explained are not with certainty explained by the concept of "continuing creation," and that to do so must involve some supernatural agency. All this ultimately entails agreement with the limits of Pius XII on the dialogue if the radical harmony of faith and science is to be fruitfully enjoyed. In a word, the discussion today, theologically speaking, stands exactly where it stood after *Humani Generis*. The only question to be pinpointed is this: are there any grounds: scientific, metaphysical, theological for preferring the terminology suggested by the pope, or for insisting on something closer to that of St. Bonaventure?

Equivocal Assumptions and Their Clarification in a Third Option

In the rest of this essay, I am not so much interested in answering that question or in detailing how so many so easily overlooked both the directives of Pius XII and the actual direction taken by scientific study. Nor do I intend to try to explain how so many among better educated Catholics, clerical as well as lay, either accepted some or all of the major premises of theistic evolution (not necessarily in its radical Teilhardian format) considerably prior to *Humani Generis* and failed to correct these in the light of the encyclical; or overreacted in favor of some version of "special creation," viz., of the species.

Rather I wish to point out the equivocal assumptions which sympathy for or acceptance (and sometimes the rejection) of theistic evolution reinforce. The existence of these assumptions in great part accounts both for the ease in which evolutionary theory spread among Catholics and for the difficulty in persuading Catholic clergy and theologians of the falsity and danger of evolutionary theory. Any realistic hope of bringing about a recognition of the true theological status of evolution as this was commonly set out *circa* 1950 must effectively expose and refute them.

No doubt there are many ways of formulating the offending equivocations. But for the purposes of this conference, in formulating and replying to the question: are creation and evolution friends or enemies, the following three headings seem to me crucial: (1) the priority of science and the equivalency of change and evolution; (2) the priority of becoming in all human knowledge; (3) time as continuing creation or creative evolution.

> [An additional problem this section could address: how to correlate the notion of species or essence, absolutely unchanging in the mind of God with that of common nature existing outside the mind of God, which is found only in a singular mode (*in genere suo*) and which indeed according to Bonaventure is relatively qualified by mutability either toward something more perfect or less perfect. This is the question of the relation between the metaphysical and empirical, one controlling interpretation of what is observed to have happened or to be happening.]

First Assumption: The Priority of Science and the Equivalency of Change and Evolution

By science here is intended "empirical science" in the modern sense, or physical or natural science in the Aristotelian, not science as a generic term for organized knowledge of any kind. And by priority is meant not that this is the only kind of science, or that the methodology of this science is absolutely normative for all other types of science (though often enough this is the popular understanding and the practice in academies of learning), but something more basic. The validity and perfection of any other science, metaphysics and theology included, are conditioned by the relative perfection of the empirical science, whose character determines the context in which all other reflection on the world is conducted.

The equivocation behind the assumption is this: because change and development are a universal feature of all the observable phenomena of the world, and this activity or motion is the primary concern of empirical science, therefore change or evolution or becoming must be the fundamental feature of any non-scientific explanations of the origin and end of that activity, or such non-scientific knowledge of reality is illusory. If the non-empirical forms of knowing fail to reflect this empirical-evolutionary context of the *real*, they thereby fall into the category of *imaginary* or *mythical* knowing. The premise is equivocal and the conclusion is false.

> [However, the problem still remains: metaphysical knowledge of being (the species as such) does not directly explain what appears to be the radical mutability of singular as type imbedded in matter.]

Thus, the equivocation often appears in the context of an objection to the five ways of St. Thomas for recognizing the existence of God: how can these be fully trustworthy if the "science" of St. Thomas is so primitive vis-à-vis the sophistication of its modern counterpart? Or how can creation theology based on the literal (and unscientific) character of the first chapters of Genesis be valid, if such an approach rejects evolution as such, or substitutes the *non-empirical*, pre-conceptual, mythical science of the primitives for the *critical*, empirical, realistic science of the moderns?

The simplest and most effective answer is to deny the assumption. It is simply not true that such disciplines as metaphysics or theology have but indirect or mediated contact with experience and with the real or "objective," and so depend essentially for their cultivation and validity on the mastery of empirical science by the metaphysician or theologian, or on the degree of perfection of science in any given culture. Nor is it true that the man untrained in the sciences is incapable of knowing reality as such, but only in the form of *myth*: pre-conceptually or symbolically. That capacity to truly know reality, easily verified in the simplest of persons, obviously explains why one does not need three advanced degrees in science and philosophy to tell the difference between man and ape, and why we spontaneously doubt not only the fact, but the possibility of the descent of man from the brute. There may be other reasons, however, why the theologian or metaphysician or historian or man in the street should be acquainted with questions of science. A good case can be made for such in view of the confirmation and support sound science gives to creation theology. But one of these reasons is not his initial and direct and objective knowledge of being *a parte rei* (as it is extra-mentally: stable being [*esse permanens*] as well as being undergoing change [*esse decurrens*]).

[A remaining weakness of this response: non-scientific knowledge of the empirical or physical (operative, in motion) world
is pre-conceptual in the sense of pre-rational or scientific. Is it
metaphysical? Metaphysics prescinds from the physical totally
to be metaphysical. Hence, if there is non-scientific knowledge
of the physical, it can only be, so the critic will argue, a kind of
mythical knowledge, that of archetypes, symbols. The theologian
dealing with the created can do so only via interpretation of symbols (aesthetic-ethical experience) or in terms of a scientific hermeneutic articulated about the concept of motion or "evolution."
It is here that the importance of the ontological argument is to be
discovered, and the contributions of Scotus to a theory of matter,
motion and recapitulation in "Adam" through "the Virgin."]

   This is why the theological doctrine of creation does not exclude, as
it is so often falsely accused of doing,[88] evolution as a generic synonym for
change (e.g., microevolution, development, etc.) but only evolution theory
as the explanation of the origin of finite being and the differentiation of the
species. This theological certainty does not depend on a scientific proof of
creation, which science alone cannot give, nor does it depend on a rejection
of evolution as scientific, which science can give. In a word: experience of
reality does indeed include the element of change. But the objective possibility of change, as well as its explanation is not primarily a matter of empirical science, for the simple reason that the content of observable experience
and its knowability transcend the limits of empirical science, viz., precludes
its priority, or better posits the priority of the stable in experience over the
(relatively) unstable or changeable. Hence, change or becoming does in fact
(in the extramental realm or *a parte rei*), as well as in theory, rest on the unchanging. For that reason, explanation of that change based on the changeless or stable or "fixed," far from being a form of aprioristic rationalism or
imaginary literalism, is not an unrealistic imposition of ideology conflicting
with the formal concerns of empirical science or a denial of change itself
(generation and corruption of individuals of established species).[89]

   [This comment needs to be complemented by the reflections of
   Scotus on the basis of the exemplars in divine mind, viz., the
   role of the divine will and its rationality. This in turn explains

   88. Under the heading of "fixism," a term often used by evolutionists to ridicule the
perfectly sane concept of stable nature, *esse permanens*, in the thought of St. Augustine
and St. Bonaventure.
   89. Kant in his classic denial of precisely this possibility, not only failed to provide
an adequate response to the anti-scientific casualism of Hume, but paved the way for
the radical philosophical evolutionism of Hegel.

why the theoretical possibility of macroevolution as defined earlier is an *a priori* of science and of finite existence, even if such never occurred in fact. Once postulated hypothetically (in a voluntarist perspective of common nature), then a second question may be raised: in view of the perfection of the universe, or of the re-creation, is it fitting that the "continuing creation" (after the first moment which is purely creative) include a kind of macroevolution, the figurative *substratum* of what terminates in recapitulation in the Creator become (second) Adam? This is what is meant by exemplary or personal causality at the root of all secondary causality, efficient and final, a type of causality present in the universe from the beginning, cooperating with the Spirit Creator.]

On the other hand, the possibility of empirical science depends on the logically antecedent validity of the second and third degrees of abstraction, viz., of mathematics and of metaphysics, the former being dependent on the latter. The reason is this: what is identified at the first level of abstraction, the actual or real in the form of motion and change (natural processes) rests on form and proportion (the real identified at the second level of mathematics) and in turn on being, general and specific (identified at the third level of metaphysics). The priority of science in the interpretation of experience and of the observable rests on an identification of extramental reality with change (or evolution) and stability with the intramental (or the metaphysical), which are false premises.[90] Just as change in fact is not possible without stability, so neither is science possible except in dependence on the validity of metaphysics and mathematics. Hence empirical science cannot exhaust the content of experience and of the observable. Therefore, it cannot enjoy an absolute priority in regard to the resolution of questions not properly scientific.

We may add that a full metaphysics ultimately rests on theology, as St. Bonaventure saw so clearly in his little masterpiece of pedagogical theory, *De reductione artium ad theologiam*. One may cultivate all these branches of learning without adverting expressly to these lines of dependence (called *reduction* by the Saintly Doctor), but unless one adverts to them, there remains

90. This peculiar prejudice, a consequence of the repudiation of scholastic realism and a notion of empirical science as exclusively objective in great part undergirds the modern prejudice, namely, that if what is recounted in the first chapters of Genesis cannot be validated in terms of a textbook of physics, it is not objective and any attempt to defend its contents as objective knowledge about the origin of all things, including the objects of science, viz., natural change, is immediately branded as literalism and myth. On such assumptions the very existence of a Creator must eventually be considered mythical.

a very real danger of tragic equivocation, as in the present case where the fact of change has become *self-explanatory*, as in evolution theory.

The Origin of Knowledge, the Senses, and Abstraction

The same point can be made in terms of the old axiom: all human knowing in our present state begins factually with sense knowledge: *nil in intellectu nisi prius in sensibus*. But neither sense knowledge nor empirical observation is empirical science or physical science (Aristotle's first degree of abstraction). When that sense knowledge takes the form of scientific or organized intelligence or understanding, it does so implicitly (objectively) or expressly in dependence on two givens: (1) the relation between all sense objects and the divine exemplars, and (2) their relation to the the light of reason.[91]

It is one thing to observe the present moment and note how all objects of sense perception are subject to change and development—and, if one desires, speak of this phenomenon as the evolutionary character of the world. It is quite another to reflect on this and to organize one's knowledge of this scientifically, or critically in order to understand the nature and purpose of the world: its origin, its inner structure, its goal. The questions arise naturally. If the scientist is aware of them and if in some way these questions cannot help but condition his work as scientist, the methods and formal object of empirical science or physics in the broad sense will be understood as dealing directly only with the present operation of individual agents in the world. That the experience of reality should include an awareness of questions concerning origins and ends which science neither treats nor answers, is but an indication of the priority of metaphysics in the mental realm and the priority of being and the immutable in relation to the phenomenal and changeable in the extramental realm.

The object of metaphysics (that which transcends the natural), at the very heart of reality and of the spiritual experience of reality, from the start is precisely the object of a discipline that makes it possible to attempt an answer to the questions of origins and ends, answers only presented in a complete manner when that metaphysics is perfected by theology and theological history. The fathers and great scholastics saw this clearly. They did not imagine Genesis to be a textbook of empirical science of any kind, because they realized Genesis dealt with the presuppositions of science and of the current

---

91. These two givens refer to the capacity of the human mind not only to (1) abstract or prescind from the sense characteristics obscuring the intelligible as such, but (2) to judge, viz., critically esteem, why a particular is true, that is, what its relation to Truth as such is.

operation of the world. And since with the help of revelation they understood that the work of creation comprised not only the initial act of calling
something from nothing into existence, but the specific differentiation and
correlation of the various beings within that created world, they realized that
metaphysics dealt not only with being in general, but with what Scotus called
its disjunctive transcendentals,[92] infinite and finite being.

Equivocations on Being and Species

Finite being is not merely being, nor merely this individual being, but "specific" being. The notion of species of the neo-scholastics, or common nature
of Scotus, or *ratio seminalis* of Augustine and Bonaventure, is neither a universal (a mental reality) nor the individual form determining the potential of
matter to this or that, but precisely the metaphysical aspect[93] of each finite
being qua distinctive being. Modern usage fails to appreciate this feature of
the traditional Christian essentialism: the perfections or formalities (*rationes* in Augustine and Bonaventure) which are neither mental constructs nor
the forms of existing individuals, yet that which in the individual, so long as
it is there, accounts for its intelligibility and stability. Rather modern usage
tends to confuse species or common nature with the individual acting and
changing and tends to conclude the stable or fixed species is merely a mental
construct, no longer particularly useful. For Augustine and Bonaventure,
the *seminalis* qualifying *ratio* means not an individual seed, but the power
of a finite organic essence or species to reproduce itself in individuals, not a
capacity to originate itself or anything else.[94]

92. *Disjunctive transcendentals*: the *common* transcendentals are properties of being
as such, whether perfect or imperfect. The *disjunctive* are properties of being as such,
but not in being of every degree of perfection. In the thought of Scotus, the disjunctive transcendentals play a key role in the elaboration of the notion of being and the
primary proof for God's existence (that associated with the name of St. Anselm). To the
contrary, in the metaphysics of St. Thomas, with its repudiation of the theory of divine
illumination, the proof of St. Anselm and the formal distinction, they play no key role.

93. *Metaphysical aspect*: in the Augustinian-Bonaventurian-Scotistic approach the
metaphysical constitution of any specific being connotes initially not a concept, however objectively valid, but an extramental reality (*a parte rei*) real, objective, prior to any
intellectual reflection on it.

94. As noted above neither Augustine nor Bonaventure hold for a "special creation"
of the species on one of the days of the first week. Rather all the species were "concreated" with matter before the first day. Augustine holds their concreation and their
full distinction or "first perfection" *in esse permanens* were simultaneous; Bonaventure
holds that the full distinction of the *rationes* followed upon their concreation in the
beginning, a distinction effected by the Creator alone, not however *ex nihilo*, but via a
formation from the preexistent *rationes seminales*.

[This is true, but does not finally resolve question of the possibility of macroevolution before the formation of Adam or first recapitulation and of this "macroevolution" providing the symbol or figure of subsequent types of development (not in the biosphere, but in the historical and then spiritual, all terminating in a second or new recapitulation, this time in the divine Adam through the virgin Woman-Eve). To be noted: in recapitulation the theory of multiplicity of forms is crucial to the possibility of macroevolution and final disappearance of plants and animals in final recapitulation.]

Science indeed does deal with the origin of the individual and with hylomorphic theory, for this is a physical question. It does not deal directly with the origin of the species any more than with the origin of being as such because this is a metaphysical-theological question. For Scotus the theory of matter and form explains the physical composition of what actually exists and so comes under scientific study as well as metaphysical. But the antecedent composition of the species in terms of finite perfections is a metaphysical question. The failure to appreciate the distinction has led many theistic evolutionists—not necessarily always scientists[95]—to interpret the Augustinian *ratio seminalis* in hylomorphic terms, as though the progression of time (evolution) could lead to an eduction of the various species or forms from the potential of the original creation (unformed matter).

And the same failure to appreciate fully the metaphysics involved in definition of the species or *ratio* and the distinction between *ratio seminalis* and *ratio naturalis*, between the work of God before the seventh day and the work of the universe thereafter, has led them to jump to conclusions about a "special creation" and a strictly twenty-four hour day, not warranted scientifically, nor accurate theologically, and fail to appreciate the difference between a seminal process activated by the Creator terminating in a distinct species and a natural process activated by a created agent and terminating in the reproduction of the same *ratio seminalis* or species. The first is not a special creation, because it is a process, but neither is it an evolution from a less perfect *ratio seminalis* or species to a different and more perfect *ratio seminalis*. It is, rather, a change of the same *ratio seminalis* as an active power, being fully realized in its *esse permanens*. In state and appearance, it is incapable of activating that power to a state in which both in condition and appearance it is so capable. The difficulty is not in

95. There have always been excellent scientists who have accepted this traditional Catholic approach, e.g., as set forth by Scotus, but also by St. Thomas. This is particularly true in the field of taxonomy. Cf. Thompson, "Systematics," 493–99; and by the same "Evolution," 549–70.

the Augustinian-Bonaventurian-Scotistic line of thought, but the currently well-nigh total unfamiliarity with essentialist metaphysics.

[Theories of special creation show their fallacious aspect when they so easily immortalize plants and animals in paradise, both first and final.]

In this line of thought the notion of being is not simply a notion or concept or idea like those so easily—and so often incorrectly—formed of the immediate objects of our senses, a mental construct, subject therefore to constant revision. The notion of being is more unlike these other concepts, and is the unique notion-concept to which all others must be reduced, which it is itself irreducible to science or mathematics, or any other branch of learning. This first notion of being, without which no other can be formed, and which is always present whenever the mind acts qua mind, is rather the first point of contact with the divine light which alone differentiates spiritual from merely material being.

It has been recently suggested in a prestigious reference work on science and faith that the *world*, not *being*, is the foundation of human thought, both in general and in a formally reflexive way (first and second intention).[96] Such a suggestion must ultimately lead, as St. Bonaventure so clearly saw,[97] to the prioritization of change in the extramental world and of myth in the mental, or in other words the idolization of empirical science and epistemological

96. Livi, "Metafisica," 1:946. The article is an interesting and informative one, yet this suggestion effectively negates what is at the heart of all patristic and scholastic understanding of the spiritual as distinct from the material. In every thought and in every volition of the spiritual creature there is, besides the experience and the relatively complex psychological process, a simple element that is not reducible to the finite, that is the tip of the metaphysical, the "supernatural." It is the notion of being so perfect that it cannot not exist (St. Anselm), the initial contact of the mind with that fontal light which alone makes intellection and volition possible to the creature (St. Bonaventure). That contact, not to be confused with an immediate intuition of the divine essence, is what makes it possible for the mind to discern the reality behind the phenomena and discover the essential or "species" which in excluding macroevolution renders a science of microevolution possible. Lonergan in his *Method* (1972) proposes that the traditional patristic and scholastic metaphysics centered in one way or another around being as essence (therefore essentialist and fixist!) should be abandoned in the light of the absolutely revolutionary character of modern culture (everywhere triumphant!) in favor of a philosophy rooted in the subjective (existential change). What is wrong with existentialism, at least from a Bonaventurian-Scotistic viewpoint centered on essence (common nature, species, etc.), was set forth in 1961 by Oromi, *Introducción* and a companion volume dealing with some theological implications by Madariaga, *La Filosofía al Interior* (1961), both unfortunately ignored by the then overwhelmingly popular existentialism in Catholic philosophical circles.

97. In many places in his *Sent.*, in the *Brev.*, the *Itin.*, *Red. art.*, *Chr. mag.*, *Hex.*, above all the *Scien. Chr.*, q. 4.

relativism under the heading of evolution and progress. For the genuine contemplation of the perfect being whose name is He Who Is, pure action and so changeless is substituted the pseudo-mystique of change for its own sake. Once adopted a curious transposition occurs: *evolution* instead of being a *scientific hypothesis* whose truth is contingent on rigorous scientific demonstration becomes a *basic principle* determining how the evidence of science, no matter how contrary to the hypothesis, must be interpreted.

It is a tragedy of our times that what is most characteristic of the intellectual, the ability to perceive being and specific differences of being, has in practice become the most dormant power of the human mind. Were this not so, it would be relatively easy to deal with the second assumption: the priority of becoming in all human knowing. It is rather theological and historical. But this cannot be recognized, let alone understood, unless the native metaphysical bent of the human intellect is cultivated. In the order of fallen nature, this can only be with the help of the light of faith, which unfortunately a considerable part of the academic world refuses—including some so-called Catholic institutions which refuse to acknowledge the role of a divinely appointed magisterium as Christ instituted it, as set forth for instance in the recent *Ex Corde Ecclesiae*.

Second Assumption: The Priority of Becoming in all Human Knowing

The prioritizing of empirical science and the consequently widely accepted identification of the objective or observable reality with change has not a little to do with the *a priori* plausibility attributed to evolution theory as the foundation of all reality over its reputed opposite, creation theory.

> [This paragraph needs qualification in light of comments inserted above. The following needs qualification in terms of experience, consciousness and deliberation. At the heart of this is the Marian factor: acceptance or rejection.]

This in turn contributes not a little to the popularity of a second error: that the unity of human knowledge, or gnoseological unity, without which our understanding of the real cannot escape the confusion, doubt and intellectual paralysis induced by the various disciplines and methodologies in contradiction to one another, is based not on a metaphysical "ideology" of being and fixed species (Plato's world of ideas), but on change or becoming or "evolution." Not being, but a consciousness or sense of evolution or time or history as the fundamental dimension of all reality, of the dynamic as opposed to the static, constitutes the principle of unity prior to and underlying any distinction of sciences. Therefore, it functions as the hermeneutical principle of all interdisciplinary activity, as in the case of the question of origins, involving both empirical science and theology. Whence to the wonder of many excellent scientists and theologians, even if evolution is disproven theologically and scientifically, the theistic evolutionist will counter by saying that the underlying unity of human understanding requires both theology and science to be so adjusted as to rest on the truth of evolution.

Third Assumption: Science Can Know the Origins and Ends of the Material World

Intimately linked to these false assumptions about the changeable as the basic constitutive of the objective world and becoming as the radical context of all gnoseological unity and cultural interchange, is a deeply rooted assumption concerning what science can know about the material world, directly or indirectly, viz., everything knowable about it, including its origins and ends. Nothing so predisposes the mind to naturalism, to the rejection of miracles and the supernatural than these assumptions.[98]

Spiritual Realities

In fact, not only are the invisible, spiritual world of angels, of the intellectual and affective life of human souls, and the infinite being of God beyond the range of scientific study, but a great many aspects, indeed some of the most fundamental of the visible world are also beyond the reach of scientific scrutiny and analysis. Examples include the singular, in particular the personal as distinct from nature; the historical; the miraculous, including miracles which are "physical," e.g., the virgin birth of Jesus, the resurrection of Jesus, eucharistic transubstantiation.

Material Realities

But even those aspects of the sensible world which fall under the direct scrutiny of the scientist cannot be known fully by way of such study. In Aristotelian terms the scientist operating within the limits of the first degree

---

98. This includes the very possibility of creation *ex nilhilo sui et subjecti* by a simple act of the will of an omnipotent and omniscient God.

of abstraction deals with the motion or activity or operation of natural agents[99]—I repeat natural in the sense of physical, not intelligent, rational, free, personal agents.[100] What the formal object of empirical or physical science[101] permits is the knowledge of generation and corruption. This knowledge is extraordinarily valuable and useful. But it is a knowledge by reason of an object and method restricted to what observation of present natural processes can yield, directly or indirectly. It can tell us something about the origin of individual natural agents which is observable in the process. It can tell us something about the nature of the agent or species operating. But it can tell us nothing about the origin of the species, much less of finite being as such. This is a direct matter of theology (metaphysics) and history.

Examples

A few examples will help to make the point more exact. A chemical analysis of the eucharistic species (bread and wine) before the consecration during the Canon of the Mass and of the sacred species veiling the body and blood of Christ after the consecration will fail to identify any difference. But this does not prove nothing happened, or that the change is merely in the perception of the believer. It means only that while transformations can be studied scientifically, transubstantiation is totally (directly and indirectly) beyond the ken of science, yet perhaps nothing in our world so affects matter as this miracle. In this instance theology and metaphysics instruct us directly about some of the most basic aspects of the material and sensible world.

Another example: The chemist can study the inorganic and the organic. He can recognize important differences and identify some of the operative features of the living organism. But chemistry cannot determine the nature of life, nor of its specific variations, much less account for its origin or produce the living out of the non-living. Whatever applied science may do in terms of the organic, it always requires a living *terminus a quo* or point of departure. Life may be modified in a test tube; it cannot be produced therein.

The discovery of DNA was heralded initially as a major scientific breakthrough in favor of evolution, whether theistic or atheistic, as the indispensable frame of reference for all understanding of existence and

---

99. The *agens naturale* or creature as vestige of God.

100. The *agens intellectuale* or creature that is the image of God and not merely a vestige.

101. Not merely modern physics, a branch of science restricted to certain motions of natural agents.

life. It has been presented as the agent of macroevolutionary change. In fact, it is nothing of the kind. Its function rather is conservative of the species in the production and development of individuals whose entire *raison d'être* is not to produce other species, lesser or greater, but to continue in existence, i.e., conserve the species precisely by maintaining limits within which microevolutionary changes can occur and so blocking any "macroevolution." Any artificial intervention to circumvent this, far from inducing a change of species, will only effect its corruption. The concept of endangered species has force only on the assumption that macroevolution does not and cannot occur.

The origin of the world, of the species and of their differentiation and interrelations is not in the first instance a scientific question, and any attempt to approach it as such must inevitably yield not valid scientific hypotheses, but false theology and history. Set out in scientific garb in an age which tends to adore empirical science and to endow it with the attributes of divine omniscience, such ideology functions in fact as the pseudo-mystical side of pantheism and naturalism.

This equivocation, similar to the first, is not, however, identical with it, but complementary. The first assumed that because change is a universal feature of all observable phenomena, therefore change must be the fundamental explanation of everything, including the origin of what changes. Whence the radical instability of the species. This equivocation prescinds from the validity of this illation and argues in terms of the necessary unity underlying the different sciences or disciplines, including theology. Duration or *becoming* rather than *being* provides the basis for gnoseological unity and hermeneutic consistency. In this sense evolution, not viewed as a theory "reductively" or purely scientific, but as the basic "global" view of reality suggested by the primacy and "omniscience" of science in regard to the temporal, connotes the point of departure for dealing with interdisciplinary questions such as the relation between the Creator and his creation. On this assumption a theory of origins which is not radically evolutionary is simply irrational.

Catholic Theology Rejects Total Evolution: Origins is a Question of Theology

Traditional Catholic theology denies precisely such a concept of evolution as a "global" vision of reality which does not permit a rejection of evolution scientifically as false. The possible truth or falsity of some scientific hypothesis must be decided primarily on scientific grounds. But the question of the unity of knowledge has other premises, quite independent of the fact of change or evolution. One of these is the hierarchical subordination of all the arts and sciences (disciplines) to theology[102]—and not inversely, hence excluding the possibility in this life of a kind of grand synthesis (Leibnitz or Hegel) or a terrestrial "beatific vision" made possible on the basis of a "global theory of evolution" conditioning all intellectual methods.

> [Here must be added some consideration of a twofold sense of evolution: (1) as denoting merely a scientific thesis directly applicable to processes under actual observation; and (2) as denoting a metaphysical thesis concerning the *a priori* possibility of the finite-temporal and its relation to the *signa voluntatis divinae*. Dissatisfaction with the absence of such an *a priori* in creation theory on the part of a large number of sincere scholars is surely an indication that the Holy Father's recent observations (1996) must be taken seriously.]

Therefore, the Catholic tradition in theology holds that origins is a question of theology. This is because the origin of all being outside of the Creator and the origin of its specific differentiation is the Creator or Omnipotent God. Origins is also a question of history because the question of origins is a question of what that Creator freely chose to do by a simple command of his will. And since the Creator is the only credible witness and hence only historian, we can only know what he did in fact, how he did it, not by reasoning from the present to the past in terms of what is possible or what is necessary,[103] but by consulting the account the Creator gave of his creative work, an account of the work of the six days eminently readable and intelligible.

> [The foregoing is true, but leaves untouched the obvious question: what constitutes the intelligibility of pre-history (before the first recapitulation in Adam) and history (before the recapitulation in the New Adam)? The differentiation of species within the unity of material world is a formative process, not a creation out of no pre-existence, one which radically includes the principle of active cooperation terminating in recapitulation. This means, at least minimally, some kind of specific or macro development, at the non-personal and at the personal level, constituting a kind of elevation to a new order (sphere). In so far as this elevation

---

102. The classical formulation is that of St. Bonaventure, *Red. art.*, not without parallels in Cardinal Newman's *Idea of a University*.

103. Human science and philosophy can theoretically contribute to our understanding of these points.

always includes cooperation in principle of the subject elevated (a point denied by protestant creationism), do not such terms as élan vital, creative evolution, progressive creation have a legitimate use as well as an illegitimate caricature?]

Personally, I think it is possible to demonstrate the inherent contradiction and so impossibility of total or global evolution, but I also realize I am quite incapable of making this conviction prevail at the moment. One of the weaknesses of pre-conciliar anti-evolutionism among Catholics was a tendency to over-rely on argumentation of this kind and not attend to the far more effective two-pronged approach of tradition (revelation *and* reason, not revelation *or* reason) in regard to the question of the eternity of the world, so similar to and indeed bound up with evolutionary theory of origins: of being in general and specific being in particular.

St. Bonaventure[104] is well known as a supporter of the view that an eternal world could not have been created by God, and that this proposition can be demonstrated metaphysically. St. Thomas[105] (and it seems Bl. John Duns Scotus[106]) differ, not on the first part of the proposition, but on the latter. They hold that the impossibility can only be known with certainty through revelation. Without faith it is impossible to prove the impossibility of an eternal world, but they also add emphatically neither is it possible in the light of reason to prove the possibility of an eternal world. On this point, at least in practice *pro statu isto*, in the state of fallen nature, reason alone yields no firm conclusions, and because a certain answer is indispensable for our eternal well-being, we very much need the testimony of the Creator as guide to our reasoning on this point. But it is also important to note the correct line of reasoning on this point: questions touching origins can only be grasped adequately when knowledge of eternity and what the Creator in fact did is the starting point, not inversely where observable activities of creatures are the initial grounds for speculating about what God might or might not have done.

So, too, with attempts to determine the origin of the world, how the Creator might or might not have initiated and organized his work. The differences between the mode of producing on the part of creatures once created and that of the Creator are greater than the likenesses. Hence, any

104. *II Sent.*, d 1, p. 1, a. 1, q. 2. In agreement with the Seraphic Doctor are St. Albert the Great, and the 17th century Jesuit patrologist, Petavius, and the vast majority of the Fathers. Cf. Mondraganes, "De impossibilitate aeternae mundi," 529–70.

105. *ST* I, q. 46, a. 2; *De Potentia* q. 3, a. 13; *Quodlibet.* 3, a. 31; opusc. *De aeternitate mundi contra murmuratores*. Since the Council of Trent, a larger number of theologians have opted for the opinion of St. Thomas.

106. *Ord. II*, d. 1, q. 3.

attempt to determine *a posteriori* what is characteristic of the creative action of God, whether *ex nihilo* in the strict sense or in the broad sense formative, must rest on a comparison of the creative to the non-creative, of the perfect to the imperfect, and so entail a misrepresentation of what in fact occurred.

> [Here a caveat: the possibility of macroevolution is what un-derlies the intelligibility or *decuit* of what the Creator actually did. Hence Scotus' corrective of Bonaventure on the eternity of world and the Bonaventurian arguments for its impossibility.]

For example, a prior knowledge of "concreation" and seminal production of the species during the *Hexaemeron* can be a great help for the understanding of natural reproduction of the species thereafter without in anyway substi-tuting for the need to study such reproduction scientifically. However, no prior scientific knowledge of such processes can alone provide a sure and inerrant basis for a theory of origins. This is also why radical departures from such traditional (and reasonable) interpretations of Genesis, as those of St. Bonaventure, solely to accommodate scientific hypotheses or philosophic speculation, is a very risky and so imprudent enterprise.

The discussion of the possibility/impossibility of evolution or creation or a combination of both can be useful, but in practice it can never be apo-dictically decisive except to the degree it provides a confirmation of what we already know from faith to have occurred. For the question of the origin of being and of the origin, differentiation and graduation of the species is a theological-historical one in fact. The testimony is of God himself as that has been preserved for us in the unchanging tradition of the church and that tradition embraces the following points:

- an initial creation out of nothing of the visible and invisible finite worlds;
- the organization of the visible world over a period of six days[107] with the differentiation of the species, their graduated organization, culmi-nating in the formation of Adam from the slime of the earth and Eve from the side of Adam;

---

107. On the length of each of the six days Bonaventure would have said (using cur-rent terminology) that his view was solidly probable, viz., that each day was given by God a duration divisible into twenty-four hours, a duration at the basis of our measure of the day as composed of twenty-four hours. He would have further noted that this is a determination of the divine will, not a postulate of some theoretical possibility, whether Augustine's or that of the modern evolutionist. All the evidence points to the correctness of the majority opinion of the fathers.

- the functioning of the visible world on earth placed under the charge of Adam and Eve;

- the rest of God on the seventh day, viz., the commencement of the relatively autonomous operation of the visible universe as a whole;

- the catastrophe of the universal flood which according to St. Peter (2 Pet 3:3–7) radically altered the functioning of the universe (as it will be radically altered again on the last day by fire), thus rendering inconclusive the arguments of those affirming an eternal universe on the basis of present modes of generation and corruption.

St. Bonaventure is right: we should be able to see that an eternal world (and so evolutionary *origin* of the world and species) is a contradiction in terms. But so are St. Thomas and Bl. John Duns Scotus: in fact, only the believer sees the point. One of the reasons is the believer's freedom from a prejudice: viz., the question of origins in all its dimensions is a scientific one, or at least dependent on the resolution of the question qua scientific. A majority of ecclesiastics today are not necessarily enthusiastic about evolutionary theory. But they are afraid to exclude its possibility absolutely, lest they and the church be branded as obscurantist, of planning another "Galileo case" and the persecution of science and scientists. Hence, to be on the safe side they believe they must allow for a purely symbolic or mythical interpretation of Genesis and so for an evolutionary account of origins compatible with belief in creation. Because so few have a genuine understanding of modern science, they fail to see this is no longer the concept of creation found in the tradition of the church. The development of doctrine tends to be seen in terms of "macroevolution," which is one reason so many professional theologians incline to be process theologians or as they are known in Europe neo-Hegelians.

But demolish this assumption and I believe many will return to traditional creationism, a doctrine not at all the enemy, but the support of genuine scientific progress. Scholars have more than once noted that neither Francis Bacon, nor Copernicus, nor Galileo, nor Descartes, nor Newton laid down the basic principles of a fruitful empirical science, but the great scholastics in their teaching on creation and metaphysics provided this grounding.[108] In the long run the belief that the work of creation is principally the work of God alone (whether creating in the strict sense, or forming from preexisting matter), not evolution, can guarantee that progress.

---

108. For example: Duhem, *Système du monde*, especially vols. 3–4. Also, the many studies of Meier on medieval science.

And in insisting that the question of origins in all its dimensions as traditionally understood in the work of the six days as the Creator's work, not creation's, there is no intention to deprecate the importance of the scientific contribution, but simply to point out that empirical science neither defines nor resolves the question. Rather, once the question has been properly formulated scientific study can provide valuable pointers in confirmation or rejection of one or another line of argumentation and solution.

What these pointers are and what they mean does not depend primarily on science, but on theology and history. The question of origins is first of all a question of fact, of history, what happened. That means a recognition of the importance of the old axiom: *a posse ad esse non valet illatio*.[109] Unless one could demonstrate some kind of metaphysical necessity for evolution as an instrument of creation, an impossibility, there is no way of demonstrating apodictically—not the possibility—but the fact of evolution in any form, except by tinkering with the obvious sense of the only available historical testimony and converting it into a myth. Mivart clearly and correctly saw that evolution could not be proven purely on scientific grounds. What he did not grasp in asserting the fact to be certain, even if the scientific riddles of evolutionary "mechanics" were never fully expounded, and which so many others since still do not seem to understand, is that the so called certain historical fact of evolution then rests either on blind choice or fictitious myth.

Those subscribing to theistic evolution recognize the priority of the question of historical fact when they criticize the atheistic evolutionist who attempts to justify his position by an appeal to apodictic scientific proof as indulging reductionism (since no such final scientific proof exists), and so as resting his atheism on very weak grounds.[110] But the gratuitous assertion of global evolution as a fundamental characteristic of finite existence, and the further confusion of natural history (e.g., paleontology) with true history (involving the interaction of free agents and unpredictable contingent choices) in an unbroken linear continuum consequent upon a failure to acknowledge the dissimilarities between the human body and that of the brute, between human procreation and animal breeding as greater than the similarities and constituting an unbridgeable divide for natural processes, deprive the theory of theistic evolution of even minimal probability.

> [This needs qualification. Macro-evolution in Scotistic terms is a viable, indeed necessary construct. What must be distinguished is the difference between macro before and after the first Adam,

109. In matters touching the contingent one cannot argue from possibility to fact.
110. Cf. Galleni, "Evoluzione," 1:584–87.

and then brought into relation with a correct notion of recapitulation and the relation of the great archetypes, male and female, to the vertex of created and uncreated in the Immaculate and Word Incarnate. Further, exemplary and physical causality must be distinguished and exemplary shown to be prior to physical and inherent in matter from the beginning, reaching its most perfect form in the virgin earth. So too, what follows. Evolution as scientific fact cannot be proven. But evolution as a theological construct correctly defined may come to be acknowledged as part of Catholic tradition, even if under less clear titles.]

Once this is grasped, then it should not be too difficult to realize that evolution as a fact will never be proven, why at the moment to so many scientists all the available scientific pointers tend to exclude evolution and favor creation, and why there are no theological reasons postulating evolution whereas there are many such reasons postulating just the contrary.[111] Correct the prejudice and most persons will be willing to admit this. But if the prejudice is left uncorrected, both the promoters and the subscribers to the myth will be unmoved by the lack of scientific proof, indeed by any overwhelming scientific disproof of evolution as scientific, because for them the truth of evolution is not consequent on scientific proof, but on a simplistic faith in a preference for change over stability, development over permanence.

Needless to say, there is no discernible difference between this (prejudicial) faith and the philosophic evolutionism (sometimes called historicism) condemned by name in *Humani Generis*, though without mentioning by name the then best-known proponent, the Jesuit Teilhard de Chardin.[112] How that faith might be shaken requires the examination of one further assumption, the one perhaps lending theistic evolution its greatest plausibility.

Time as Continuing Creation or Creative Evolution

The concept of becoming as the overarching context of the unity of human intellectual endeavor, including the theological, complements and reinforces a key feature of theistic evolution. This is the concept of time as "continuing creation" or "the revelation of evolution as the heart of creation" bearing it

111. E.g., the unicity of the first human couple, original sin, the typology of Adam and Eve in relation to Christ and Mary, the entire vision of the world as functioning in terms of mediation and recapitulation, as will be noted in the next section.

112. For the influence of such "historicism" on some well-known Catholic theologians and philosophers just before, during and after Vatican II, cf. Siri, *Gethsemani*.

dynamically to its goal, not fortuitously, but in virtue of an immanent finality energizing that continuous progressing from imperfection to perfection.
It is this notion of creative evolution which confers both on an impersonal
science and Hegelian idealism and on a rigid theology a dynamic, personal,
existential mystical *elan*, one which *de facto* has fired the imagination of
large numbers of people, believers as well as unbelievers.

Ambiguities in the Notion of Theistic Evolution

One of the major problems of evolutionary theory is its inbuilt proclivity
to divorce any concept of final causality from the operation of efficient
causes, agents of change. All change, macro and micro, is therefore arbitrary or blind, a matter of chance. One need only advert to the popularity of
J. Monod among persons who believe in evolution to recognize the magni-
tude of the difficulty. Or one need only consider the relative defensiveness
of evolutionists confronted by the very effective exposure of this weakness
on scientific grounds in M. Behe's study, *Darwin's Black Box*:[113] unless a
species is what it is in its entirety at the inception of each new individual of
the species, the individual will never be or enjoy any "micro-development."
This is nothing but a scientific verification of the very ancient concept of
entelechy, and it is easily grasped, as Behe notes, in the development of the
eye. Either all the parts of the eye are present from the beginning, even if
not obvious to superficial observation, or they will never develop. What
is originally not an eye seminally, but something else, cannot produce a
whole eye as a consequence of a graduated mutation of parts. For the parts
of the eye cannot function so as to grow into a mature eye, unless they
are all present at the inception of such growth as parts of a complete and
"fixed" essence, the *ratio seminalis* of St. Augustine and St. Bonaventure.
Far from providing a traditional and ancient theological basis for theistic
evolution "immanent" finality divorced from "fixed" species defining the
limits of growth positively excludes this.

    This immediately raises the other major problem of theistic evolution:
the lack of any objective *theological* reason for accepting the possibility of
evolution let alone "the fact" as a basis for "rereading" Genesis. If there is
no scientific basis for evolutionary theory and if there are no easily identifi-
able and cogent theological reasons for finding a way to avoid the obvious
meaning of the Genesis account and unanimous patristic and scholastic
interpretation thereof, why should anyone indulge in exegetical acrobatics
to show that Genesis does not objectively mean what most intelligent people

---

113. Behe, *Darwin's Black Box*.

normally understand it to mean, or why the good Lord would reveal such basic truths in a way calculated to deceive all but modern exegetes?

Theistic evolutionists, in their efforts to show that evolutionary theory as such is not radically atheistic or irrational, but indeed eminently reasonable and theological, have tried to counter the problem by describing evolution as the instrument of the Creator, not in the first moment of creation, but in the subsequent work of structuring and organizing the development of the world in view of an ultimate goal, because it is the primary postulate of any theory of cooperation of the creature with the Creator in the return of all things to the Father. Hence aside from any lack of scientific proof, or even the impossibility of scientific proof in the strict sense, evolution is a necessary first principle of all empirical science, if it is to be reconciled with theology and faith. For change or development or evolution, macro as well as micro, is a part of creation from its beginning, before day one, and which in this form continues to the present, linking alpha and omega, beginning and end. This is the third, and perhaps most potent equivocation behind the attractiveness of theistic evolution to so many: the priority of a continuity between all stages and aspects of creation from beginning to end, to be explained principally not in terms of an agency superior to the natural,[114] but principally in terms of energy or powers immanent to the less perfect becoming more perfect.

Creative evolution is synonymous with continuing creation and is neatly opposed to the traditional concept of reaching the goal of creation via a system of mediatory reduction or recapitulation of the lower grades of perfection by the higher and highest: for instance, man in relation to the natural, Christ in relation to redeemed mankind. The traditional notion of the general sacramentality of the created world in reference to the supernatural order (sometimes discussed under the heading of type and anti-type) is based, not on linear progress as postulated by evolutionary theory, but rather on a hierarchical vision of the various grades of being, within which the mediation of the higher agent is foreshadowed by the less perfect. This relation, mistaken as a proof for the existence of an upward evolutionary *elan*, in fact is an aspect of exemplary causality supporting a traditional view of creation.

Time, then, or the duration characteristic of created being is seen as radically univocal and linear, whereas in the traditional view it is analogical, with a coordination and finality not based on a univocal *elan* immanent in each species, but by the mediatory action of a more perfect agent on a

---

114. E.g., the supernatural dynamic of intervention, of mediation, of elevation from above, of recapitulation.

less perfect and the recapitulation effected thereby in the return of all things to the triune Creator. St. Bonaventure calls this the hierarchical[115] structure of the world effected by the Creator alone in the work of the six days. The hierarchization of this world instead is what is effected by the process of recapitulation in the return of all things to the Father.

Whereas the theistic evolutionist posits a uninterrupted continuum between coming forth and return and calls this "continuing creation" in which things developing enjoy a truly creative energy to produce and to rise above a given grade of being (*gradus entium*) established in a stable way by the Creator, the traditional view championed by Augustine, Bonaventure, Thomas, and Scotus posits only an analogical continuity based on the possibility and degree of supernatural intervention in the actual operation of the finite world. Without such that operation not only is merely conservative and not creative in any sense, but ultimately exhaustive, a devolution in accord with the laws of thermodynamics rather than evolution.[116] Instead, the traditional view makes possible an elevation to a higher level via mediation, as Bonaventure points out in his discussion of human nature as essentially mediatory of the corporal in relation to the spiritual.[117] The concept of "continuing creation," blurring as it does the clear distinction between the "six day" creative work of God now over with the subsequent development of that hierarchically structured work by creatures themselves, tends to reintroduce features both of the Aristotelian "eternal world"[118] and of the neo-Platonic notion of creation by way of graduated steps—upward rather than downward. The simple, linear,

115. Hierarchy, hierarchical: in current usage generally associated with social ranking of equals and unequals (as an alternative to an egalitarian approach to order). Etymologically, however, the term means a ranking by God (a sacred person) in a sacred order (such as the church). By analogy St. Bonaventure employs this Augustinian concept of order to the world in general to express his belief that the Creator not only brought into existence the various finite beings, living and non-living, plants and animals, but himself directly gave them their relative degree of perfection and rank within the cosmos as a whole. With this Bonaventure rejects in principle the neo-Platonic explanation of world order via the graduated cooperation of a demiurge and subordinates, but at the same time affirms a basic principle of cooperation of creatures in the return of all things to the Creator: not by way of evolutionary ascent, but by way of hierarchization of the less perfect by the more perfect creature, or mediator, viz., via elevation to a higher order beyond the limits of the lower species.

116. Science conducted without benefit of evolutionary theory would agree. Cf. Thompson, "Work," 62–70.

117. *Brev.*, p. 2, cc. 1, 9–12.

118. What reason other than the dogmatic creed of the church have theistic evolutionists for exempting the existence of the world, of angels and persons as end products of an evolutionary *elan* (as in the thought of Teilhard)?

uninterrupted continuum of "continuing creation" fuses what the tradition maintains cannot be fused with a resulting confusion, not only mentally, but extramentally in the disappearance not only of fixed and unalterable differences between species, but between the natural and personal, natural and supernatural, and indeed the temporal and eternal.

Whereas Catholic theology rejects both, insisting that the graduated degrees of being (differentiation and coordination of species) are solely the work of the Creator in view of future creaturely cooperation in the work of return, a cooperation only ultimately effective to the degree it is open to the supernatural. Thus, whether the world exists, how it is structured and ordered, and to what end it comes, depends first on the divine counsels and will, not on any immanent process of continuing creation.

Underlying this new concept of "continuing creation," then, is a fusion of what in the past was clearly distinguished: the work of creation was principally the work of the Creator and ended on the sixth day. Thereafter the work of "re-creation" or development began, which is not a continuation of the *exitus* of all things from God, but of their *reditus* or return to God. Whereas in the neo-Platonic theories of origin, the cooperation of lesser "demiurges" with the Demiurge is located in the *exitus* or emanation of the various kinds of being from the first being, at root a kind of devolutionary pantheism underscoring not the teaching of the fathers, but the heresies of Arius. In Christian theology the origin of the universe is the sole work of God, the Word being not a lesser demiurge, but equal to the Father. The cooperation of creatures, each according to its nature and relation to beings more perfect than itself, begins only with the completion of the work of creation and the onset of the *reditus* or return of that creation to God. Scripture indeed speaks of the accomplishment in the age of grace as a "new creation," as a "re-creation." The usage of the term creation here, however, is analogical: not the creation or formation of a new species, but a perfecting of the first in the consummation of the work of mediation of the Word Incarnate.

This cooperation, further, requires in the traditional view the recognition of a certain discontinuity between the work of the six days and its conservation, between natural and spiritual, between natural and voluntary, between natural and supernatural, a discontinuity not to be transcended via a linear or univocal progression, but only by way of a mediation from on high. On this point St. Bonaventure notes that such a mediation postulates an analogical or recapitulative-recirculating notion of time and history. Otherwise, each natural grade of being continues to operate conservatively, not creatively or innovatively, within the limits pre-set by the Creator of the species (*ratio seminalis; natura communis*).

Whatever this postulate of theistic evolution is, it is not science, but a kind of pre-scientific faith. Whether it is true on grounds other than scientific, e.g., metaphysics or theology, must be examined before any conclusions about the overall certainty of a universal evolutionary perspective can be made. And if it coincides with the "evolutionism" condemned outright by Pius XII in *Humani Generis*, then it must be repudiated as contrary to the truth and unable to be demonstrated by sound science.

Such a theory rests first on the premise that before man, the final work of creation, is formed on the "sixth day," the creatures already formed are in some way actively (not merely passively as matter from which the Creator forms them) involved in the gradual emergence of more perfect species at a higher level of existence. This requires that the biblical account in terms of six twenty-four-hour days is merely symbolic, having nothing to do either with the actual measures of time or sequence of times in this graduated increase in perfection from imperfection and order from disorder (of the big bang perhaps). Obviously, if it is shown that in fact the six days really were six days, and that by divine choice, not necessity of nature, only six days were needed by the Creator to accomplish all this by himself alone as sole efficient agent,[119] evolutionary theory is finished as a viable scientific theory.

But aside from this point, far more telling against the possibility of theistic evolution is the indisputable fact that nowhere in the biblical account of the work of the *Hexaemeron* is any other effective agent of the work of each day noted except the Creator. Nor does the work of creation begin to function as a whole with a relative autonomy, until the whole is completed and functions or malfunctions (as a consequence of sin and punishment) as a whole, a kind of model of the entelechy found in every species. Thereafter, i.e., after the sixth day, the work functions at each specific level of existence within the limits of each species (or common nature) with a regularity reflecting the limits of the species, a regularity strictly conservative, not evolutionary.

This points to a second mistaken premise, one absolutely fatal for theistic evolution. This second premise holds that the finality which can be observed in the order of the world and in the disorder resulting whenever that finality is not respected, is inherent in the natural processes as autonomous. Translated this means that the creature at a lower level of existence, e.g., non-living, can actively elevate itself to a higher level, e.g., living, or in its most radical form to the very level of divine existence as in the Teilhardian notion

---

119. Because no creature can enjoy the power to effect being as such or define a finite essence as species.

of Christogenesis. Thus, God himself in some way is not only the author, but becomes instead the end product of natural processes.

Theistic evolutionists often point to this "immanent" finality in the evolutionary process as touching all aspects of finite existence including the religious as the "global" approach to all reality as the outcome of process, first fully articulated by Teilhard de Chardin, as opposed to the "reductive" Darwinian approach attempting to justify evolution on scientific certitudes. This "global" approach, they claim, renders irrelevant the older patristic-scholastic notion of fixed or changeless species as the basis for change or development in individuals, or in more general terms process is dependent on and limited by the priority of reality or essence.

In order to make this transposition (essentially Hegelian) from *being* to *becoming* as the first ground of reality it is necessary to understand priority merely in temporal terms and, as Scotus would say, in terms of an "accidentally" ordered series. That is just what genuine Christian metaphysics in terms of the notion of being, and theology on the basis of the first article of the creed deny. The priority here is that of the eternal, of the exemplars in the mind of God according to which the Creator has determined the essence or *ratio* or species of each created type, and which in the material, organic order has endowed with the power (seminal) to reproduce. The priority is not "accidental, but essential," as Scotus so neatly puts it,[120] thus asserting the fixity of the species and of being, not in a phenomenological way, but metaphysically *a parte rei*.

This is particularly clear in Scotus' understanding of the concept of being as univocal, the first concept of the mind constituting as it were the first point of encounter with the light of truth (the divine illumination of St. Bonaventure), a concept unlike any other and to which all others are compared (reduced in the language of St. Bonaventure), a concept of being including its basic modes, infinite and finite, the disjunctive transcendentals. The structure of that concept of being as univocal reflects in fact the dogmatic formula for the incarnation coined by St. Leo the Great: one person, two natures, one infinite, the other finite, united in the unity of one person, therefore undivided, but also not confused (*indivise et inconfuse*), whose appearance is the appearance of him who said: I am the light of the world. The absolute primacy of Christ, in the mind of the Creator as well as in history, is the reason for insisting that the reality which is prior in the finite order, which antecedes any process, and which determines in a fixed manner the grades of being analogically—*indivise sed inconfuse*—is unchanging, and so

120. *De primo omnium rerum principio*, his brief treatise perfecting the classic argument of St. Anselm and St. Bonaventure for the existence of God.

is truer. This primacy of Christ, in fact, makes change and history possible and intelligible: *id verius quod prius, non id verius quod posterius.*

Translated into a discussion of finality this means that the finite or created world was created in a way to make possible a return of all things to the Father via mediation and recapitulation of the lower by the intervention of the higher. The so-called immanent finality to be observed in the operation of the cosmos is not that of evolution, but supernatural mediation, ultimately of God himself, based on the absolute supremacy of the divine will and divine freedom, a sovereignty not to be confused with the immanent finality of natural processes. For that is what stands at the heart of the supernatural: the intervention of the higher or super-agent in a lower order limited by the species defining that order. Recapitulation does not proceed from the action of the lower producing the higher or truer. Theistic evolutionists, in trying to meet the charge that evolution as such is merely a matter of chance, fail to allow for this key distinction and so end by excluding the natural substratum of a world created for the sake of hierarchical mediation. Simply put, evolution and mediation are two completely opposed versions of how the world functions: the first insisting on the absolute priority of the natural, the other on the absolute priority of the transcendent divine will in explaining the differentiation of the species.

Evolution and Mediation as Cooperative Hierarchization

The Bible, the fathers, the scholastics, and the magisterium of the church have always insisted on the mediatory vision in the functioning of the cosmos, created for the sake of Jesus and Mary. It is clearly apparent in the priority of grace over nature and explains St. Augustine's horror for the errors of Pelagius. Evolution as a substitution of becoming for being in general and the being of the species or *ratio seminalis* in particular, in any form is but a version of the opposite: naturalism, or Pelagianism. A view of the world based on the mediation of the Incarnate Word postulates an origin of the world, not by way of neo-platonic devolution, nor Hegelian evolution, but one created, structured and coordinated by the Creator alone in the work of six days. This is why there are no theological reasons for evolution in the sources; this is why there are so many reasons, above all in the typology of the work of the *Hexaemeron*, for creation. Considered apart from this it is perhaps not possible to demonstrate apodictically the incompatibility of creation and evolution; it certainly is when we consider the mediation of Christ as the global approach to all intellectual endeavors of man.

The discussion of creation versus evolution has often been bedeviled by a simplistic opposition between the two, as *a priori* evident, with the implication that one must choose between faith and science, should evolution prove to be a viable scientific theory. It is perfectly true that creation and evolution are mutually exclusive, not because evolution is a scientific theory possibly true, but because it is demonstrably untrue. In this sense the church in permitting the discussion of theories of evolution by competent scholars is simply continuing the stance of the Fathers and great scholastic theologians: the Magisterium and theology have no direct authority over legitimate scientific investigation or hypothesizing, so long as this does not contradict the truth clearly and certainly known on other grounds.[121]

But when evolutionary theory is shown to be (1) unscientific, because it is attempting to deal, not with the subject of empirical science, and/or is (2) clearly contradictory both of a hierarchized, mediatory vision of the world, and of its intellectual counterpart, then the real source of the opposition emerges: the conflict between a Pelagian autonomy and dependence on divine grace vis-à-vis salvation and beatitude. In the first instance, evolutionary theory extends itself beyond the relatively autonomous and conservative functioning of the world, once the creative work of the six days is completed, and concerns itself with the work of God which is the subject of theological history. In the second instance, evolutionary theory denies a hierarchized order of sciences, the lower reducible to the higher.[122]

The option of Pelagian autonomy supposes an evolutionary version of the world, while the recognition of salvation's dependence on God's good pleasure supposes a creationist view. Once that is seen, to the man of good will, it should be clear: assent to the first is an irrational, blind, absurd choice of an illusion at the heart of the mysticism of Teilhard. Assent or belief in the second is eminently reasonable as well as a wise choice, a choice which sound science in its own way will support.

Unfortunately, in the century or so before Vatican II little attention was given to this point in Catholic discussion of creation theory and the

121. Far from being an obstacle to genuine science, according to many competent scholars this very attitude made possible the birth of modern science, e.g., the well-known Duhem, *Système*, in particular volumes 3 and 4. Only five of the planned 10 volumes were completed by the author. The great scholastics, like the Fathers, on the origin of the human body are relevant because the question is primarily theological, not scientific. And all of the greats: Alexander of Hales, Bonaventure, Thomas, Duns Scotus come down on the side of immediate formation by God of the bodies of Adam and Eve, whereas the nominalism and voluntarism of Ockham opens the door to evolutionism. Cf. the bibliography in Sagüés, *De Deo Creante et Elevante*, 671n29.

122. To be clear, such a hierarchy is not the grand synthesis of Hegelianism or a gnoseological unity of the sciences as a kind of worldly equivalent of the beatific vision.

inherent weaknesses of all evolutionary theory. A full presentation of the Catholic doctrine of creation must give due consideration both to the origin and to the end of the world: to the last week (Holy Week) as well as the first week.[123] In that doctrine the origin of the world, or its *exitus* (coming forth) from the hand of God out of nothing, the differentiation and coordination of the various species is the exclusive work of the Creator. The cooperation of creatures,[124] of each of the species in a certain order of subordination of one to the other in the *reditus* (return) of all things to the Father through the Son in the Holy Spirit is the work both of the Creator and of the creatures, is not a work of evolution, but of mediation by which the lower is recapitulated in and by the higher and the highest (angels and man) is elevated by the mediation of the Incarnate Word of God to communion with the Blessed Trinity. Recapitulation, recirculation (as it is described by the early Fathers such as Justin and Irenaeus) is the mindset of the Lord himself. What St. Bonaventure calls hierarchization, or sacred ordering in view of an end, is not evolutionary—this would be simply another name for Pelagianism, or do it yourself sanctification—but rather mediatory. Only the supernatural agency is capable of breaking the sound barrier which contains or defines the limits of all specific action and change.

Perhaps of the three equivocal assumptions discussed here, this is the one most difficult for the modern mind to grasp, for we have all been conditioned by what in the tradition might have been termed Pelagianism, namely the self-sufficiency of an autonomously functioning natural order (i.e., the secular as such) to reach beatitude. The difficulty of communicating the importance of the current discussion of Marian coredemption and mediation even to the clergy is symptomatic of the loss of any sense of hierarchy and mediation: not in respect to the original creation, but in respect to its functioning

---

123. The importance of this for theology, liturgy and spirituality cannot be underestimated. One of the merits of St. Bonaventure is to have explained this so clearly, e.g., in *Itin.* and *Hex.* Cf. Fehlner, "Martyr of Charity," *CE* 6, chapter 17.

124. The cooperation of creatures in the work of salvation, viz., the concrete form which the return of creation to the Father through the Son takes, was the precise point affirmed by Catholics and denied by the Protestant reformers, a denial given classic formulation in the famous *solus* or alone: God alone, Christ alone, grace alone, Scripture alone, faith alone. The repudiation of the very possibility of such cooperation is at the core of the Protestant rejection of Marian mediation in the accomplishment of salvation and of that of the church in the application of the fruits of Christ's salvific sacrifice, that is to say of a hierarchized vision of the entire creation, thereby preparing the ground for an interpretation of the creative work of the six days on a basis quite different from the traditional Catholic one, one more and more tending to resemble in reverse the neo-platonic gradualism in which no fixed distinction between uncreated and created, natural and personal, eternal and temporal orders exists, where becoming is substituted for being.

in terms of final causality. That is why, to borrow the phrase of Dietrich von Hildebrand, it functions as a "Trojan horse in the city of God."

No wonder there is so much confusion concerning the literal and spiritual senses of the first chapters of Genesis. An anti-evolutionist as staunch as the late Cardinal Ruffini completely overlooks the spiritual sense of the six days and reduces the literal to a kind of metaphor for ages of development. Far better is the traditional exposition of St. Bonaventure, which Fr. Jaki claims makes no sense. Quite the contrary: God made and organized the visible world in a work of six days, because he alone wished thereby to set the measure of all time (day and week) before the ages began to course, and because he wished thus to reveal the intelligibility of divine providence guiding the succession of times or ages, and because he wished in this as in all else affecting the purpose of creation to provide a type in his original work of creation to understand the anti-type in the restoration and fulfillment during the last week of the world (Holy Week) and its fruit, the initiation of the eighth and unending day of the resurrection.

> [Scotus and Evolution: How *id verius quod prius* (origins in relation to the *nunc fluens*) needs to be complemented with the *id verius quod posterius* (the *nunc fluens* out of origins) in relation to the "not yet" of the future or hope, or in more scholastic terms, the created *ens* or *verum* or *bonum* is governed in the orders[125] of real existence by the principle of finality (will) understood as the immanent root of all created possibility in God (*signa voluntatis divinae*) and immanent core of all actuality (*sive in actu primo sive in actu secundo*) outside God: *quod prius in intentione* (*origo activitatis immanentis seu vitalis*) ultimum in executione (*finis activitatis immanentis seu vitalis*). This means that in its utterly incomparable beginning in time, creation and all creatures are the term of a free, creative act of God alone (*actus primus*). However, by that fact creation and its inhabitants are fully in act only in so far as they are in continuous or progressive creation or secondary action as theistic evolution progressively realizing and revealing the order of final causality in the mind of Creator.]

This activity of progressive creation converges upon either a secular end (not divine) or on God himself (*homo fit Deus* of St. Maximilian in the Incarnation), where only the initially *posterius* will ultimately, in realization, explain the origin. Such an explanation of the origin of the species (that is the relatively stable natural order now) is radically evolutionary

---

125. Or *spheres*: *cosmosphere* or extramental world; *noosphere*; *etho* and *polispheres*; *hagiosphere* or of the hypostatic union.

because dynamically teleological, placing the concept and reality of the present state or sphere in relative vertibility in reference not to form at origin, but in reference to the end of all change once it is achieved. The truth about origins and species in terms of special creation is radically skewed because it regards present species or natures as absolutely fixed, both *a parte ante* (in view of what these were at origin) and in view of what they will be (at point of arrival, e.g., mortal body and immortal body: how they are different and how the same is impossible to answer on this basis). The evolutionary approach in terms of final causality is radically the correct one. This is the case provided one's evolutionary approach is "from above." Such an approach unites the *signs* or *order of ends* in the divine will and, hence, the source of divine ideas of the created (the above) with that which is the basis of unified order outside the divine mind at the origin of creation (term of the exclusively creative act of God). This where the divine will, as creative, coincides in some way with all created reality, material as well as spiritual, as the inner *elan* of secondary activity or development.[126]

> [Evolution is nothing but the distinctive intrinsic mode of finite being (to an end) in the extramental world, perceived in the noetic world as the univocal notion or concept of being, incomparable in its first moment to any other, so only fully known as finally realized in the practical order if the Incarnation is willed, and not secularity as the final end of time. Univocal being is situated in the *nunc fluens* of experience (subject to doubt, despair, and guilt) between the original univocity of the original creative act, including in one way the immutable (*ordo essentialis*, distinctive subordinations willed by God) terminating in the *ordo accidentalis* or *contingentis*[127] continuing and revealed precisely in its evolutionary character toward an end. This latter point is denied by the deist or atheistic evolutionist, who reduces all efficient causality to chance, or rejects the principle of dynamic finality as formulated by Scotus, as the root explanation of all other forms of activity: the will as self-moved.]

126. Evolution in/through time as the essential cypher of created beings or specifically distinct natures in operation (*physis* as generative inanimately and vitally).

127. Whether we are concerned with an extensive finite or infinite is irrelevant to its creative character and dependence on an essential order centered in perfect unity and unchangeableness.

True and False Notions of Evolution

This long summary is necessary to appreciate the importance of the long treatment of Bonaventure as the first great opponent of the bases of false evolutionism (atheistic, theistic in Kantian-Transcendental Thomist form), why the discussion of *rationes seminales* of Augustine is not germane,[128] and why the critique of false evolution does not necessarily prove special creation as correct, or even tenable for Catholics. Rather, despite its short-comings, the merit of Bonaventure's position, as developed by Scotus is, paradoxically, to point in the direction of integrating a true understanding of evolution in Marian mediation.[129]

The relation between creation,[130] attained by a circulation solely divine and including nothing else,[131] and re-creation, or the tending to an end (God or the secular) by steps, each one higher than the prior, ultimately involves a recapitulation. However, this recapitulation occurs only via a recirculation. The exemplar of this movement of recapitulation through recirculation is the Immaculate-Creator Spirit, whose full operation only begins in the Virgin Mother.[132] Without this recirculation (evolutionary character of world as created) there can be no realization of the end or recapitulation and so no full knowledge of origins *in actu primo*, or *secundo* (species).

In symbolic-typical language (dynamic equivalency): circulation and capitulation or exclusively creative action out of nothing is revealed primarily by the male archetype by which conceptualizations of this mystery must be interpreted. Recirculation and recapitulation as creative or procreative activity are revealed primarily in the figure of the virgin earth as contributing to the emergence-formation of Adam. Hence, they are revealed by the feminine archetype in terms of which generation as active source of a new

128. Either for or against evolution.

129. This is evident in the Kolbean adaptation of both Bonaventure and Scotus in terms of Newton's law of action and reaction: the action being exclusively creative, the reaction, not repetitive, but inherently creative, first of all, in Mary. Action and reaction are from within, directing the process toward ever more perfect ends not only secular but divine. Hence, in the church, Kolbe's *Militia Immaculatae* describes the whole of Catholicism (grace) under a new form or species. This dynamic structure grounds the possibility of specifically new forms of Franciscan life evolving out of older forms (*ordo semper reformandus*) until terminating at a final form reflecting total incorporation of the Immaculate into common life, adumbrated in Bonaventure. This is a plain description of ecclesial existence *in via* in terms of already-not yet, whose type in the first creation must also be evolutionary.

130. Capitulation or originating of creation terminating in a head, Adam, male and female, joint patriarchate, or father and mother as one before distinct.

131. Symbol or archetype in creation the masculine.

132. Symbol and archetype the feminine.

man is procreative. This activity is not merely productive of new individual of species (breeding), but of a new person, specifically transcending the merely corporal, or evolutionary. In both the formation of the first Adam as well as in the procreation of his descendants the role of the feminine signals the essential character of secondary causality, to cooperate in the progressive elevation or hierarchization of the world. Whence it comes about that the perfect secondary causality of the Immaculate Conception (all the love and will of creation in a single person) precisely as perfect finite Fiat is both evolutionary (finalizing) and mediatory, bringing the created into the divine order by bringing the divine into the human-created: the hominization of God and the divinization of man, realized in the body of Christ which is the church (fullness of Godhead).

Reformulating the Problematic: Three Approaches

From the foregoing it is clear that there are only three types of hypothetical approaches: (1) purely evolutionary, (2) purely creationistic out of nothing directly, and (3) a fusion of the two: theistic evolution or progressive creation.

The first is clearly atheistic. It excludes any notion of a Creator transcending the world who accounts for the origin of the world as a whole before any distinction of species or categories of creatures and for the radical dichotomy between spiritual and material being (*prope Deum* and *prope nihil*), a differentiation which only exclusively divine power can achieve.[133]

The second excludes any creaturely cooperation in the progressive finalization of the world ordained by God and would seem to impose on secondary activity and motion a natural determinism. The latter would exclude any genuine free or moral element in the progressive development of the world in one or more different directions (except by chance). Physical premotion becomes the name of the game, or pure occasionalism disguising the exclusively creative efficient causality of the omnipotent. This is Calvinism.

The third alternative, indicated by the name theistic evolution or progressive creation, is in fact a general category, containing many explanations of the origin of the species at various levels of existence. Each explanation shares in a similar preoccupation: that the creature might genuinely contribute to the ever more perfect structuring of the world, viz., enjoy procreativity. In what sense this might be called evolutionary or not differs

133. Hence spirit cannot be from the material, and what is called spiritual matter is only metaphorically such.

from theory to theory, which reject either an exclusively evolutionary or exclusively creationistic interpretation. Among the theoreticians we do not find any fathers of the church, not even Augustine, because the question was not asked in this fashion in discussing the origin of different organic species. Only in St. Bonaventure do we find hints of the possibility of an evolutionary sense to the emerging of distinct species from indistinct seminal species. But here the difference is more between express and impress, not between non-existing and existing out of less perfect species via the activity of the earlier species. In his reflections on the critical problem, he suggests the role of the will (finalistic evolution) without drawing any conclusions. In insisting on the realism of common nature outside the mind, on the role of the unchanging ideal reasons (species) as primarily governing the character of creaturely activity, he seems to preclude theistic evolution as explained on Kantian premises (denial of the eternal ideas of Plato), but he does not thereby subscribe to special creation.

Scotus on the other hand with his insistence on the priority of the singular rather than the multiplication of individuals, on the univocity of being and the contingent character of the finite, together with his notion of the absolute primacy of Jesus and the Immaculate, and above all his insistence on the primacy of the will and final causality, divine and created, in the explanation of all efficient or physical causality, opens the door to the development of a theory of Marian evolution-mediation from within the creature. Scotus' hypothesis is fully elaborated by Maximilian Kolbe on the basis of his formula for the Immaculate Conception: two persons in two natures whose natures or essences compenetrate in such wise that creaturely activity of perfect love is creative and the Creator Spirit's activity is evolutionary. In a word, personal or voluntary causality, final causality as dynamic rather than static, is the heart of spiritual-Marian evolution, or what the John Paul II calls continuous creation: recirculation terminating (finalizing) in divinization of the body, rather than a merely secular end.

Conclusion: Marian Mediation and Marian Evolution

I have sketched a number of assumptions, each of which and all together, in the minds of believers, especially Catholics, effectively function so as to make theistic evolution in its Kantian form (Thomistic transcendentalism) seem more plausible than creationism, a view I found very attractive as seminarian and during my first twenty years as professor of systematic theology. Those holding these assumptions take vertibility, rather than fixity, as the essential coefficient of all finite being, possible or actual. They are prone, therefore, to believe *becoming* rather than *being*, viz., evolution, is the existential *a priori* of all thought. They also tend to hold that the continuation of the original creative act, either in the conservation and cooperation with secondary agents *capable* of acting, or *in fact* acting, is qua creative also evolutionary. Hence, they take active creation to be progressive toward an end, and active development or progress to tend toward a higher stage and not merely repetitive multiplication.[134]

In this scenario the primary sense of the definition of *species* passes from that of something primarily extramental to that of something primarily intramental, an object of the mind. The extramental noumenon at the starting point of thought appears merely as undifferentiated matter (quantifiable according to degrees of velocity). Hence the noumenon appears capable of multiplication (microevolution) extramentally and specification (macroevolution) intramentally via conceptualization. Whence, the *a priori* of all understanding and future development of the material via technology (praxis) to meet the desire of thinker or ego (use or praxis as a function of desire) is evolution, not as a scientific theory verifiable or falsifiable on scientific grounds, but on meta-scientific grounds. The extramental can only make sense in an evolutionary context of consciousness. But at the same time, this evolutionary context functions as the radical origin both of ego and of object of the mind. It postulates a creative and not merely physical efficiency. Whence the mystical aspect and personal dimension of evolutionary theory, making it so persuasive, on the one side. And, on the other, the impersonal, purely objective dimension of the merely logical (including dogmatic formulations) makes pure reason or pure dogmatic faith seem so repulsive.

On Kantian premises theistic evolution in theory avoids the atheism of so many evolutionists (e.g., Darwin), but it also depends for its ultimate objective validation on the possibility and probability of scientific verification in the biological as well as cultural orders. There, the evidence is zero, leaving evolutionary theory as the basic *a priori* of corporal-organic existence a purely arbitrary construct, dangerous for theology as well as philosophy and ethics, leaving it merely a possibly useful theory of artistic creativity.

On realizing this most people find themselves attracted to assent to the traditional hierarchized view of the world as leading to a recognition of the priority of *being* over *becoming* and *stability* over *change* and so of the illusory character of all evolutionary theorizing about origins. Almost as a corollary, this approach interprets the differentiation of the species as

---

134. A difference perfectly evident in the artistic experience: creative rather than reduplicative.

an exclusive work of God before the emergence of man and including the emergence of man, whence the term special creation. But this tendency is also a feature of Platonic thought in all its forms, whether non-Christian (e.g., neo-Platonism, Hinduism) or Christian (e.g., Origen, Augustine). It leaves the doctrine of creation the only plausible and sensible approach to the question of the origin and end of the world, and in a very special way to the "miraculous" formation of the first Adam from the virgin earth and the still more supernatural origin of the new Adam, the Incarnate Word, not only in but by the Virgin Mother, the Immaculate, or as the fathers call her, the new "Virgin Earth." Whence the attractiveness of theories of special creation as the explanation for the origin of the different species, graded in order of perfection.[135]

Yet, the validity of this approach cannot withstand critical analysis. Special creationism depends not simply on metaphysical principles, but on a willingness to reduce the genuine productive activity of creatures to a point that their efficiency is non-existent. Gilson noted that this was for him a prime reason for supporting some form of theistic or teleological evolutionism as the only sane guarantee of respect for the autonomy of nature and the contemporary understanding of motion.

There are serious problematic features in special creationism. Like Kantian forms of theistic evolution (as proposed by Jaki, for instance), it depends on some kind of probable scientific evidence, not merely that evolution is false, but that special creationism is the only alternative scientifically speaking. This raises the first problem: there is no such evidence, less than there is for evolutionism. The concluding verses of Chesterton's *To a Holy Roller*, pointing out the impossibility of such definitive proof go like this: by rolling on the ground like a beast, the fundamentalists strive to prove there is no genetic resemblance between man and beast (special creation), as foolish as that of those (evolutionists) who try in the name of reason (science) to prove there is no difference.

This points to a second major difficulty, scientifically speaking, with which theistic evolution is not encumbered, the need to posit an Aristotelian concept of motion (circular), no longer scientifically valid, as nonetheless true and the modern notion of movement,[136] since the thirteenth century with the origin of modern science on the basis of rational belief in a Creator (Duhem, Meier, Jaki) false and without validity (as in Galileo, Newton, Einstein). All this eventually introduces the worst features of

135. A position to which I was for a number of years strongly attracted after abandoning my earlier Kantian approach to philosophy and science.

136. Linear and progressive or finalistic, potentially infinite in duration as an accidental or evolutionary series.

Neo-Platonism, so lamented by Gilson: in the name of science to affirm the unreality of nature scientifically understood.

Theologically speaking, in denying any creaturely cooperation (evolution or transformism) in the origin of Adam, there is a clear tendency to deny the active virginal contribution to the incarnation or formation of the second Adam, truly man as well as God. In non-Christian form this also leads not only to a kind of tendency for created operation to merge with the uncreated, but ultimately to a denial of the reality and truth of time qua successive and progressive. This is similar to philosophical and theological systems that deny true efficiency to creatures (occasionalism of Malebranche), or, more extreme, the very reality of the creature as being (e.g., Berkeley, Christian Science). This understanding underlies the classic Protestant denial of the possibility of human cooperation in the work of redemption and salvation[137] ending in the pantheism originally this theory of origins was intended to avoid, viz., God alone exists, therefore everything, me included, is God.

Such for the theoretical underpinnings of one form of private judgment in place of that of the pope, now a prominent feature of "sedevacantism." Hence, it is, despite its appearance of super-orthodoxy, anti-Marian. For this reason, I became more and more repulsed by special creationism and its traditionalist supporters among Catholics, in striving to defend the formation, and not creation of the first man and woman, and I became convinced of the necessity of taking seriously the pope's public approval and promotion of some form of theistic evolution as the preferred basis for a Catholic approach to origins and the relations not only of faith and science, but above all the church and the world. Hence, my rejection of special creationism as a Catholic theory.

Is there an alternative? or is the debate totally sterile from a practical point of view? I have suggested that there is an alternative, genuinely creative and genuinely evolutionary or historic, but not in terms of a *Deus solus* of the special creationists. Nor is my suggested alternative conceived in terms of a theistic evolutionism which does not escape the ultimate irrational mysticism of its best-known proponent, Teilhard de Chardin, whatever its appeal in terms of modern science and subjectivity. I propose Marian evolution. This proposal is a spin off from the mystery of Mary as perfect finite mode of being: not immaculately conceived, but the Immaculate Conception, unchangeably identical with herself, yet immanently engaged in all other change, as universal mediatrix, an *a priori* both for all other finite existence

---

137. As for instance in Calvinism, whose supporters were the first in the seventeenth century to propose the hypothesis of special creation.

and for all science and for all action. This applies whether we are considering *frui* or *uti*, before the *nunc ultimum* of all history in the center of history, which is the mystery of the cross and redemption. This Marian evolution includes pardon of sin and divinization of man in the cross and resurrection, whose mediation is at the core of all activity at any stage, however primitive. It represents the degree of spiritualization or personal influence fueling from within all efficient or physical causality, rendering possible a transfinalization which is progressively from within (immanent), elevating to the point that man becomes God (*homo-Deus*), a term or head capable of recirculation and recapitulation, for which the original creation (solely divine and transcendent) was produced from nothing.

Recirculation is the reversal in direction (finality) of the solely creative and so is defined best as creative evolution, or mediation of the Immaculate. It is the point at which personal or moral "causality" rooted in the will as personal, productive act outside the person makes possible physical or efficient causality (developmental), of which the fullest examples are (1) the virginal conception by power of the Holy Spirit, and (2) sacramental causality. The first in being personal (consent of the Virgin) leads to an effect in the biological or natural order, the procreation of a divine person by a human person, primarily a spiritual action, but also eminently physical. In the second case of sacramental causality, primarily spiritual or personal, there is effected a transfinalization of the symbols in the sensible or corporal order together with their finalization. This is accomplished, therefore, not simply as an action of the head, Christ, but also of the Immaculate Conception, Holy Spirit and Virgin Mother together, and hence the visible contribution of minister and church. All this because of the unique mediation involving the uncreated and created Immaculate Conception, united as two distinct persons and two distinct natures or principles and modes of operation, yet fused as one from within, a kind of consubstantiation in contrast with the transubstantiation in the Eucharist. Yet, it is this premise or dynamic (real evolutionary or personal) operation which is the *a priori* of all other operations of Christ or of the church and her ministers.

Whence, according to St. Maximilian, total consecration to the Immaculate is a radically new form or basis not only for theology and spirituality, not only for metaphysics,[138] but for science, for psychology, culture, politics, especially as these bear on the point of departure both for conversion and holiness, for the pursuit of the beautiful, and for the problem of communion in the one church of those baptized. In effect, in

138. Pre-existence in the counsels of God as *primum volitum* and basis for the possibility of all other finite being in an orderly manner: teleological evolution in the mind of Creator as basis for initial creative act.

taking seriously the critical problem of the *nunc fluens* of the person and community in relation to the *nunc permanens* already in history, the experience of Marian mediation in total consecration as the existential *a priori* of every aspect of human and personal experience, it is shown to be at once the radical and immanent source of the charismatic aspect at the basis of the genuinely mystical-religious. It is the immanent guarantee of truth in thought, both in the ego and the cogito, in the intramental-subjective of consciousness and in the extramental-objective as the existing of the ego sum, and the rightness, justice, *recta ratio* and inner drive of all action, whether technological, artistic or moral (fruition-use), whether preceding or recapitulated in perfect charity, as that same Spirit of truth, the Immaculate Conception, created and uncreated, unfolding or evolving by leaps in each successive now, for better or for worse.

In a word: orthodoxy—genuine consciousness and growth, even in the man-Jesus—is within the embrace of orthopraxis, understood as the Immaculate Conception, and the difference between merely secular or solely evil forms of evolution on the one hand and on the other beatifying (the great question of Luther and Kant) is the difference between the presence or absence of the Immaculate Conception as actual acceptance or rejection by the heavenly Father via the loving sacrifice of Jesus. In this sense we can say that we are justified and saved by faith alone if by faith alone we mean by the operation of the Holy Spirit, impetrated by consecration to the Immaculate, effected sacramentally (personal or spiritual action in sensible form), and manifested in good works, above all those of ministry in the sacramental order.

I insist now on the term *theistic*, or better *Marian evolution*, so as to make clear why creation in theory, and then in practice includes in some way a mode of creating which is progressive and historical, not as an accident of the mode of operation, but as its essential mode or *a priori*. Hence, the importance of the contribution of Scotus and its adaption to current expression so affected by the success of science and by the triumph of the personal and subjective, both psychologically and sociologically and religiously. These advances do not constitute the final triumph of the Immaculate Heart. But neither are they *per se* evil, or merely neutral. The so-called secularization of the world, whereby it becomes ever more different from the institutional forms of the church and earlier forms of Christian culture, need not be rejected wholesale, if we approach positively and imaginatively (artistically as in the aesthetic theory and practice of Hopkins) the most generic *a priori* of all this: evolution.

This in brief is why the address of the pope on evolution to the Pontifical Academy of Science is important, *not* for an assessment of a biological hypothesis as law, but for a correct understanding of evolution as an *a priori* of all *scientific* meaning, even if there is not, in natural or physical causes, any indication of macroevolution. The truth about evolution, rather, is seen in the birth of consciousness, in the *ego cogito, ergo sum*, as a radically new identity. Yet, this occurs with origin and coming to be (memory) that is immanent yet, not from within. It is realized consciously (intellect) with and through the presence within of first principles formulated by me (ontology), yet with one concept from without and from above me, yet within me (univocal being). This univocal being is both the transcendent light illumining and the transcendent good stimulating and ordering my own spontaneity and freedom as an autonomous origin of new acts. It is the eternal Spirit, within as one with Mary Immaculate, yet remaining distinct in person and nature from her.

The resolution of the debate over the origin of the species in Marian evolutionary terms will entail a great deal of patient "re-education": not the condemnation of science—for genuine science has served and continues ever more so today to illustrate the unsubstantiated and unsubstantiable character of macroevolution in any form, but the restoration and prioritizing of the metaphysical thrust of the intellect as that most essentially expressive of the what and the why of the intellect in the definition of a non-material, spiritual being. That restoration can only be complete in the supernatural order of grace under the tutelage of the one master of all, whose magisterium is only made accessible to us through the *Mater et Magistra*, mother and teacher who is the Virgin Immaculate, of whom the church is the extension, or in the words of St. Francis of Assisi: *Virgo Ecclesia Facta* (the Virgin made church, in his *Salutation to the Virgin*). This is because the church is the body of Christ formed in the virginal womb of Mary. May she, the perfect fruit of a perfect redemption by a most perfect Creator-Redeemer, her Son (Bl. John Duns Scotus), enable us once more to regain that true perspective of creation and the Creator which we profess in the first article of the creed.

3

Theistic Evolution or Special Creation[1]

During 1988, *Christ to the World*, then under the editorship of the late Fr. Basil M. Arthradeva, F.I., published in three installments a study of mine entitled *In the Beginning*.[2] This study was an attempt to assess current dispute over creationism and evolutionism in the context of the ancient tradition of the church concerning the right understanding of the first article of the creed. On publication it met with considerable interest in various parts of the world, including Rome itself where various groups of theologians made it the subject of their reflection on the mystery of creation.

Special Creation or Theistic Evolution:
Mutually Exclusive Alternatives?

Informative on a question of interest to all believers and missionaries, though long and involved as it may have seemed to many regular readers of this journal, it hardly covered every aspect of the question. Indeed, the printed version of the study was only a considerably abbreviated version and did not include one very important section on the meaning of "literal" sense in biblical studies, and on the error of "literalism," common both to certain groups of creationists and evolutionists alike. With hindsight, that omission may have had something to do with the subsequent misinterpretation of the article, particularly in certain Catholic creationist circles sympathetic to what is called "geocentrism" and "special creation" *ex nihilo sui et subjecti* of every different living species, then and now, including the human. These are theses often associated with advocates of a literalist interpretation of the Bible typical of certain forms of Protestant exegesis. These theses are often

1. This essay was originally published in 2005 as a series of three short articles in the Roman journal *Christ to the World* 50 (2005) 342–53, 329–40, 427–37.

2. *Christ to the World* 33 (1988): 56–72; 150–164; 237–248. Chapter 1 of the present volume.

conjoined to another, clearly contrary to Catholic belief, on the "immortality" of all living beings (i.e., of all animals and plants, and not only Adam and Eve) before the fall. Such methodologies are also typical of those who, in the name of a "literal" reading of the Bible on such points as the length of a day during the *Hexaemeron*, would minimize the Virgin Mother and deny the Eucharistic real presence and transubstantiation.

For quite some time, viz., for at least five years, *In the Beginning* has been often cited in support of such approaches, for example, as an authority for the novel hypothesis that "special creation" was defined *de fide* by the Fourth Lateran Council and in virtue of this definition all forms of theistic evolution, progressive creation, or continuing creation, including that supported by the recently deceased pope (as a personal opinion) have been condemned as heretical. To put it mildly this is a strange opinion: a solemn condemnation completely forgotten by everyone in the church for nearly eight centuries! Not only is this view absurd. It is but a mere hairbreadth away from damning the pope as a heretic along lines known today as *sedevacantism*, a type of condemnation historically indicating the accuser to be himself near heresy or schism. During this period, I pointed out to persons who inquired about this that the article, far from supporting such theses, did just the opposite. Further, where I was aware of misquotation, I requested that such "misquoting" or quoting so as to leave the impression that *In the Beginning* supported the non-Catholic positions mentioned above cease.

Needless to say, I do not and never have regarded "special creation" as anything but a rather odd opinion, certainly false as regards the formation of Adam and of Eve. And I certainly never claimed Lateran IV condemned a scientific hypothesis now known as theistic evolution or progressive creation, for the plain reason that said hypothesis, apart from being non-existent in those days, does not directly contradict any point solemnly defined by that Council. The most that might be done with the dogmatic definitions and anathemas of Lateran IV, in the light of subsequent developments not envisioned by the Council, is to use these as basis for the construction of some kind of *theological argument*. Such an argument would aim at showing how no version of theistic evolution as a scientific interpretation of the surviving phenomena bearing on the original differentiation of the species as we know them can in principle be reconciled with what God has told us about the *Hexaemeron* or work of six days. But by no stretch of the "properly formed" theological mind can it be imagined that an argumentation can prevail over a fact, in this case that Lateran IV simply made no such condemnation as certain creationists pretend to argue. *Contra factum non datur argumentum.*

In the published article (discussing Lateran IV and Pius XII) I adverted to the hypothetical possibility of such an argumentation for a limited end. But I also noted at the same time that theistic evolution as such had not been condemned by the church. Only selected theses called theistic evolution, instance by instance, had even been condemned, because in each instance the theory had contradicted some point of doctrine declared certain by the magisterium, not because it was an instance of a condemned general concept known as "theistic evolution." Ecclesiastical condemnations deal with precise errors. The precise error involved in every instance where in some way the magisterium has disapproved some theory called transformism or theistic evolution, is not the fact that said theory is evolutionary, but that it presumes to explain the origin of the species by *exclusive* reference to natural processes.

But the generic concept of "theistic evolution" is much too imprecise to qualify for the kind of condemnation the "special creationists" imagine the church has issued. For the rest, in more than one place, I noted the normative "patristic consensus" guiding the subsequent exercise of the Magisterium, I made it perfectly clear that aside from the immediate creation of souls, the unique formation of the bodies of Adam and Eve and the singular, individual character of the first human couple, revelation and church doctrine do not directly deal with the scientific question commonly called the "origin of the species." Even if the fathers and great scholastics did not use this terminology, they were not so naïve as to think theological and scientific approaches to the known facts about the origin of the world perfectly matched one another. The ease with which special creationists read their pet theories into Lateran IV matches, if not outdoes, that of theistic evolutionists who discover theirs expressly formulated in great Fathers such as St. Augustine and St. Gregory of Nyssa.

But there is another difficulty with this novel theory. A theological argument, as necessarily complex as a dogmatic definition is necessarily simple, unless the *Magisterium* of the church as it were, canonizes that argumentation, viz., makes it normative for all Catholic theological reflection, is only another fallible opinion, subject to correction. In the light of the Holy Father's 1996 address to the Pontifical Academy of Science, whatever further significance this address may have, such an argumentation cannot presently (and it would seem for some time to come) oblige the assent of anyone in the church. One may disbelieve theistic evolution and perhaps think its advocates unenlightened, and in some instances heretical; one would sin grievously to damn a theistic evolutionist as heretic, merely because he does not accept "special creation" as revealed by God and so beyond question.

The favour accorded hypotheses such as "special creation" by many Catholic creationists reveals them to be just as subtly influenced by one or another form of contemporary rationalism as their opposite numbers among Catholic proponents of theistic evolution. Rationalism here means a hyper-confidence in one's own argumentation, the exact contrary of a universal scepticism about the ability of science or theology to reach any certain conclusion about anything. Science can and does yield certain and valid knowledge about the beings of this world and the laws governing their operation. But that certainty is conditioned by the relative necessity of the objects known and the necessity of the link between premises and conclusions. It is one thing to know the laws of nature; it is quite another on the basis of this knowledge alone to determine how these laws might operate in circumstances quite different, and perhaps unrelated to those familiar to us and subject to our control.

This is certainly the case where we know all arrangements of this kind depend on a maker who acts freely. The freedom of the Creator in creating does not mean God in working a miracle, for instance, cancels or contradicts the laws of nature. He merely suspends them. But that also means that in knowing the laws of nature theoretically I cannot before the fact deduce what God will do, or might have done in the past, in circumstances scientifically unknowable with certainty. What is true of the limits of empirical science in resolving questions concerning the origin of the species is also true of our metaphysical knowledge of God. It is one thing to deduce conclusions about the necessary essence of God. It is quite another to attempt to do the same in respect to the contingencies involved in creation. Lateran IV insists on the theological-metaphysical principles imbedded in the facts revealed about creation in the beginning of time. It is quite another matter to deduce conclusions from these principles in respect to questions involving contingencies not elucidated by the Creator, or conclusions apparently contrary to things he did reveal about the formation of Adam and Eve.

The old axiom of logic: *a posse ad esse non valet illatio* [existence cannot be deduced from possibility] sums up nicely the point made by Bl. John Duns Scotus. We can only know for certain what God has done, or will do, viz., what is beyond our observation and control, if he tells us or if we can witness it. The facts we do know we can understand better through science, but no amount of scientific hypothesizing can alter, much less disprove what is simply factual. But it is also true that when contingencies of history are not known directly, no theory, even the most certain, whether metaphysical or physical, can substitute for certain knowledge of them via historical verification. Certain knowledge of possibility, of laws governing operation, by themselves do not provide a basis for deducing with certainty whether certain things happened in the past or determining how they happened. The Creator is the only witness of the work of six days.

In the case of the origin of the species, the Creator has told us some facts, but precious little to reveal how his omnipotence accomplished what in fact is described in the first chapters of Genesis. Only in the case of Adam are we given some detail about the process, detail which fits neither the special creationist scheme of things tending to affirm an origin of each species immediately out of nothing, nor the theistic evolutionist tendency of ascribing the upward thrust in the work of "six days" to an immanent dynamism of the subject evolving.

One must carefully distinguish then, as I did in the study partly published in 1988, between (1) evolutionism as a philosophical-religious theory, rejecting the first origin of the present world, visible and invisible, via a creation immediately out of nothing, viz., solely by an act of the divine will and not formed out of a pre-existing subject, and rejecting as well as the origin of each angel and human soul in the same way, therefore condemned as heretical, and (2) theories of evolution purporting only to explain either the gradual structuring of the material world between the initial creation and the formation of Adam or its subsequent conservation and development by the Creator with the cooperation both passive and active of created agents, more or less perfect. The first have long since been expressly condemned by the church, practically from the beginning of her history, in proclaiming and expounding the first article of the creed. The second have not been condemned in principle. The most that can be said negatively about these to date is that some versions of "theistic evolution" have been the object of warnings, as involving notions neither scientific nor unscientific, but heretical. From the fact that some instances of theories called theistic evolution have been frowned upon, one cannot conclude that a notion as generic as "theistic evolution" has been condemned in principle.

Because the term "evolution," theoretically legitimate, has become a kind of loaded term, triggering associations with atheistic denials of the first article of the Creed, I tended *not* to favour its use to describe what in the sources of revelation clearly is not an instantaneous act of creation out of nothing, but some kind of process involving succession at the phenomenological level. Rather, I preferred one stressing more the part of the Creator rather than that of the creature. I still do prefer such, because most of those persons, including members of the clergy, who think theistic evolution as a scientific hypothesis probable, or erroneously believe it to be proven fact, do indeed tend to subscribe to any number of theological propositions long since damned as heretical. But in opting so, I certainly did not, and do not now imagine that the question of the origin of the species had been decided in the dogmatic way in which the question of the origin of the world and of spiritual creatures has been long since defined.

On rereading the published article I believe these points were made with sufficient clarity. It has been suggested that, "properly expounded," Lateran IV might seem to exclude any kind of "theistic evolution." But there is the catch: whose exposition is the "proper" one, short of formal magisterial approbation? And what is the exact definition of "theistic evolution" in principle? It is presumptuous to assume one's own theological argumentation is the proper exposition merely on the basis of private judgment. In any case "proper theological exposition" is not a synonym for dogmatic anathematisation and no such "proper exposition" was attempted in *In the Beginning*.

Final Causality and the Origin of the Species

One may also argue that perhaps greater stress should be laid on the creaturely cooperation, that indeed a case can be made for the theoretical validity of the term "theistic evolution," provided it can be sanitized, as a foreshadowing of procreative activity in the various spheres of human enterprise.

This last observation is linked to another serious misreading of *In the Beginning*. In distinguishing between the activity of creatures before the completion of the work of six days and their activity afterwards, viz., after the formation of Adam and Eve, I described that of creatures during the work of six days as "instrumental" cooperation with the sole principal agent, the Creator. By contrast, with the "rest" of the Creator on the seventh day that cooperation became a form of principal causality. Some have taken this to mean, therefore, that the many kinds of creatures formed by the Creator during the work of the six days had no activity at all (in the sense of natural or physical efficient causality in *actu secundo*) until the formation of Adam and Eve.

Such an interpretation misses the point being made in confusing the operation of the cosmos as a whole with the operation of each single kind of creature as an individual. It is one thing to discuss the efficient or physical causality of natural created agents apart from their relation to the overall end of the cosmos. It is quite another to discuss this in the context of the relation of this natural or physical activity to a higher form of created agency, viz., that of the "intellectual" or personal agent, and the manner in which the less perfect agent and its form of activity is subordinated to and recapitulated in that of the higher, ultimately looking to the recapitulation of all things by and in Christ, the Son of God and Son of Mary. In medieval times this theme was discussed by such Franciscan luminaries as St. Bonaventure and Bl. John

Duns Scotus under the heading: plurality of forms in a single organism, the less perfect such as the vegetative, being capable formally of existing merely as a plant, or of being recapitulated (without loss of formal identity) in a higher mode of existence, e.g., that of an animal. A more familiar example might be that of sacramental causality, where the material or natural elements are subordinated to a higher form of personal causality, that of Christ and of his minister, in view of an end or effect transcending the limits of physical causality, but not excluding it.

My observation touched only upon the universe as a whole and the types of causality which might be involved in creaturely cooperation with the Creator in the work of the six days, and then in the subsequent conservation and return of that creation to the Creator through Christ in the Spirit. While one may argue that what is connoted by certain forms of theistic evolution appears to exclude any such distinction, one can hardly argue on this basis that theistic evolution, employed as a generic phrase to denote the possibility of some kind of cooperation with the Creator as principal agent of the work of the six days, is false in principle. To do so would seem to exclude *a priori* any subsequent cooperation with the Creator in the work of re-creation, exactly the thesis of radical Calvinism: *Deus solus, Christus solus*, thereby excluding *a priori* the possibility of Marian mediation and the sacramental-hierarchical mediation of the church. So argue the current crop of Marian minimizers: some people misinterpret the title *Co-redemptress* as making Mary equal to her Redeemer Son, as some in times past argued that the title *Immaculate Conception* denies original sin. *Abusus tamen non tollit usum.* Abuse does not of itself invalidate use.

This leads me to add here, a point I did not touch, let alone develop in any way in the earlier essay, *In the Beginning*. The strong point of so many versions of theistic evolution since the end of the Council, e.g., as presented by Etienne Gilson from a philosophical perspective[3] is their attempt to deal not only with evolution from the point of view of efficient causality (the weak point in theories of theistic evolution), but from that of final causality. Whether these teleological versions do so successfully is another question. That they are making an important point is beyond question. It is this point which I suggested should be treated by creationists, not solely or primarily from the point of view of the four causes as expounded by Aristotle and somewhat glossed (though not abolished) by the theory of contemporary empirical science, but rather in the context of what in the Franciscan school, especially as articulated by Bl. John Duns Scotus, is known as personal or terminal causality and which constitutes one of the metaphysical supports

3. Cf. Gilson, *Aristotle to Darwin.*

of their theology of recapitulation (of which at the level of physics appears as the theory of multiplicity of forms).

We might pinpoint the relevance of these formal subtleties by noting the distinction between biological reproduction and personal procreation. The first is a purely physical procedure, as Aristotle so accurately noted, directed to the preservation of the species via the multiplication of individuals, who never attain the level of personal existence and never exist for their own sake, but merely to conserve a species or essential type, so long as this is useful to the cosmos as a whole. Human begetting cannot reductively be identified with reproduction, even if certain of the qualities or formalities of this biological process appear in natural generation of human persons. Rather these formalities at the empirical level are subsumed or recapitulated in a higher order, rightly called in Catholic theology not reproduction of the human species, but procreation of persons whose primary reason for being is to be found in the personal dignity of each, not in the preservation of a species in the physical or empirical sense. What is primary and principal in procreation is not the production of a new individual nature similar to that of the parents. Rather in the communication of a part of the father's nature to the child through the mother there is established a relationship of paternity-filiation, that is, the begotten is a *person*. The difference should be fairly obvious: contraception as a purely natural phenomenon is unheard of, because fidelity has nothing to do with mere reproductivity. It has a great deal to do, like infidelity, with the ultimate fruitfulness or less of procreation. The essence of marriage, unlike reproduction, consists not in its use, but in the mutual vow of fidelity effecting an unbreakable covenant "until death do us part." Infidelity to spousal love, rendered totally efficacious in contraceptive form, nullifies entirely the procreative action differentiating human begetting from animal breeding.

Special creationists seem utterly oblivious of a hypothetical possibility which cannot be excluded by some kind of *a priori* argumentation about what Lateran IV might or might not have said had the fathers of that Council known of theistic evolution. The omnipotent Creator might have employed some kind of organic reproductive process (presently unknown to us, and perhaps never to be known short of the beatific vision) as an instrumental agency for the formation of Adam's body from the "virgin earth." In this hypothetical scenario the non-personal instrumental agents do not become parents of Adam, nor can they, precisely because to be father or mother of a person one must act over and above the reproductive process, that is, personally or procreatively. Mere plausibility, however, cannot determine a question of fact: did the Creator use such a process in the formation of Adam. Theistic evolutionists have no grounds for concluding such, even as a weak probable opinion.

Obviously, this reflection requires also some ability to deal with analogical predication, a mental habit over which neither special creationists nor theistic evolutionists demonstrate much mastery.

In what follows I want to add a number of considerations bearing on the difficulty of the question. They are intended to show why, even if evolutionary explanations of the origin of the species are unconvincing scientifically, such a judgment does not constitute grounds (1) for canonizing "special creation" or (2) for denying that from a theological point of view the phrase "theistic evolution" might be a legitimate expression (among many others, perhaps far better) of an insight into the development of the world, but with no apodictic bearing on scientific discussions.

The legitimacy of combining or not combining evolution with the term *theistic* hinges about the notion of "species" or kind as used respectively in science and in theology. And the correspondence or lack thereof in the usage of this term in two quite distinct fields of study is very much linked to the problem of the *literal* meaning of Genesis in recounting the work of the six days (or *Hexaemeron*), and to the vice attendant on failure to understand what is meant by *literal* in theology, viz., the vice of *literalism*. My comments will be organized about three disputed points: the problem of literalism in theology; the problem of defining species in theology and science; the problem of differentiating macro and micro-evolution, to be followed by some considerations bearing on the work of the six days as it appears in the Fathers and theologians of the past.

Literal, Literalistic and Spiritual.

When the great Fathers and Doctors of the church refer to the *inspired* literal meaning of a text of Scripture, basis of its *inspired* spiritual or mystical sense, what they mean dogmatically and theologically by literal and spiritual must be carefully distinguished from what is meant by the same or matching terms in logic (univocal and analogical) and in philology or grammar (literal and metaphorical). Use of these terms at different levels, theology-metaphysics, logic and grammar, involves no necessary contradiction. Indeed, theological use in biblical exegesis presupposes logic and grammar (because God reveals mysteries beyond our natural ken and speech in concepts and language drawing on logic and grammar). But by the very fact that he communicates to us mysteries beyond our natural powers of thought and speech, the technical sense of literal and spiritual in the study of the inspired text must be carefully differentiated from that of similar terminology in logic and grammar. Literal sense of a biblical text is not synonymous either with univocal in logic nor with literal in grammar, but may also be analogical and/or metaphorical. Similarly, spiritual or symbolic sense of a biblical text is not synonymous either with analogical or with metaphorical.

First, a definition and exemplification of terminology. Univocal predication of terms in logic means that a notion or word has the same, identical meaning in its every usage or predication of a subject, for instance, human of every descendant of Adam born of woman. Equivocal or ambiguous usage indicates use of the same notion or word in a manner totally diverse each time it is predicated of a subject. Homonyms are a good example. Analogical use indicates that a notion or word has a meaning partly similar and partly dissimilar in each usage, for instance, create. It may mean make something new out of something previously existing or something new entirely out of nothing. If we restrict the term to one or the other possible ways of making, and use it thus consistently, it is known as a univocal concept/term. If on the other hand we use this term to refer to both ways, it is said to analogical. Science often employs the term univocally to denote making something new out of something pre-existing, and so regards the strict theological meaning of create as making out of nothing as not literal, whereas the theologian holds just the contrary. There is nothing wrong *per se* with this difference of usage. There is something wrong with the claim that what is not literal scientifically is not literal theologically.

Analogical predication has many forms, all of them useful, but not always under the same conditions or for the same ends. Metaphor is a form of analogy sometimes identified in modern discussions of Genesis with myth. Mythical language certainly employs metaphor, but the use of metaphor to describe the creation and structuring of the world does not of itself imply a mythical account. Metaphor is a form of speech whereby two things simply different in essence are compared and given clear expression on the basis of a common quality. For instance, we may speak of a "smiling field" or a "lion-hearted" person. In order for such usage to be effective we must know independently what is a smile and what is a field, what is a lion and what is a person. It is not false to say that fields smile, but it would certainly be false to say that smiling men and fields are the same in kind. They are simply different in nature and not comparable in terms of their nature. So, too, with lions and men. By nature man and beast are specifically different and not comparable. Analogical terms in the strict sense, however differ from metaphorical. They permit us to compare different beings, not merely in terms of some identical shared quality, e.g., pleasantness in the case of smiling persons and fields or strength in the case of lions and courageous men, but directly in terms of their natures. For instance, in the case of lions and men: both are truly living beings, but life in each is different both in nature and relative perfection. Life is said to be an analogical term. Not to acknowledge this is to put man and beast on the same level, patently false. Man and beast are simply different before they are compared as like.

Analogy in the strict sense is particularly important in theology, where uncreated and created being are truly beings in the proper sense and not merely metaphorically, yet not in the same way. Whereas metaphors tell us nothing directly about the nature of the things compared, analogy in the narrower sense often does. What we know about the nature of things analogically, e.g., the doctrine of creation in Genesis, can be given more concrete and effective expression in metaphor or in scientific form, but only if in fact we know analogically and metaphysically what is meant by creation. When St. Augustine states that Genesis tells us precious little directly bearing on empirical science either in the ancient or modern sense, he does not mean it tells us nothing about the essence of the Creator or creature metaphysically or analogically. All the holy doctor means is that our metaphysical and revealed theology is in this vale of tears no substitute for the study of empirical science, even if the latter can only be successfully conducted over the long haul in harmony with the truths of faith. Precisely because theological analogy as defined by Lateran IV rather than mythical or purely symbolic discourse is entailed in the account of creation and the work of the six days, the metaphorical style employed to explain this does indeed "literally" tell us something about the world which science prefers to explain "literally" in another style. Evidently, "literal" is not at all a term free of ambiguity, viz., is not univocal.

Another example, bearing more on grammar than logic. "Star," grammatically speaking, is a word which in the literal sense, viz., as denoting a concrete object of the senses, ultimately capable of measurement, indicates a particular celestial being. Metaphorically, however, it may also designate a famous person, human or angelic, as in the phrase "a third of the stars of heaven" were cast down in the defeat of the rebellious angels (cf. Rev 12:4; Jude 13). Or where "star" connotes saint, as in the phrase: "star differs from star in glory" (cf. 1 Cor 15:41). Whereas in Genesis the biblical literal sense of "star" is also literal grammatically, with St. Paul and St. John and St. Jude the biblical literal sense of "star" is grammatically metaphorical. But to conclude, as so many theistic evolutionists do, that the meaning of the metaphor depends on some scientific theory ancient or modern concerning the stellar physics, or that its use implies the persons so designated or events like the fall into sin and the battle in heaven were merely mythical and not historical is a tribute to ignorance of the elements of theological discourse. Or to affirm as special creationists often do that without acknowledging the *de fide* character of "special creation" one is predestined to deny the historical character of the fall of Adam and Eve or the fall of the angels or the reality of the glorified body in the final resurrection is a similar tribute to ignorance of the elements of theological discourse.

Another instance might be "battle." In the literal sense it connotes armed conflict between groups of men. In the metaphorical sense it connotes spiritual struggle between single persons or groups of persons. Some would say that in theological usage of this term the respective designations of literal and metaphorical are reversed. Error arises when one claims that the literal sense of any passage of Scripture is confined to what is meant by literal in grammar, in which case (as many modern philosophers erroneously maintain) not only theology in the Catholic sense, but Christian metaphysics based on the analogy of being becomes, as it does in Kantian inspired thought, meaningless, except as a way of interpreting the literal or real symbolically or mythically. Whatever speculative hurdles are involved in mastering biblical hermeneutics, the reasonable complexity of the term "literal," yet equally reasonable possibility of avoiding "literalism" should be apparent from the examples. The metaphorical "star" of Hollywood is no less real than the literal "star" in the sky. But they do not have the same natures. The need of analogy to relate material and spiritual in this world and to speak of each intelligently should be obvious. That is why God made use of it in revelation to relate the world and ourselves to him as Saviour.

Something similar occurs when we must deal with historical facts and their interpretation. Both accurate factual information and correct interpretation are not only legitimate, but necessary to the cultivation of history. Mere chronological knowledge of names dates and places is not history; and explanations of history without factual basis are fairy tales or myth. Factual accuracy requires a sense of the univocal and literal, whether fruit of personal witness, or found in human records, or given in divine revelation. Interpretation requires an ability to visualize the key facts in a coherent whole, at least relatively complete, whether the result of philosophical speculation or still better the fruit of divine revelation and faith. This is but another use of the analogical sense, or perhaps symbolic sense. We find this in all the Fathers and great scholastic Doctors, e.g., St. Bonaventure, when speaking of the nature of historical knowledge. We need not credit modern idealistic philosophy (e.g., Hegel) with the invention of these distinctions, but only with their abuse.

When we come to the applications in the first eleven chapters of Genesis the church has assisted us in understanding the essentials: what historical facts are to be taken in the literal sense, and what principles of their interpretation are sound, viz., lead to no kind of historicism which would reduce the facts merely to the status of a projection or theory. Among the facts so guaranteed are those of Adam and Eve as single persons in the strict sense, of original sin and its consequences, of the flood, etc. Among alleged facts not so guaranteed are the exact procedures followed in the structuring of the material world from its absolute beginning in time to the formation of Adam, the exact measure of time indicated by the term "day" during the *Hexaemeron*, viz., whether twenty-four hours to the second, or less or more, etc. The opinions of Augustine, Bonaventure, and Thomas are interesting, but only opinions. Neither "young earth enthusiasts" (special creationists: six days only in the most literal sense, so rendering "impossible" any form of theistic evolution) nor "old earth enthusiasts" (theistic evolutionists: billions of years) have any grounds for resolving what is not in the first instance a speculative question: what could God have done (and unless someone is omniscient, he cannot resolve this question), but one of fact or history in the first sense: what did God do (and only the Creator can tell us because he is the only witness, the remaining evidences being insufficient for drawing any firm conclusion). A great many discussions of special creation versus theistic evolution are fruitless, because the participants on both sides are totally innocent of these distinctions and their implications for the formulation of the problematic.

Next, some applications very much germane to the present discussion. In the very first verse of chapter one of Genesis the word ordinarily translated as "create" (out of nothing) could also be translated as "made" (out of something). The theologian understands the original Hebrew word analogically, viz., as admitting of several different meanings, partially alike, partially dissimilar. In this case the word may mean make out of something, or out of nothing. In both instances there is a genuine action of making or exercise of efficient causality, though in two quite different ways. "Make out of something" is a notion familiar to ordinary experience. "Make out of nothing" is not a concept corresponding to any natural experience of ours. The closest, but still quite different, is that of the Roman military commander praised by our Lord (cf. Matt 8:5–13; Ps 33:6, 9 for the metaphysics of creation behind Christ's comments), whose mere "word" is sufficient to produce results. Faith in divine revelation, tradition and the apostolic magisterium guide the theologian to realize the inspired literal meaning in Genesis is that of "make out of nothing" or create, an analogical concept whose validity rests on the validity of what the church calls "analogy of being." The person who insists that the inspired literal sense is identical with the univocal meaning of the word "make" accessible to our senses will, mistakenly, consider the theologian's analogical use of the term not the literal meaning, but a purely symbolic or mythical interpretation.

Another example is in the second verse of Genesis 1, where the Spirit is said to be drawn over the waters in order to bring order out of disorder, form out of formlessness or chaos. The theologian will say that this literally means educing form from the potentiality of matter, but with terminology, grammatically speaking, metaphorical. The literalist will insist that because the figure of speech is metaphorical rather than "grammatically" literal, therefore the literal meaning here is mythical, or from the exact opposite viewpoint of certain creationists, therefore the verse describes something that can be immediately translated into scientific terminology.

Or again, what is the literal sense of Adam and Eve? Do these names connote single, individual persons, a very concrete, non-repeatable historical couple, the first and therefore unique origin of all other persons claiming to be human? The church has defined this as the literal sense. Atheistic evolutionists, supporters of polygenism, etc., reject this and claim the literal sense is merely a symbolic one: Adam and Eve are code words to designate the simultaneous appearance of many couples which can be classified under the heading of a species known as human. Traditional Catholic theology would see this as a confusion of the spiritual or typological sense of Adam and Eve with the literal. Adam and Eve are types (another aspect of "kind") of Christ and Mary, but they do not for this reason cease to be historical personages in their own right. In this instance the misreading of the spiritual sense as a kind of poetic expression of evolutionism reveals in those promoting this interpretation a form of literalism.

How do tragic misunderstandings come about? By way of a kind of "literalism" shared with the adherents of the old Calvinism by many of our contemporaries, even if they claim not to be Calvinists. "Literal" sense theologically is confused with grammatical usage, viz., where literal denotes sensible object, and then with scientific usage where literal denotes a subject capable of measurement. Since Adam is not used scientifically here, therefore, so the theory goes, the name must be understood metaphorically or symbolically. Another example: water, or light, or land, etc. According to the modern evolutionist, since these words are not used literally or scientifically, therefore they are merely symbolic and do not connote anything individual and concrete. The special creationist tends to read on exactly the same premises, but with contrary results: since "water" in the inspired text must have a literal sense, therefore it tells us something about "water" scientifically considered. And so on for each "kind." The evolutionist confuses the symbolic meaning with the literal; the special creationist simply ignores the typological as unreal. Both are in error.

In speaking of the inspired meaning of sacred writ, the fathers and great doctors intend, rather, the relation between the meaning conveyed by text written under inspiration of the Holy Spirit and the human language or words used to convey what God intends us to understand, but which these words (apart from this inspiration) naturally do not, indeed cannot connote except under the inspiration of the Holy Spirit (who speaks through the prophets) and which under his inspiration they do connote. That is why St. Peter tells us (cf. 2 Pet 1:20–1) biblical revelation is the fruit not of private judgment or opinion, but of divine inspiration and therefore by implication only a divinely appointed authority can definitively determine the meaning of that revelation or prophecy. Attempts to do this privately, apart from the apostolic magisterium, whether from left or right, are doomed to misunderstanding, and the perpetrators of these attempts show themselves to be "false prophets" (cf. 2 Pet 2:1–2).

The literal sense, without which no understanding of the mystical or supernatural revelation is possible, is precisely that which the words chosen by the hagiographer under the inspiration of the Spirit *immediately* connote. The spiritual or full sense of the words: that which is *ultimately* intended by their inspired use in Scripture, is always linked to the literal, but not necessarily identical with it. Where the literal and the spiritual are not identical, the literal is the indispensable gate to the spiritual. Thus, to hold that the virginal birth of Christ is merely the spiritual sense of the accounts of Luke and Matthew is false and heretical. It is the literal sense of the account, on whose truth the spiritual sense (and therefore all accommodated senses as well) of the text depend.

However complicated this may seem, a simple example familiar to everyone (and often employed by the fathers in explaining these basics of Bible study) is that of the human voice and the meaning conveyed by it. The voice: or word (oral) or letter (written), is not simply a physiological phenomenon. It involves a spiritual, or immaterial factor really distinct from and independent of the corporal organs by which the voice is produced. Without the faculties of the spiritual and immaterial soul no voice is any different from animal grunts or inanimate noise, and no music can be other than cacophony. To adapt a witty observation of Chesterton on materialistic anthropology in his study of George Bernard Shaw,[4] any theories to the contrary "may be taken to hell or to Oxford." In the same way the spiritual sense of Scripture is related to the literal. This is an admission of the existence of spiritual substances and their priority and perfection vis-à-vis purely material beings, of the difference between form and matter, quality and quantity,

---

4. Chesterton, *George Bernard Shaw*.

and of their perfect coordination in the union of soul and body to constitute a single, complex human nature in Adam and Eve, male and female (cf. Gen 1:27–30). St. Bonaventure accurately calls man the creature whose role by nature is to mediate or bring into harmony within the cosmos the spiritual and material, so pre-figuring a most perfect realization of this mediation or recapitulation in Christ and Mary and the church.[5]

For the same reason, the literal sense of the Bible (in theological usage) can never be reduced to a philological or logical or scientific analysis of terms or concepts. We should be guilty of the crudest form of rationalistic scientism, if we imagined that any kind of empirical biology, whether Aristotelian or modern (that having its origin in the late Middle Ages and renaissance), could directly define and verify the integral reality (and not merely tangible, but scientifically unexplainable aspects of the mystery) denoted by the terms virginal maternity and virginal birth of the Savior-God. A similar difficulty exists with the mystery of Christ's resurrection, Our Lady's assumption, and the miracle of Eucharistic transubstantiation and real presence. Chemical analysis before and after the consecration will reveal no difference in the appearances or species (theological, not biological usage) of bread and wine. Yet it would be not only an error, but heresy to conclude no radical change affecting the total substance of bread and wine occurred in the extra-mental order or real world. Quite obviously, what the theologian means by literal sense is not identical with what the chemist means by the same word. There is no necessary contradiction. Indeed, the knowledge of the miracle in all these instances may well, at least indirectly, help the scientist in his own field to discover new and fruitful approaches. And no doubt the theologian can benefit in considering scientific reflection on related aspects of a mystery. But in no case can we do without an appreciation of analogy, or what the ancients called the sacramental-hierarchical structure built into the very essence and operation of the cosmos as a whole. One of the great disappointments in the current discussion of creation versus evolution is to find so little recognition of these so basic and not so difficult to grasp principles.

Hence, what cannot be done is to define the literal sense of a divine revelation by employing the methods and criteria of empirical science: observation of sensible phenomena and their subsequent organization on the basis of mathematical measurement. This is what is known in theology as the vice of literalism. It has always been the temptation (1) of those whose appreciation of Christian metaphysics and dogma is insufficient and/or who often enough deny the use of "analogy of being" as a genuine means

5. *Brev.*, p. 2, c. 1, nn. 9–12.

to knowledge of the reality; or (2) of those who on rejecting the divinely appointed magisterium anchored on the successor of St. Peter are per force condemned to seek certainty in their reading of the Bible, either via a private mystical experience of the Holy Spirit, or in the prestige of the academy and its professors. Unfortunately, a great many creationists as well as evolutionists, at least in practice, seem to have contracted the vice in their approach to the problem of the work of the six days.

It is perfectly true that the revealed account of the origin of the world as we know it is historical, and contains true information both about the material as well as spiritual. But what this account means when translated from theological to scientific language using the same words, e.g., species, kind, day, etc., is very difficult and sometimes impossible at present to determine, as it has always been recognized to be difficult by great fathers (St. Augustine) and doctors (St. Thomas, St. Bonaventure). For this reason, the church, even when condemning philosophical evolutionism denying the first article of the creed, has always refused to define the exact sense of day in the work of the six days, thus acknowledging that something is to be said for each of the divergent opinions of such great saints and thinkers as Augustine, Bonaventure, and Thomas Aquinas.

As the curious opinion: viz., that literal is a synonym for sensible and for what is measurable mathematically, a philosophical error closely related to the Protestant theory of private judgment based on personal experience (whence the exaggerated importance of the literal sense in exegesis and the ridicule of Catholic stress on the mystical, symbolic and typical), gained ground throughout modern thought and became the intellectual basis for popular piety, there took shape what is called "literalism." Literalistic reading of the scriptures, a failing shared both by evolutionists and creationists, equates the literal meaning of Genesis with "the sensible and scientifically measurable." What is not literal in that sense is mythical or fictional. The only difference between both warring camps is one of faith: the creationist believes the literal sense of the Genesis account of the *Hexaemeron* tells us something immediately relevant to scientific theory and practice. The evolutionist holds, that because it does not, therefore it is pure fiction or myth bearing only on the way we think or do not think about the material.

Both are wrong. Those who call themselves "theistic evolutionists" generally tend to assume, and are wrong in so assuming, that what they know as a scientific hypothesis constitutes a direct and reliable basis for saying anything about how the "species" as we know them came originally to be differentiated. For this reason, use of the term evolution to describe what is in fact a theological reality or process not falling within the ambit of scientific study as such is highly ambivalent and therefore misleading. Similarly, special creationists who place an equal sign between the theological notion of species as essence (category in the Aristotelian sense) and the modern scientific notion of species as general class, are guilty of the same sophistry: that of equivocation, otherwise known as the fallacy of the "undistributed middle." That was a major point of the section of *In the Beginning* not published. The editor, now deceased, a saintly and highly intelligent priest and creationist, trained as a philosopher of science at Oxford, subsequently told me privately it had been a mistake on his part to omit, for reasons of space, the long section dealing with this central problem.

Species

From the foregoing it is clear that species or kind as it is used in the Scriptures and theology and species as it is used in modern science are not synonyms. Coordination of these various uses is not a simple task, and surely requires some mastery of analogical thinking, viz., of how to coordinate similitude and dissimilitude in multiple, diverse usages of a single term, like species. Here only a sampling of the problem can be given.

Any worthwhile dictionary of any modern language, and of Latin and Greek over the centuries, will usually point out that the meaning of species widely differs in theology, metaphysics and epistemology, logic, science and aesthetics. In theology and biblical study, it means type or figure. In metaphysics it means a definite kind of essence, in logic a mirror image (*species impressa* and *expressa*), mode of predication, or fallacious (specious argument), in science a class of beings capable of reproducing in kind, and in a seemingly unrelated field such as aesthetics beauty.

Only a brief reflection suffices to illustrate the complexities which the term species poses for the scholar. *Species* in Latin, Christian and pagan, as in the phrase *mulier speciosa* means beautiful woman, but the ignorant literalist of today might translate *speciosa* here as meaning "specious" woman, perhaps suggesting something fraudulent, as in a logical usage (e.g., specious argument), and above all in science. And even within the restricted field of theology *species* can indicate either the essence (as in study of creation), or the proportions or figure appropriate to that essence (as in the Augustinian phrase describing various relations to the creature to the Creator: *modus, species et pondus*), or the accidents of a thing (as in study of the Eucharist). No doubt a study of etymology will reveal how these very different meanings are historically linked to a single Latin root, but this does not change the fact that the same word can bear multiple meanings, sometimes not at all related to one another. The correct meaning of *species* in each instance can only be determined by a divinely appointed authority.

In discussions of the origin of the species the same problem exists, this time without much by way of "infallible" pronouncements as guides in settling disputes over definition of terms. Except for two questions alone: (1) in that concerning the passage from inorganic types to organic "kinds," viz., the question of the appearance of living organisms on the fourth day, and (2) in that concerning the formation or process by which the human organism came to be on the sixth day, there is not a single instance in the use of the word "kind" with reference to the appearance of various species of animals in Genesis, which use has any directly discernible implications either for or against scientific hypotheses favouring "theistic evolution."

Very simply, whereas one may stigmatise this or that specific hypothesis supporting evolution of the species as *de facto* contrary to some defined truth (such as the creation of the soul), one can find in the biblical use of the term species or kind no basis for condemning wholesale the very possibility of a legitimate meaning for the phrase "theistic evolution." Parallelwise, the biblical-theological use of the term kind or species does not constitute an argument for what is called the theory of "special creation." As middle term of the argument for special creation species is equivocal or a form of the "undistributed middle," i.e., a term not used in the identical sense in the major and minor propositions of the argument, so rendering the argument inconclusive.

This is further confirmed when we examine the use of the term species in science as a term of classification. Whereas certain types of scientific classification are objective and measurable (e.g., chemical compounds) those used in taxonomy are notoriously subjective, viz., depending on the mental categories of the taxonomist. One can arrange living species (and fossilized remains) in an evolutionary framework or creationist with equal logic and with equal inconclusiveness. On both sides there is exemplified the Kantian *a priori*, at the heart of so much of the modern epistemology of empirical science. Whether this tells us anything about what actually happened in the past or provides an adequate basis for explaining how it happened, or whether the actual cooperation of creatures in the formation, and then development, of the world can be appropriately termed "evolutionary" in a technical, scientific sense, is highly dubious.

The theological (and metaphysical) use of the term "species" is very different. The theological usage of "species" is neither "subjective" nor "objective" as these latter terms are commonly understood (often under a Kantian influence) in empirical science. "Species," theologically speaking, designates the essence of a thing, what makes it what it is and so different from all other beings not characterized by what makes the essence of this existing thing a species distinct from all other things, namely by what in scholastic philosophy is known as the "specific difference." That which differentiates, for example, the essence of man from that of the animal is "rationality" or in more Christian language "spirituality" or "the quality of being pneumatic" in Christian Greek, translated in Christian Latin as the perfection or formality of being "rational." "Sensibility" is the quality which differentiates the animal from the plant. Curiously, the further one moves along this line of reflection from what is most clear, viz., the specific difference between man and all other lower or less perfect species, the more difficult it becomes to draw an exact line between what today is called macro- and micro- differentiation of species.

Objectively (as this is understood in science, viz., something accurately measurable by a standard independent of mental constructs), the taxonomist can describe quite accurately and in great detail the appearances of each item he then classifies on subjectively chosen grounds. Whereas the metaphysician is often hard put to identify in detail how for instance the bovine essence differs from the canine at the level of being, the taxonomist becomes vaguer and progressively more subjective and arbitrary in his judgments as he proceeds in the contrary direction, viz., as these touch on the question of essence and specific difference rather than on the classification of observable phenomena.

Only where the theologian is dealing with the difference between inanimate and animate, between impersonal and personal life, can he become as it were more specific and comment directly on empirical or phenomenological discussions of the same questions. Conversely the scientist on the basis of his "ambivalent" usage of the term species cannot arrive at any final judgment concerning even the hypothetical possibility of an evolutionary origin of the species, much less the fact of such. A fortiori the scientist cannot conclude metaphysics and theology are irrelevant to the question of origins. But neither on the basis of what is known theologically about this question can the theologian conclude that every scientific evolutionary hypothesis purporting to explain the differentiation of the "species" is impossible. This is exactly what I pointed out in In the Beginning, in the form of two questions still to be resolved: (1) just how much light does church doctrine and theology shed on questions concerning the origin of the species raised in scientific form; and (2) just what can science tell us, either directly or indirectly, about those historical facts already known from revelation and theology?

That the complete answers to these two questions are after so many millennia still unavailable to us should make it clear to the crusaders on both sides of this polemic that the kind of exhaustive resolution being attempted, either in terms of theistic evolution or special creation, is hardly a prerequisite for faith and for the conduct of Christian life in the church. We already know what we need to know to keep our intellectual and moral balance in these matters. Further research and reflection both theologically and scientifically is commendable, but let us beware of exaggerated and indemonstrable claims from any quarter.

Evolution: Macro and Micro

Because there remains at best an over-lapping in the theological and scientific usage of the key term "species" in discussions of the "origin of the species," it is extremely difficult to arrive at a universally acceptable definition of evolution. The creationist will insist that he does not deny what is commonly known as micro-evolution, viz., variation of a species within already determined limits, but only macro-evolution, viz., the determination of such limits by the action of any agent other than the Creator.

But the theistic evolutionist can easily reply (and this was noted by John Paul II in his 1996 address to the Pontifical Academy of Science) that aside from the passage from the non-living sphere to the world of living organisms, and from this world of living organisms to the human sphere of personalized organism, there is no sure way of determining where the line between micro and macro-evolution among living, non-personal organisms is to be drawn. That some "species" only existed to make possible the emergence of higher species and disappeared without a trace is plausible, even if not provable. This is the scenario proposed by some theistic evolutionists who point to "junk DNA" as leftovers from a time, viz., not that time involving the conservation and development of the world by man after the formation of Adam and Eve, but from the time or "week" preceding human history, viz., of the structuring of the initially chaotic visible world. Other species of greater or lesser perfection survived and reproduced in order to contribute to the conservation of the world.

Such theistic evolutionists (did they know the views of St. Bonaventure and St. Thomas) might even cite in confirmation the teaching of those two theological greats on the formation of a new heavens and new earth on the last day. According to these great doctors, summarizing an ancient tradition, when generation or reproduction of individuals to conserve a "species" no longer serves any purpose, the remaining plants and animals as we know them will disappear without a trace, except as perfections recapitulated in the glorified bodies of the saints. In the heavenly paradise there will be neither plants nor animals, which does not mean paradise will be a desert devoid of ornamentation and beauty. The teaching of these saints merely means the beauty of heaven as a garden of delights will be beyond compare and so beyond classification as we now know it, whether metaphysical or scientific, so as to render them irrelevant. Whether the parallel is valid I do not know. If the theory comes to be proven scientifically incoherent, the theological point remains valid, but it hardly confirms what has been shown on other grounds to be unintelligible. Presently, however, we are hardly in a position to damn the theoretical possibility of some form of "macro-evolution," or to claim *de fide* that every evolutionary theory of the origin of the species is by definition atheistic. The reason is sufficiently clear: except for the difference between living and non living and between personal and impersonal it is not possible to define exactly the difference between macro and micro evolution.[6]

Historical considerations.

It is often asserted that St. Augustine was a theistic evolutionist in the modern sense. He most certainly was not. But neither was he a creationist in the sense of supporting a hypotheses of "special creation." His thesis about the immediate creation of all species in a single day, viz., in a single, instantaneous moment (without process) if taken in this sense obviously conflicts with what he says about the formation of Adam and Eve, not from nothing, but from pre-existing matter, so entailing a passage of time (as St. Thomas and St. Bonaventure clearly saw). St. Bonaventure rightly remarks that St. Augustine does not deny a passage of time described either literally or symbolically as six days. Rather, he simply does not deal with the question, except as a basis for what St. Bonaventure calls the *rationes seminales*, the various types or forms of physical causality, including the reproductive and organic, embedded in the non-organized first matter created before the first day out of nothing by the Creator. Such simultaneity, however, does not include actual distinction or differentiation. This

6. But whether or not any given theory of evolution, whatever qualifier is given it, is inherently plausible, is primarily a scientific question. The current state of the question gives no grounds for thinking it is plausible and many reasons for thinking it is not. On the other hand, the question of origins, whether of the world or of the structuring of the world, is primarily a historical-theological question. Whatever valid meaning the word evolution might have in such a context, its use in such a context cannot serve as a primary proof for the validity of a scientific hypotheses of evolution. These must stand on their own ground scientifically. Theological and historical study of origins, conditioned primarily by the possibility that some form of evolutionary science might be proven valid, is hardly sound theological or historical method.

occurs, according to the Seraphic Doctor by way of a progressive eduction by the Creator of types or kinds from the potency of the primitive "seed bed." The primitive matter is the seed bed, or *seminarium* out of which each thing according to its kind emerged, principally under the influence of the Creator Spirit drawn across the chaotic waters (Gen 1–2).

St. Bonaventure does not tell us whether this process is restricted merely to the use of pre-existent matter, or includes (as Bl. John Duns Scotus seems to imply and St. Thomas deny) some kind of instrumental, active cooperation of creatures in the order of efficient causality. Theologically (and metaphysically) one can only say that this is a possibility, but perhaps it never happened in fact. In any case, the great medieval scholastics had a far more sophisticated appreciation of the problem than many who have come after them in the modern world, whether creationist or evolutionist in preference.

Only in one instance, that of the formation of Adam, male and female, from the slime of the earth or from the virgin earth, might something more be suggested. In so far as the virgin earth is a type of the Immaculate Virgin, mother of the New Adam, who does indeed contribute actively as well as passively to the realization of the incarnation, might the role of the earth in the formation of Adam be something more than passive? This surely is the case if we admit the objective and effective character of exemplary causality. But precisely this mystery is least amenable to the kind of hypothesis normally described as evolutionary in biology, and the thinking associated with it in theology, e.g., that of Teilhard de Chardin.

The reason is, neither Aristotelian science nor modern science deal with what is one of the primary considerations of Christian metaphysics and theology: the notion of personal action and personal causality, (1) on the part of the divine persons as the presupposition for the creative act bringing the world into existence from nothing, and (2) of the formal cooperation of rational creatures, both men and angels, with the work of re-creation. Empirical science in itself prescinds from all this. Theology, on the other hand, must begin precisely here (while still making use of a language first developed in view of science), though not neglecting the four causes of Aristotle. It is this difference which largely accounts for a variety of opinion on exactly how to assess the juncture of the two approaches.

Pope John Paul II comments that creationist and evolutionist hypotheses in biology are equally probable. He then goes on to say that as an *a priori* of scientific thought theistic evolution is more than a hypothesis. This may be taken, as many take it, in the Kantian sense, a view whose correctness is open to serious question. Or it may be understood from a theological perspective as a way of affirming that the possibility of creaturely cooperation with the Creator, above all the human creature, is a presupposition for all reflection, theological and scientific, on the created world and on the reason for its existence. So interpreted the pope does not indicate that evolutionary hypotheses in biology are more probable than creationist hypotheses. But he does indicate something which is true theologically (and denied by the strict Calvinist): the radical possibility of an Immaculate Conception and the active cooperation of the Woman, viz., the Virgin-Mother of the Creator, in the re-creation, beginning with the Incarnation and redemption.

Whether this premise should be described as theistic evolution is open to question for the reasons given above. The pope himself prefers "continuing creation" or "progressive creation." Personally, because the term evolution has acquired so many associations which are anti-Christian, I would prefer to designate this premise with some term related to procreation, viz., to the power in a created agent, not merely capable of reproduction of a species, but of procreation of persons, brought into existence, not primarily to conserve a "species" or kind but to complete the number of the citizens of heaven, viz., of the partakers of the delights of the heavenly paradise. A living organism with the power to procreate is one evidently also a personal agent. How does such an organism come to be? This is the great mystery of conception: a process involving pre-existent living matter, yet procreation of a person who did not pre-exist conception. But before the formation of Adam and Eve, the mystery of conception as we know it did not yet exist. What kind of process, if any, preceded the personalization of Adam's body with the infusion of his soul? I offer no solution; I merely raise the questions to be addressed in formulation of the problematic: if the created instrument was not already personalized before the process began, how could it in any sense be described as a "procreative" process (the question for theistic evolutionists)? And if there were no "procreative" process, at least typologically, then in what proper sense of the term can it be called formative (the question for creationists)?

Conclusion

I would want to make clear at this point (1) that I am personally convinced theistic evolution as a scientific hypothesis is false: as a personal view, not a dogmatic conviction; and (2) that even if in some sense theistic evolution should be validated scientifically, I would not use such a term with so many unfortunate associations to describe what is a theological truth or rather insight, on some points suggesting possible links with the scientific. The dangers involved are perfectly evident in the parallel case of virginity or *parthenogenesis*, considered theologically and biologically. What the biologist means by *parthenogenesis* does not coincide, except in some few points, with what the theologian means in dealing with the miracle of Mary's virginity before, during and after childbirth. The attempt to put an equal sign between these is a hallmark of modernism in theology and rationalism in science.

Surely, all these riddles of theology and science dealing with the question of origin of the species will be resolved in heaven. But here below the missionary and pastor need only be concerned with that which God has chosen to make certain to us concerning the basic structures of this world, of the interaction of the spiritual and material, of the origin of life, and human life in particular, and how every conception, like every marriage and family, is related to the Immaculate Conception, to the virginal marriage of our Lady and St. Joseph, and to the possibility of procreating potential new members of that family, to be reborn of water and the Holy Spirit. This is why the church wisely refuses to become dogmatically involved in pure scientific hypotheses, like theistic evolution and special creation, for their own sake. Both creationists and evolutionists who abound in the careless use of terms and who are quick to damn their opponents either as heretics or as fools should strive to emulate this prudent caution before leaping to conclusions much too apodictic in view of the arguments on which they rest.

That is also why I have thought it necessary to correct misinterpretations of my earlier study, *In the Beginning*. These misinterpretations almost always rested (at least implicitly) on the following claim. There is found in the solemn decisions of Lateran IV and Vatican I condemnation of atheistic evolution: viz., of the false and heretical claim that the world, material and spiritual, did not originate with a simple act of the Creator's will calling this world and each distinct species in it into existence immediately out of nothing, but by way of an immanent evolution out of an eternally existing matter. This condemnation, it is claimed, translates automatically into a condemnation of the abstract term "evolution" as atheistic by definition, whether applied to the origin of the world as a whole, or to the differentiation of the species. On such grounds any theory of theistic evolution as an explanation of the origin and differentiation of the species in the work of the six days would be *a priori* contrary to faith.

Such a claim is dangerous, because it tends of itself to a denial of the very possibility of creaturely cooperation in the work or re-creation, and of the return of all things to God by whom they were first made. That denial is the basis for repudiating the title of our Lady as Immaculate Mediatress of all graces, Mother of God and Mother of the Church, mother indeed of the Creator and so able to cooperate with him in the salvation of the world.

In a word, it is a denial of the classic thesis formulated by St. Anselm, of the very possibility that the *Fiat* of the Creator might be complemented by that of the Immaculate Virgin in the formation of the New Adam and work of re-creation, remotely envisioned (typologically) in the work of six days leading to the formation of the first Adam.

One final observation. The proponents both of "special creation" and of "theistic evolution" as explanations for the origin and differentiation of the species seek to confirm their own preferences and invalidate those of their opponents by an appeal to scientific proof. Strictly speaking empirical science neither proves nor disproves any theory of origins, for the simple reason that this question is not a direct object of scientific study, but of history and theology. Scientific hypotheses or interpretations of surviving evidences of what may or may not have happened in the distant past may be offered as possible contributions to an understanding of what is otherwise known. But the truth of the first article of the creed, as the church has always understood and continues to understand it, does not rest on a successful demonstration of the Creator's role in the origin of the species, apart from the formation of the first man and woman. Creationists weaken their defence of saving truth when they overstate their case scientifically, attempting to impose on scientists a flawed theological theory known as "special creation," claiming for it the highest degree of doctrinal certainty and anathematising in principle any scientific hypothesis dubbed evolutionary, merely because atheists have found the term useful to promote what is not science, but false theology dressed up to look like science. Conversely, theistic evolutionists would do well to take note of the incredibly heavy dose of pantheism mixed up with a great deal of shoddy speculation commonly known as "theistic evolution" or "process theology" (a la Whitehead), neither good theology nor sound science. The craze to justify faith by an appeal to science, inspired often enough by exclusively apologetic preoccupations, can only end, as it does in the writings of Teilhard de Chardin, in an orgy of pseudo-mysticism. *De hac re salva nos, Domine!*

Teilhard de Chardin Ambiguity by Design[1]

CURRENTLY A BOOK ON man, evolution, and the universe, *The Phenomenon of Man*, by Pierre Teilhard de Chardin, S.J., translated by Bernard Wall and published by Harper's in 1959, has aroused much interest and comment not only in the Catholic press, but secular as well. Generally favorable comments and reviews have been made. None that we have so far seen in the Catholic press have noted the substantially objectionable character of the work, which was published in English without ecclesiastical permission, but with a glowing introduction by none other than the British agnostic, Julian Huxley. It is unfortunate that such popular Catholic reviews as *Jubilee, The Critic, Commonweal* have seen fit to lavish praise on the book's merits without sufficiently indicating the very questionable orthodoxy of the author's views and the danger which the book constitutes for a reading public untrained in theological method.

The Man Behind the Book

It is our intention in this brief article to indicate who Pierre Teilhard de Chardin was and what questionable, if not down right erroneous opinions he propounds in *The Phenomenon of Man*. We believe that this résumé will make abundantly clear the objectionable features of Teilhard's work.

Pierre Teilhard de Chardin (1881–1955), a French Jesuit, was a renowned paleontologist, famous in scientific circles for his discovery of the Peking man. Admittedly a brilliant scientific scholar, he has not achieved the same renown in theological circles, especially among those who are careful to follow the teaching of the magisterium of the church and to obey its directives. He was almost always requested to relinquish the many professorships held by him in Catholic institutes of higher learning, because he

1. This essay was originally published in *The Homiletic and Pastoral Review* 50 (1960) 709–17.

was either unable or unwilling to give a clearly orthodox sense and expression to his opinions. Except for some strictly scientific essays, he was unable during his lifetime to obtain from his religious and ecclesiastical superiors the necessary permissions to publish his writings. Some of these writings had been circulating in France and elsewhere, in manuscript form, sometime prior to 1950. They lacked ecclesiastical permission, but in all fairness to the Jesuit writer, who always protested his orthodoxy and loyalty to the church, this circulation was against his wishes.

As a result, Fr. Teilhard was involved in the controversy that took place just before the publication of the encyclical *Humani Generis*. No one, of course, was personally condemned by Pius XII in that document. Nevertheless, Fr. Teilhard's writings continued to be suspected of containing certain errors, or at least erroneous tendencies toward evolutionary relativism, reproved by this encyclical. Under pressure he left Paris in 1951 and came to New York where he worked for the Wenner-Gren scientific foundation until his death, Easter day, 1955. He is buried at St. Andrew-on-Hudson, Poughkeepsie, New York.

Both the French and English editions of *The Phenomenon of Man* have appeared without ecclesiastical approbation and without the permission of the superiors of the Society of Jesus. It seems that anonymous friends prevailed upon Teilhard de Chardin before his death to leave his manuscripts to them. These friends (whose identity has not been revealed) are publishing his work on their own authority. The apology of Julian Huxley in his introduction to this work to the effect that the manuscripts of a priest can "be published after his death, since permission to publish is only required for the work of a living author," is certainly original, if not exactly canonical. Neither the standing of Huxley nor the book's method of publication recommends it to Catholics.

Man: Evolution Become Conscious of Itself

It is not so much the apparent lack of docility to the authorities of the church on the part of the literary heirs of Fr. Teilhard which constitutes the principal danger of this work. It is rather to be found in certain themes, and methods employed in expounding them. Fr. Teilhard is not concerned merely with the question of the evolution of man's body from pre-existing inferior species. In his view, the question of transformism takes its place in a larger vision of evolution as the historical unfolding, perfecting and return of all creation through man to that point from which all originally came forth, the Alpha and Omega. His perspective is not only that of man's past in terms of a continually evolving space-time, but of man's future in terms of fundamental laws governing the progress of creation toward fulfillment. Man is the principal agent of this process.

Nor is his perspective merely that of the detached scientist; rather it is that of a man who is himself a part of the evolutionary process, so much so that he regards the very discovery of the laws of evolution as a landmark in the progress of the cosmos. His view, in brief, is that of an existentialist describing man in terms of an evolving spacetime, in which the very stuff of the cosmos contains the germ of life, and life contains the germ of consciousness. Teilhard holds that the same laws of entropy and complexity, the same forces of divisive (tangential) energy and unifying (radial) energy governing the initial biological development of the world, govern also its further development at the higher level of thought or the "noosphere." Thus, the birth of life (biogenesis) saw a further change and development that prepared lor the birth of man and consciousness (anthropogenesis and noogenesis), while the discovery of the evolutionary process itself marks the beginning of a further perfecting of the world through the socialization of human thought. This process can only culminate when each thinking center or monad, namely man, is perfectly turned in upon itself and upon that center of centers at the heart of the world, namely Omega, from which the entire process began. Then and then only will the "noosphere," or realm of mind, exhaust the centripetal and centrifugal energies at work in the world, because then perfect unity in totality will be acquired in the perfectly centered activity of reflective consciousness. "Man is nothing else than evolution become conscious of itself," and the Incarnation and Redemption are "a prodigious biological operation."

A Fundamental Error

We have no quarrel with Fr. Teilhard on the question of transformism, except that he seems overly sanguine in his conviction of its truth and its necessity for salvation. Revealed truth does not stand or fall on this point. The church does not forbid prudent investigation of this problem. On the other hand, she recommends that the arguments in favor of biological evolution of the body of Adam properly consider the necessity for a special intervention of God in the process; that serious difficulties still to be solved be indicated by those treating the question of transformism. We are not sure whether Fr. Teilhard regards evolution as a hypothesis or as an absolutely proved fact. If the latter is the case, then he has certainly exceeded the bounds of prudence laid down for Catholics in the encyclical *Humani Generis*.

We are not unmindful of the many valid observations which Fr. Teilhard notes in the course of his exposition, especially the irreversible character of history and the necessity of a historical or evolutionary perspective in studying any aspect of this world. Nor can one do ought but admire the objectives which have inspired this study of man and the cosmos in an evolutionary framework: the consideration of the human phenomenon scientifically and at the same time not impersonally; the attempt to indicate the harmony of a generally evolving universe with Catholic theology and especially the hopeful prognosis for the future based on the laws of evolution.

What seems to us most objectionable and dangerous is *the method by which these objectives are pursued in this work*. Although others have criticized, as questionable, various assertions of the author concerning God, Christ, evil, the supernatural order, no American Catholic review has yet indicated this fundamental error of method which renders Fr. Teilhard's protestations of orthodoxy forced and unconvincing. This error of method coupled with a revolutionary terminology gives rise to an ambiguity which is practically insuperable. This ambiguity in the fundamentals of the faith is not of small importance. But of even greater importance is the error of method. We think that it consists in a misunderstanding of the relations between empirical science, phenomenology, and related disciplines, on the one hand, and theology and metaphysics on the other. We think that Fr. Teilhard has overreached the limits of science. As a result, many of his assertions are untenable both from the point of view of science and from the point of view of theology. These assertions are precisely those which are of fundamental importance to Catholic doctrine.

Fr. Teilhard repeatedly states that he is writing merely from the phenomenological point of view, i.e., concerning what appears to scientific inquiry, and therefore that his work ought not to be judged theologically or metaphysically. While his description of the whole phenomenon of man in terms of the principles of cosmic evolution goes beyond physics as it is commonly understood, he does not wish this "hyperphysics"—as he describes it—to be identified with metaphysics, and much less with theology. While Fr. Teilhard asserts that "complete liberty is not only conceded but offered by the phenomenon to theology," nevertheless he introduces subjects into his phenomenology, namely God, evil, Christ, faith, etc., which cannot be considered merely from the standpoint of phenomenology. These realities either are not phenomena, i.e., objects of the senses, or at least they are not principally such. To treat these matters without reference to the judgment of metaphysics and theology, even in a merely "phenomenological" work, is to court disaster to the cause of truth. This "hyperphysics" of Fr. Teilhard seems to us very much confused with metaphysics; it is also very much confused with theology, for, when introducing truths of faith, "hyperphysics" fails to distinguish the natural from the supernatural, the evidence of reason from the foundations of faith. Fr. Teilhard does indeed affirm that, as they approach the poles, phenomenology and metaphysics "merge" without ceasing to remain distinct. We deny that they merge. Where there is overlapping, we affirm the subordination of science to the judgments of metaphysics and theology. We deny, therefore, the need and possibility of a pure "hyperphysics" or phenomenology that presumes to study God, thought, Christ faith, the supernatural, evil, without any reference at all to a metaphysical or theological critique.

Some Strange Reversals

What we are saying is that the first principles and final conclusions of our theology and metaphysics are not linked essentially to the latest scientific cosmogony any more than they were linked to the cosmogony of the ancient Hebrews or that of Aristotle. Theology does not need the "liberty" of science. Theology does not need an authorization it already has and cannot be deprived of.

Nor do the first principles of metaphysics depend on the sufferance of science. But the opposite is true: the first principles of science depend upon metaphysics. Metaphysics, if valid, will certainly not deny to science the right to exist; neither will the knowledge of metaphysics ever be a substitute for the knowledge of the empirical sciences. But if a scientist should wish to provide the epistemological justification for the first principles of his science, then he would have to have recourse to a discipline more primary than science. The truths of metaphysics are not generalizations from the phenomenological sciences; they are a penetration of reality at a level deeper and more intelligible than that of phenomena. To ignore this is to ignore the subordination of one intellectual discipline to another.

When Fr. Teilhard attempts to introduce, for example, finality into the total cosmic phenomenon on the basis of phenomenology alone, he is overreaching his science. There *is* finality in the world; phenomena *do* have a direction. But to understand the direction of the world to its last end, one must introduce the notion of finality established by metaphysics. Rightly to consider the direction of man toward his supernatural end, one must introduce the data of revelation and concepts of theology. It is impossible to treat these matters in a "hyperphysics" which prescinds from the norms and judgments of theology and metaphysics. Such a procedure can lead only to confusion and error where confusion and error are fatal.

Pseudo-Philosophy and Hyperphysics

In what we believe to be a very significant statement of the basic principles governing his synthesis, Fr. Teilhard asserts that evolution is a light enlightening all other theories, a condition of knowledge to which all other disciplines must bow.[2] We do not affirm that theology and metaphysics are substitutes for the observation of the empirical sciences. Nor are the observations of the scientist without value in illustrating the truths of theology and metaphysics. But theology and metaphysics do not thereby depend on or submit to the relative and changing elements in evolution for their validity. As this assertion of Teilhard stands—and nowhere does he make any further distinction in his stand—it seems to us that it is not much different from the cardinal principle of the philosophies of becoming and evolutionary pantheism: viz., that no truth is absolutely valid, because all truth ultimately rests on the relative basis of an ever changing reality. J.B.S. Haldane, in a passage cited approvingly by Teilhard,[3] though with reservations, arrives at quite explicitly Pantheistic conclusions, beginning with the same data as Fr. Teilhard and submitting them to this universal condition of all knowledge. It may be said that J.B.S. Haldane is writing pseudo-philosophy, but Fr. Teilhard, with his "hyperphysics" that supposedly arrives at a view of the world acceptable to a Catholic, is doing the same. The conclusions of neither are supported by the phenomena studied phenomenologically, because both have overreached the possibilities of phenomenology as a source of truth.

His Religion of the Future

What is fatal in philosophy is worse in theology. If evolution is a light enlightening all theories, what possible objective, permanent meaning can be attached to the truths of revelation, valid for all places and times? Fr. Teilhard asserts that Christianity (we trust he means Catholicity, although under "defenders of the spiritual" he apparently includes anyone who has ever written anything in favor of religion, no matter how erroneous) is the religion of the future, because it will fulfill all the conditions of the "religion of science" of Renan, minus Renan's materialism.

He asserts that evolution will be the means of spiritual perfection by a fusion of mysticism with science in a kind of blending of the personal, subjective truths of religion with the objective truths of science. When he says these

2. *Phenomenon*, 217–18.

3. *Phenomenon*, 57n1.

things, we think he is reintroducing the evolutionary, subjective and naturalistic concept of religion and faith propagated by the modernists at the turn of the century. We find that when, in Teilhard's work, physics and theology do finally "merge" at the poles near the end of his book, the resultant "religion of the future" is as questionable as the "hyperphysics" on which it is founded. At the very least—granting possible clarifications which escape us—we do not think phenomenological "hyperphysics" a sound basis on which to discuss the relations between the cosmos and the supernatural.

It is with pleasure that we here make a pertinent observation of St. Bonaventure. He writes: "It is the right of the highest contemplatives, not natural philosophers (we would also say "scientists"), to read the book of nature as revealing God, because the natural philosopher knows only the nature of things, not the nature of things as the vestige of God."[4] Lest anyone misunderstand the Seraphic Doctor, "contemplatives" here include the theologian and metaphysician; "natural philosopher" means cosmologist and scientist. While a scientist may also be a contemplative, it is not as a scientist that he ascends the heights to a knowledge of God. This may seem very obvious, but Fr. Teilhard does not seem to make the necessary distinctions when speaking of the religion of science and that fusion of mysticism and "research" in which scientific research becomes "adoration."

Had he perhaps consulted and cited a few holy doctors of the church and a number of saintly theologians, rather than Haldane, Huxley, Brunschvig, Poincaré, Einstein, Jeans, *et al.*, he would have realized that evolution is not the universal light. Although material things, which provide us (via the senses) with the first objects of our knowledge, are subject to change and becoming, that which our intellect knows most profoundly about them as knowable is their being, not their becoming. And in this knowledge of being we transcend, in a certain sense, change. So also, *mutatis mutandis*, the same is true of the light of faith. Both lights are superior lights, and the knowledge they convey of the world in no way is dependent on an evolutionary "hyperphysics" for verification. If phenomenology is to contribute anything to our knowledge of religious experience, then it cannot presume to reject theological and metaphysical criticism for the simple reason that by itself it knows nothing about God, Christ, faith, grace and a host of other items considered by Fr. Teilhard.

4. *Hex.* col. 12, n. 15,

Specific Criticisms

We submit, therefore, that the following positions of Fr. Teilhard are ambiguous and questionable, at least until they are corrected in a proper theological context, or else are formulated in such wise that they are not open to an interpretation that can easily lead to evolutionary pantheism.

1. We think it most objectionable to describe animals as thinking; to speak of the biological properties of thought; to distinguish the thought of animals from that of humans merely by the criterion of reflection, as Fr. Teilhard does. We hold that it is not the psychologist who determines the essential notes of thought, but the metaphysician. The psychologist studies its existence in man. Man thinks because he can know being as being. This is something an animal cannot do. In virtue of this apprehension of being as being, human reflection is unique. We do not see how one can borrow the "concise" expression of Julian Huxley that man is "nothing else than evolution become conscious of itself." It implies that thought is nothing else but the perception of the flux of becoming, and hence relativistic. We consider the questionable nature of this position of Teilhard's an illuminating commentary on his ambiguous *noesis* and in particular this remark made in his preface: "There is no fact which exists in pure isolation, but . . . every experience, however objective it may seem, inevitably becomes enveloped in a complex of assumptions as soon as the scientist attempts to explain it. But while this aura of subjective interpretation may remain imperceptible where the field of observation is limited, it is bound to become practically dominant as soon as the pale of vision extends to the whole."[5]

We think Fr. Teilhard has tried too hard to force thought into the context of an evolutionary vortex as its "terminal"; he has tried too hard to make "room" for thought in reality, from which it could never have been validly excluded by science. By means of his "hyperphysics" he has blundered from valid scientific hypotheses into a position whose ambiguity leaves it undistinguishable from subjectivism and relativism.

2. The continual emphasis on: the "physical oneness of everything in change"; life preceded by pre-life and consciousness by pre-consciousness; spiritual perfection and material synthesis as "two aspects or connected parts of one and the same phenomenon"; religion and science as "two conjugated faces or phases of one and the same act of complete knowledge"; the single energy operating in the world, which physics is not sure is pure energy or thought; the stuff of the universe become personalized and the stuff of the universe become interiorized in thought; the biological properties

---

5. *Phenomenon*, 30.

of love, coupled with vague and unqualified phrases about a noble human eugenic in the evolution of the "noosphere"—all these expressions are not far removed from the language of monism, either material or spiritual. Indeed, although Teilhard disassociates himself from communism, many of his assertions have a totalitarian tinge about them. For instance, he writes that "we are faced with a harmonized collectivity of consciousnesses as equivalent to a sort of super-consciousness. The idea is that of the earth not only becoming covered by myriads of grains of thought, but becoming enclosed in a single thinking envelope so as to form, functionally, no more than a single vast grain of thought on the sidereal scale, the plurality of individual reflections grouping themselves together and reinforcing one another in the act of a single unanimous reflection."

3. The ambiguity and impression of a radical pantheistic tendency is even more disconcerting when Fr. Teilhard discusses the subject of God, or "Omega." The consideration of God is not incidental to his "hyperphysics." In a brief summary of his theme, Teilhard says: "To make room for thought in the world, I have needed to 'interiorize' matter: to imagine an energetics of the mind; to conceive a noogenesis rising upstream against the flow of entropy; to provide evolution with a direction, a line of advance and critical points; and finally to make all things double back upon someone."[6] But while maintaining that this "someone," Omega, is transcendent, Fr. Teilhard places him at the center of the world, closing the entire process of change by fusing and consuming all things into himself. And this despite the fact that all things become more distinct the closer they come to Omega! We are told that this is not contradictory, nor is it the pantheism condemned by the church, but rather a legitimate and superior form of pantheism.

Fr. Teilhard is riding his horse in two directions at once. The distinctions by which he attempts to distinguish his theories from pantheism simply cannot be made phenomenologically. Had he been more specific about the limits of phenomenology, he would not have introduced into a purely phenomenological work a consideration of God, except with the help of theology and philosophy. God is simply not a phenomenon and he simply is not at the center of the world as that term is understood phenomenologically. In short, we deny the possibility of a "hyperphysics" that can prescind from theology and metaphysics and still make orthodox statements about God. And because we think that a "hyperphysics" is an impossibility, we agree with the *Saturday Review of Literature* (Jan. 30, 1960) that there must be something wrong with a work whose "text . . . is so ambiguous that people whose views on its subject matter are diametrically opposed can

6. *Phenomenon*, 289.

read it with equal enthusiasm. . . ." This ambiguity of Teilhard's "hyperphysics" is fundamental and pervades the entire work, vitiating much at its root that otherwise might have some value.

4. Finality is not "groping chance," or "trying out everything" as the author says. Finality and direction play a very important part in the synthesis he proposes, but we do not think science or phenomenology can discover at this level the purpose which is operative in existing things that science studies, as it is also operative in man. As a matter of fact, we must say that Fr. Teilhard has not found the final cause or direction in becoming, if the direction which cosmic evolution follows is reduced to "groping chance." This is no foundation on which to disprove the assertions of atheists that the world can be explained without providence. Finality supposes pre-determination to one goal rather than another. "Groping chance" is not this. Had Teilhard introduced a concept of finality established metaphysically, he could very well have discussed the direction which undoubtedly is to be found in this world. But then he would not have been writing a pure "hyperphysics" that prepares the ground for the generalizations of metaphysics and provides the latter the necessary liberty to exist.

5. It is one thing to point out the harmony between the natural aspirations of men and their supernatural destiny. It is quite another to affirm that evolution is a magnificent means of feeling at one with God; that evolution has infused new blood into Christianity; that Christianity is destined to save and supplant evolution, because it fulfills all the conditions of the religion of the future. It is not perfectly clear in the system of Teilhard that the supernatural religion of Catholicity is not merely a necessary postulate of the evolutionary process; that the doctrine of the mystical body of Christ is not convertible with some form of evolutionary socialism as the final term of the entire process of evolution. The phenomenological method, as he uses it, divorced from theology, is not designed to render the truths of the gratuity of grace and its mysterious character as clearly and unequivocally as these ought to be presented.

6. In treating of evil, this author fails to distinguish at all between moral and physical evil. Evil as such, he appears to hold in a final appendix, is a necessary by-product of "groping chance" which guides the evolutionary process toward Omega. Indeed, the entire evolutionary process could not have been other than it is. We do not see how these views can be squared with elementary Catholic teaching on the radical contingency of the world and, in particular, the origin of moral evil. We are amazed that these simple truths, and important distinctions, known to any good Catholic layman, should have escaped this priest.

Nor is the consideration of evil incidental, as Fr. Teilhard claims, to his main theme. This claim is difficult to understand since he also states that evil is necessary to evolution. We think that he has quite arbitrarily selected the subject matter of his "hyperphysics," leaving out such embarrassing topics as the origin of moral evil, and that he could not have done otherwise, given the ambiguity of his "hyperphysics."

Conclusion

The foregoing criticisms are not the fruit of a morbid fear of some possible evolution of the body of the first man. Neither are they the result of a dislike for intellectual progress and a corresponding love of the "good old days." They are inspired by a concern over confusions on matters fundamental to our holy religion that so abound in this work. As Fr. Teilhard himself admits, the evolutionary synthesis he expounds goes much further than mere biology, or, conversely, biology has been extended much further than we would care to extend it, so far indeed that the author of *The Phenomenon of Man* can describe the incarnation and redemption as "a prodigious biological operation." We believe that the ambiguities and questionable assertions he makes on themes which are also treated in theology and metaphysics are not incidental to the synthesis as such. They are a consequence of a fundamental misconception of the relations between science and metaphysics and theology, coupled with a novel terminology coined by Teilhard to fit the original and rather unorthodox notions of a "hyperphysics."

It may seem that we have quoted him out of context; that our strictures are exaggerated. We should like to confess here that it has been very difficult to condense the ideas of Fr. Teilhard and our observations on him into a few pages. Neither the "inevitable blurring," nor the novel terminology, nor his *noesis* have made the task easier. We do not, however, believe we have misunderstood or misrepresented in any substantial way the basic position of the author. A close analysis, we feel, would bear us out.

Nor are we alone in judging this work dangerous, because it is confusing and misleading on fundamentals. On November 30, 1957, the Sacred Congregation of Seminaries and Universities, in a letter to all local ordinaries, ordered the book removed from seminary libraries. *A pari*, we do not think that *The Phenomenon of Man* is without danger for the faith of a Catholic untrained in the subtleties of metaphysics and theology and their relations to phenomenology. As for the non-Catholic, we think the work deceptive and not at all representative of Catholic orthodoxy, for it compromises where compromise is impossible.

We do not agree that this work of Fr. Teilhard de Chardin is the greatest Catholic book of the century or a milestone in the history of intellectual progress, as some have pretended. We have very serious reservations on the methods by which Fr. Teilhard has achieved his objectives. While he was a person well-liked and respected in non-Catholic intellectual circles, especially scientific, we nevertheless believe that in presenting Catholic views to his modern audience he has sought too much for respectability. He has been too much influenced by elements of modern thought irreconcilable with Catholic doctrine. Despite his positive achievements, he has constructed a "hyperphysics" that inevitably leads to blurring and error in fundamentals. It is, alas, ambiguity by design.

—— APPENDIX 2 ——

Pierre Teilhard de Chardin:
"Prophet of a New Vision"[1]

ROBERT T. FRANCOEUR

IN THE MAY [1960] issue of this review some opinions[2] were expressed on Fr. Pierre Teilhard de Chardin and his book, *The Phenomenon of Man*. The reason for this present article is to clarify what this writer and many other students of Teilhard believe are serious misinterpretations in the May article. We do not doubt the sincerity or good faith of Fr. Fehlner in presenting his personal opinion and reaction to *The Phenomenon of Man*. But we are convinced, in all charity, that for the most part he "missed the boat."

Judging the Whole Man

The view of Teilhard, as Fr. Fehlner sees him, has the look of an eviscerated corpse. It reminds one of the fable of the seven sages who were asked to render an opinion of a certain creature. The first sage timidly approached the creature to grasp a tail-like appendage. After careful examination his appraisal was: "A living thing in constant agitation shaped somewhat like a broom." The second scholar approached, only to bump into a massive pillar. "A very solid and immovable creature similar to a pillar." The third sage grabbed a long, proboscis and pronounced: "A type of large snake." Finally, the last sage stood back to view the whole. "Why it's

1. This piece was written in response to Fehlner's above critique of Teilhard's *The Phenomenon of Man*. It appeared in the October issue of *Homiletic and Pastoral Review* 50 (1960) 34, 36–40. Francouer was an early leading proponent of Teilhard's thought and works. He helped found the American Teilhard de Chardin Association. In addition to works on Teilhard, he was a trained in biology, serving as a professor in the field, worked in bioethics and human sexuality. In 1966, Francoeur left the Catholic priesthood and was married to Anna Kotlarchyk. —Ed.

2. Fehlner, "Teilhard de Chardin," *CE* 7, appendix 1.

neither broom, pillar nor snake. It's an elephant." The view of Teilhard de Chardin and *The Phenomenon of Man* presented in the May issue reminds one strongly of this parable.

Teilhard de Chardin wrote three hundred and seventy separate articles during his life. An authoritative list of these may be found in the biography by Claude Cuénot[3] which Helicon Press will publish shortly in English.[4] *The Phenomenon* may be the *longest* of Teilhard's works, but it is *not* the *only* writing nor the most important when dealing with his spiritual thought. Apparently, Fr. Fehlner has not perused the eight other volumes that have been published besides *The Phenomenon*. Anyone can prove Augustine a heretic *if* he takes only certain texts or even treatises alone. We must judge a man's thought by his whole work and not piecemeal.

To understand Teilhard's thought properly we must also understand his viewpoint and audience; he wrote for agnostics, atheists, non-believers, and for a scientific audience. He did not address the Catholic nor even the "believer" directly. Like St. Paul, he spoke to a pagan audience of the "unknown god" in their language. As Catholic scholars our task is to show the parallelism or divergence of this terminology with that of "perennial philosophy." (I do not say with the terminology of some Thomists who profane the spirit of Thomas by a slavish adherence to his words.)

Let us take but a few of the charges Fr. Fehlner leveled at Teilhard. And, although picking individual bones may not make for the most interesting reading, some of the pertinent facts may.

Church Authorities

Fr. Fehlner calls attention to the fact that Teilhard's religious superiors did not deem it prudent nor the proper time during his life for the publication of some of his "theological" essays. This is understandable when we realize that Teilhard began writing in 1905, some thirty years before the "Scopes Monkey Trial" of Tennessee.

> Both the French and English editions of *The Phenomenon of Man* have appeared without ecclesiastical approbation and without permission of the superiors of the Society of Jesus . . . anonymous friends prevailed upon Teilhard before his death to leave his manuscripts to them. These friends (whose

3. Cuénot, *Pierre Teilhard.*
4. *Teilhard de Chardin.*

identity has not been revealed) are publishing his works on their own authority.[5]

The common interpretations of the Constitution of the Society of Jesus and their vow of poverty is that manuscripts are not the property of the Society and may be disposed of at the author's discretion. If published during his life, double permission—the church's and the Society's—must be obtained. Hence it was not Jesuitical for Teilhard to bequeath his manuscripts to friends. If these friends decide to publish after his death, that is their affair (to which we shall come later). The "anonymous friends" to whom Fr. Fehlner refers are revealed in each of the five volumes of *Oeuvres de Teilhard* published by du Seuil—four full pages of names and the positions held by these scholars. And, further, are these "anonymous friends" for the majority non-Catholics, bound by Canon Law regarding *Imprimatur*? If the Jesuit authorities had any claim of authority over these manuscripts, surely they would have instituted legal proceedings against the usurpers. Furthermore, seven of the nine volumes published thus far in French are scientific and, even if published by Catholic laymen, would not require an *Imprimatur*. Can we then accuse this group of "lack of docility to the authorities of the church" as Fr. Fehlner does?

Fr. Fehlner objects to the statement that the incarnation and redemption are "a prodigious biological operation." I thought the term "incarnation" indicated the "Divine Word become Flesh." And if the virginal conception of Christ in the womb of Mary is not a biological prodigy, what is it? Or if the redemption of our bodies from the "slavery of this corruption" is not a biological marvel, then what is it? Fr. Fehlner also takes exception to Teilhard that there is a point in the "fusion of mysticism and 'research' in which scientific research becomes 'adoration.'"[6] Pope Pius XII told the Pontifical Academy of Sciences: "Teach others to behold, to understand and to love the created world that the admiration of splendors so sublime *may cause the knee to bend and invite the minds of men to adoration*".[7] The spirit of St. Francis in a Jesuit!

---

5. Fehlner, "Teilhard," *CE* 7, appendix 1, above.
6. Fehlner, "Teilhard," *CE* 7, appendix 1, above.
7. Pius XII, "Au moment," 394–401.

Evolution and Consciousness

But to more serious charges. "We are not sure whether Teilhard regards evolution as a hypothesis or as an absolutely proven fact."[8] It seems that Teilhard takes neither side of this "dilemma." He regards evolution as a fourth dimension, the dimension of duration, a dimension of thought and a viewpoint which helps man understand the unique instantaneous creative act. But Fr. Fehlner prefers the textbook concept of "transformism."

> For many, evolution is still only transformism, and transformism is only an old Darwinian hypothesis as local and as dated as Laplace's conception of the solar system or Wegener's Theory of Continental Drift. Blind indeed are those who do not see the sweep of movement whose orbit infinitely transcends the natural sciences and has successively invaded and conquered the surrounding territory—chemistry, physics, sociology and even mathematics and the history of religions. One after another, all the fields of human knowledge have been shaken and carried away by the same under-water current in the direction of the study of some *development*. Is evolution a theory, a system or a hypothesis? It is much more: it is a general condition . . . .[9]

Certainly, the sense of the pleroma in Hebrew and biblical thought is evolutionary or developmental. Christ could only appear in the fulness of *time*, when the world was at peace, etc. Claude Tresmontant, a noted biblical scholar, has brought this out beautifully in his chapter on Christology.[10] We often speak of the evolution of dogma without thereby denying the absolute. So, too, despite Fr. Fehlner's claim, Teilhard can be a Christian existentialist and evolutionist without denying the absolute.

The question of "consciousness" in Teilhard's thought is not an easy one. I believe the term "freedom" which Lecomte du Nouy used in *Human Destiny* clarifies a bit this difficult concept. Is man "evolution become conscious of itself?" Fr. Fehlner objects. But what does "reflection" mean? That the consciousness of plants and animals, tropisms, instincts and reflexes, is now on a much higher and different level? Consciousness bent back on itself—reflected—so that "man knows he knows while the animal only knows." This is phenomenological language, but it contains the same idea as Thomistic

---

8. Fehlner, "Teilhard," *CE* 7, appendix 1, above.

9. Teilhard, *Phenomenon*, 217.

10. Tresmontant, *Pierre Teilhard*.

psychology.[11] And if we take the development of consciousness as the main function of evolution, Teilhard is correct.

Fr. Fehlner claims that "Teilhard holds that the same laws of entropy and complexity . . . governing the initial biological development of the world, govern also its further development at the higher level of thought or the "noosphere."[12] But "the yardstick of growing complexity, which permitted us to read the direction of the cosmic process even as far as the appearance of life, from a certain moment onward, no longer suffices to help us unraveling the direction of biological evolution."[13] To understand the development of *life, consciousness* and *thought*, according to Teilhard, we must use a *new law*, the yardstick of cephalization! Entropy and complexity are of little use in this higher realm.

As for *Humani Generis*, this was as much a challenge for theologians to examine seriously the concept of evolution as it was a caution to the over-enthusiastic. Fr. Cyril Vollert, S.J., not an unknown in theological circles, closed his paper for the Duquesne University "Symposium on Evolution" (1959) with the report of a lecture on evolution given at the University of Rome with Cardinal Tisserant attending.

> Scientists here who had been consulted by the Vatican in recent days said they had gained the impression that its (the Vatican's) appraisal of the evolutionary theory was going "far beyond" the positions laid down in the encyclical *Humani Generis*.

Methodology

> What seems to us most objectionable and dangerous is the method by which these objectives are pursued in this work . . . no American Catholic review has yet indicated this fundamental error of method which renders Fr. Teilhard's protestations of orthodoxy forced and unconvincing.[14]

We wonder whether Fr. Fehlner has read any other than American Catholic reviews of Teilhard. Msgr. de Solages, Rector of the Catholic Institute of

---

11. Cf. Donceel, *Philosophical Psychology*, 35–39.

12. Fehlner, "Teilhard," *CE* 7, appendix 1, above.

13. Tresmontant, *Pierre Teilhard*, 23.

14. Fehlner, "Teilhard," *CE* 7, appendix 1, above.

Toulouse,[15] L. Malevez[16] and François Russo, S.J.[17] find little fault, danger or heresy in the methodology of Teilhard. Are we really trying to understand the methods of true phenomenology or merely, as Msgr. de Solages suggests, trying to force a new form of thought into our outdated pigeonholes of knowledge? Admittedly, as Fr. Russo points out, we would like to see Teilhard's synthesis "*more open, more unfinished.*" For "despite the care that the author took to write only within the framework of the phenomenal order, and to restrict what he has to say to that order, Fr. Teilhard—precisely because of his remarkable ability at synthesis—has presented us with a set of views on man and the world which to some little degree gives the impression of being self-sufficient."[18] And a valid criticism by Fr. Russo, though certainly nothing to compare with Fr. Fehlner's claim.

Phenomenology "cannot presume to reject theological and metaphysical criticism."[19] True, but does Teilhard do this? In the very first page of the Preface to *The Phenomenon* we read:

> Beyond these first purely scientific reflections, there is obviously ample room for the most far-reaching speculations of the philosopher and theologian . . . I have identified with some accuracy the combined movement towards unity, and have marked the places where philosophical and religious thinkers, in pursuing the matter further, would be entitled, for reasons of a higher order, to look for breaches in the continuity.

A rejection of philosophy and theology?

As for the relation of science, phenomenology, philosophy and theology, Arthur Koestler's remark in the *Sleepwalkers* seems apropos.

> Perhaps the greatest historical achievement of Albert the Great and Thomas Aquinas lies in their recognition of the "light of reason" as an independent source of knowledge besides the "light of grace." Reason, hitherto regarded as *ancilla fidei*, was now considered the bride of faith. A bride must, of course, obey her spouse in all important matters; nevertheless she is recognized as a being in her own right.[20]

15. De Solages, "Christianity and Evolution," 26–37.

16. Malevez, "Chardin et la Phénoménologie," 579–99.

17. Russo, "Phenomenon of Man," 185–89.

18. Russo, "Phenomenon of Man," 188.

19. Fehlner, "Teilhard," *CE* 7, appendix 1, above.

20. Koestler, *Sleepwalkers*, 106.

This error of method coupled with a revolutionary terminology gives rise to an ambiguity which is practically insurmountable.[21]

Perhaps some of this "insurmountable ambiguity "would have been avoided if Fr. Fehlner had taken the time to consult a Glossary of Teilhardian terms prepared by this writer for the Tresmontant study mentioned above, and which, by the way, carries the *Imprimatur*.

Other Criticisms

We can deal with only a few more charges for lack of space. After reading the careful and detailed studies of Teilhard by such theologians as Martin D'Arcy, S.J.,[22] Cyril Vollert, S.J.,[23] J. Edgar Bruns,[24] François Russo and Bruno de Solages, we wonder that they did not see the "monism, totalitarianism and pantheism" which Fr. Fehlner found. In fact, *they deny that these are there in any form.* "Those who think they see in this view pantheism, totalitarianism, immanentisic naturalism, do not understand its profound inspiration."[25] "This point of convergence which Teilhard baptizes the Omega, is it not the *Great All* of the pantheists in which fusion annihilates the individuals? Quite the contrary!"[26] We might also mention *Evolution* by Rémy Collin which quotes approvingly and extensively from Teilhard.[27]

Regarding the important decree of the Sacred Congregation of Seminaries and Universities (November 30, 1957), the letter asked that all the works *by Teilhard* be removed from the open shelves of seminary libraries. The interpretation of several canonists I have consulted is that books by Teilhard are to be removed from indiscriminate general circulation in *seminary libraries only*. The decree said nothing about seminarians keeping these works in their own libraries or about the seminary library keeping them on the "reserved shelf" where some control is made to see that they do not fall into the hands of unguided embryonic theologians.[28] It is a cautionary decree and not tantamount to "Indexing" Teilhard as some feel.

21. Fehlner, "Teilhard," *CE* 7, appendix 1, above.

22. D'Arcy, "Varieties of Human Love," 206–18.

23. Vollert, "Toward Omega," 261–69.

24. Bruns, "God Up Above," 23–30.

25. Solages, "Christianity and Evolution," 35.

26. Quenetain, "Un livre," 44.

27. Collin, *Evolution*.

28. Cf. Vollert, "Toward Omega," 268.

Thus far we have covered only a few of the misinterpretations, however unintentional they may have been, in the article by Fr. Fehlner. It is not an easy task to understand the thought of Teilhard. And, as Fr. Fehlner points out, some items must be corrected and evaluated in Teilhard's thought, for instance, evil, especially moral evil, the scientific extrapolations made and their role in his thought. But, as Jean Guitton has said, we ought to remember that Teilhard is more the prophet of a new vision than its master.

Hence, we shall end on the note struck by Msgr. de Solages:

> We must surely recognize the fact that, if on one hand these writings represent a prodigious apologetic force and have done a great deal of good among those for whom they were originally written or among competent theologians for whom they have opened up larger horizons, on the other hand, they are read with more enthusiasm than insight by young people who are insufficiently formed or who have known them only in part and therefore have often completely misunderstood them. Since I am of necessity a critical theologian, I would not subscribe to all his views. But the well-balanced synthesis which Fr. Teilhard de Chardin has now achieved contains nothing which could imperil Christian dogma.

Pierre Teilhard de Chardin:
"Leading to Confusion."[1]

EVIDENTLY, FR. FRANCOEUR BELIEVES I couldn't help but "miss the boat" for my "alleged lack of acquaintance" with the entire *corpus* of Fr. Teilhard and with the critical studies and reviews that have already appeared, especially in Europe. I should have wished, however, that Fr. Francoeur had furnished more documentary evidence for his rather gratuitous reflections on my competence to review *The Phenomenon of Man*. It is true that in the preparation of my review I did not "peruse" all three hundred and seventy "separate articles" of Fr. Teilhard, so many of these being purely scientific and not at all the object of my criticisms. But I did take the trouble to acquaint myself with his other writings which could have shed further light on the theological implications of the one work in question viz., *The Phenomenon of Man*. I likewise have at hand all the critical reviews mentioned by Fr. Francoeur, except those of Cuenot and Malevez, in addition to many others pro and con from Europe and America.

If Fr. Francoeur feels I have not adopted an entirely justifiable method of criticism in regard to *The Phenomenon of Man*, I do not think his method of replying to my review is completely above reproach. The greater part of my original review dealt with a single issue I considered *central* to any theological evaluation of quite a number of Fr. Teilhard's assertions concerning matters properly the object of theology and metaphysics. This issue is the relations between science, philosophy, and theology, and the proper method to be used in each. My point was that Fr. Teilhard, despite the best of intentions and objectives, overextended the limits of phenomenology. Specifically, his phenomenological conclusions on the existence of God, consciousness, the mystical body, and on finality (particularly the

---

1. This appeared as a part of an "Exchange on Teilhard de Chardin" in the October issue of *Homiletic and Pastoral Review* 50 (1960) 35, 40–47 in reply to Francoeur's critique of Fehlner's first article criticizing Teilhard de Chardin.

destiny of man) could not be justified in their context, however much these conclusions verbally might coincide with those of revelation. For such a method and approach opens the door not only to ambiguity, but to the very undermining of theology and metaphysics, and these Christian conclusions of Fr. Teilhard. The strength of my specific criticism rests basically not on an arbitrary interpretation or misreading of novel terminology, but on an interpretation of this terminology in a context in which I believed it could not be other than ambiguous and misleading.

To this question of methodology Fr. Francoeur devotes about one-fifth of his total reply under the heading *Methodology*, for the most part citing the opinions of others who agree with him, but without stating precisely *why* my exposition and evaluation of Teilhardian methodology is wrong. Moreover, Fr. Francoeur's remarks are made in an order scarcely calculated to clarify the principal objection of my review. Evidently, Fr. Francoeur does not give the central issue of my review central importance in his rebuttal, nor does he state why it is not of central importance. As a result, I think Fr. Francoeur has become involved in an *ignorantia elenchi*. This impression will be strengthened by the following observations.

Preliminary Objections

As to Fr. Teilhard's point of view and audience, his published works are being read "directly" by an audience of believers as well as non-believers. But even granting that the audience is the restricted one which Teilhard and Francoeur have in mind, I do not agree that the synthesis of Fr. Teilhard is objectively an apt apologetic instrument for speaking of the "unknown God" to agnostic and non-believing scientists. The parallel drawn with St. Paul is not exact. One might add that God also speaks to men in the language of men. But not any language will do. Words have meaning because they are the embodiment of concepts. There are different modes of expression following on the different modes of conceptualization proper to distinct disciplines. Scientific terminology, because it is linked to a mode of thought not of itself capable of penetrating such realities as God, the soul, etc., is not particularly apt for the expression of what is meant by these "unknown" entities. Especially in regard to revealed mysteries, words must have an exact meaning.[2] Briefly, the whole question of terminology

---

2. Although "slavish" adherence to formularies without understanding is never to be praised, the adoption of a technical vocabulary by the scholastics, approved by the church and by the experience of centuries, is by no means to be ridiculed, but to be followed. Thus, in canon 129 [= canon 279, 1983 Code] of the *Code of Canon Law* the

is linked to that of method. Unfortunately, in *The Phenomenon of Man* and in other works dealing with the same theme, Fr. Teilhard does not resolve the objection I have against his method. It is this point also which Fr. Francoeur has nicely avoided.

This same *ignorantia elenchi* on the part of Fr. Francoeur has led him to misunderstand a number of other points he adduces from my review. One case in point is the designation of the incarnation as a "prodigious biological operation." The term "biological" in the context of the Incarnation is ambiguous, i.e., open to many meanings. Understood as having reference to the flesh of Christ, it would be tantamount to docetism to assert that biology has nothing to do with Christ, or with the redemption, or final resurrection. But in the context of the phenomenology of Fr. Teilhard, I find the phrase objectionable, for it seems to reduce the Incarnation and redemption principally to a biological study. In this latter sense I intended the observation I made in my review. My sole point is that before such terminology as a "prodigious biological operation" is employed in a phenomenology such as Fr. Teilhard's *The Phenomenon of Man*, the whole question of phenomenological study of matters primarily theological must be more adequately justified. I did not, however, assert that such a phrase has no acceptable meaning, even in the works of Fr. Teilhard. I do not see that the remarks of Fr. Francoeur contribute anything to the resolution of the difficulty.

"Evolution and Consciousness"

In this same vein I might ask how Fr. Teilhard can fail to take some stand on the "dilemma" of transformism. Even the most superficial reading of *The Phenomenon of Man*[3] reveals that Fr. Teilhard is very much concerned with the development of living matter up to that point where some animal organism would be ready to become the body of man. I do not know what "textbook" concept of transformism Fr. Francoeur has decided I prefer. I do not

---

church, heeding the words of St. Paul in 1 Tim 6:20, admonishes clerics to pursue studies, avoiding, however, in matters pertaining to the sacred disciplines profane and novel terminology and pseudo-learning. Unless one is God, or an inspired writer like St. Paul, it is dangerous to make use of novel scientific concepts and modes of expression as a means to convey Catholic doctrine, without a thorough examination and understanding of the intrinsic possibilities and limitations of such a use. What St. Paul did is not always, *ipso facto*, permissible to others. It should be noted, too, that the chief aim of theology is not apologetic, but dogmatic, i.e., the determination and conservation of the exact sense of revelation. The methods and terminology of theology are linked with this aim which transcends particular cultures.

3. See *Phenomenon*, 72–152.

see, however, how anyone who maintains that evolution, i.e., in the sense of duration as a necessary precondition for the existence of anything, can fail to take a stand on the question of the formation of Adam's body through a progressive development of organic, living matter as opposed to a direct formation from inorganic matter. Some of Fr. Teilhard's expressions seem at variance with the stand enjoined on Catholics in *Humani Generis*.[4] True, the church does not forbid, indeed she even encourages research in this field; but because there is a theological state of the question as well as scientific, the church reserves to herself the right to interpret definitively on the ultimate solution. Until she does, no Catholic may affirm that transformism is a proved fact, i.e., more than his own personal opinion, no matter how personally certain one may be of this. What the church may eventually decide, I do not presume to know. Up to the present there has been no modification of the position taken in *Humani Generis*.

As regards the broader sense in which Fr. Teilhard understands evolution, viz., as a general condition of knowledge and as a fourth dimension in which everything in this world exists, certain qualifications must be made. I have no intention of denying that everything in this world has a history in the larger sense of that term, i.e., exists in time and therefore is subject to development, has a past, present, and future. What I objected to in my review was the assertion that evolution is a general condition of knowledge in conjunction with a phenomenological method that had exceeded its bounds.[5] Not *everything* in the world is subject to phenomenological analysis. Teilhardian phenomenology, according to the glossary of Fr. Francoeur, is "a science" which draws "its knowledge and facts, not from the minute studies of specialists, but from the over-all picture of concrete appearances of the world."[6] That which appears, in so far as it appears, is an object of the senses. A "science," which attempts to organize systematically on a level of *appearances* the data of appearance, cannot possibly deal with the very *being* of these appearances, much less with those things which do *not* appear. Of course, we are aware of God, the soul, etc., but by reason of formally diverse modes of knowing, namely that of philosophy and that of revelation. I am far from denying any relation of phenomenological knowledge to these superior sources of knowledge, but I *am* denying the existence of any universal,

4. Cf. *AAS* 42 (1950) 575.

5. The text from *Phenomenon*, which Fr. Francoeur leaves incomplete is as follows: "It (evolution) is a general condition to which all theories, all hypotheses, all systems must bow and which they must satisfy henceforward if they are to be thinkable and true" (218). The assertion is rather universal and is not qualified either by Fr. Teilhard or by Fr. Francoeur.

6. Tresmontant, *Pierre Teilhard*, 110.

descriptive, intellectual discipline which can extrapolate from the laws of the natural sciences, taken *globatim*, to determine the laws of beings and the development of these beings, even those not the object of the senses, and still remain on the phenomenological level solely.

Unfortunately, in the preface to *The Phenomenon of Man*,[7] Fr. Teilhard professes his intention of remaining on the merely phenomenological level. But in the summary of his thesis[8] he confesses that his method has required him to include such matters as the soul, intelligence, consciousness, and God in his phenomenology of man. It would have been more helpful on Fr. Francoeur's part to clarify my alleged misunderstanding of the apparent contradiction in the phenomenology of Fr. Teilhard, or to indicate pertinent, clarifying texts from other works of this author. Until such is done, I will stand by my original judgment.

I cannot, therefore, admit that because we speak of the evolution of dogma, evolutionary theory as practiced by Fr. Teilhard is completely orthodox. The laws of the development of dogma are not those of the natural sciences, for the simple reason that these sciences are formally diverse. In them the mind exercises formally diverse modes of thought in reaching reality. The relations between these modes of thought in treating those entities, which under formally diverse aspects are the objects of both, are not to be resolved into some generic, univocal science of evolution, because such a "science" is incompatible with the transcendental character of metaphysics and theology.

In my original review I objected to the use of ambiguous terminology in regard to questions concerning the nature of intelligence. To say, as does Fr. Francoeur, that both man and the animal know directly in the same way, but that the second does not know that it knows, equates knowledge of beasts and men *qua* knowledge. Human knowing as knowing cannot be equated with the beast's. This confusion, in the context of Fr. Teilhard's phenomenology, logically leads to psychological monism.

In his remarks Fr. Francoeur cites an article of Fr. M.C. D'Arcy, S.J., "The Varieties of Human Love," to fortify his claims that no monism can be found in *The Phenomenon of Man*. This article originally appeared in *The Saturday Evening Post*. In *The Meaning and Matter of History*, a much lengthier work, Fr. D'Arcy writes:

> This view (of Fr. Teilhard) is so all-inclusive as to bring history as well as animate and inanimate nature within its ambit. It gives a beginning and an end to history and argues that history

7. *Phenomenon*, 29–30.

8. *Phenomenon*, 289, cited in my review above.

develops on principles which are applicable to all else in the universe . . . . Such an assumption takes all meaning out of consciousness, for it has now to be applied to what is precisely its opposite. Furthermore by assuming a strict continuity between spiritual and material processes it forces history into a pattern which experience does not justify, and it skates over the very problem which underlies history, namely the conflict of liberty and natural processes . . . ."[9]

This, I believe, is what is commonly known as "psychological monism," the reduction of the spiritual to its opposite, the material. It is not very difficult to find some relation between a methodology that arrives at psychological monism and the same methodology in the use of monistic-tainted terminology concerning God. I do not know if Fr. D'Arcy concurs with me in my judgment on the gravity of such a mentality among Catholics and on the possibility of a weakening of the faith therefrom. I personally consider this very alarming, as does the encyclical *Humani Generis*.[10]

Fr. Francoeur misses the point altogether in his criticism of my "eviscerated" analysis of the laws governing Teilhardian evolution. The law of cephalization is also biological. It can no more be extrapolated to the realm of consciousness and God than the two I mentioned. Much less to the realm of dogma. This merely phenomenological extrapolation does not take sufficient account of the essentially diverse laws of superior disciplines. It is similar to an anthropomorphic approach to God and is subject to the basic difficulties of such an approach.

"Methodology"

On the principal "charge" of my review, Fr. Francoeur is unenlightening altogether. In the first place, in the peculiar process of thought proper to modern scientific disciplines, the notion of categories (into which reality is poured, as it were, and which are constantly open to revision and modification as the realm of observation to be explained by them expands) is not unrelated to the inductive method. In theology, and in the metaphysics employed by theology in its speculation, such an epistemological theory is quite objectionable.[11] Indeed, this characterization of scholasticism has a certain Kantian and Hegelian flavor about it. The concepts of scholastic metaphysics, employed instrumentally by theology, are not like the old

9. D'Arcy, *The Meaning*, 255.

10. Pius XII, *Humani Generis*, 562–70.

11. Pius XII, *Humani Generis*, 565–67.

wine bags of the gospel, unfit for new wine. They are rather our intellectual penetration and identification with the transcendental aspects of being *qua* being. And while our concepts, i.e., those penetrating being on a level transcending that of the phenomenon, are always open to further refining, this progress does not suppose a substitution of wine bags or "pigeonholes."[12] The question at issue in my review—which Fr. Francoeur again avoids—is not whether we can force the methods of theology on phenomenology. Obviously, we cannot. The question rather is just how far one can proceed with phenomenological methods in treating of matters, formally and primarily the object of metaphysics and theology. On this point the phenomenology practiced by Fr. Teilhard is, in my opinion, in error *de facto*, whatever his protestations to the contrary may be.

Secondly, even if the Teilhardian notion of moral evil and the use of scientific extrapolations in matters theological were the only faults in need of revision, I should think it obvious that the needed revisions are more than minimal.

Thirdly, the remark of Koestler is, as cited by Fr. Francoeur, most ambiguous. If the light of reason is the bride of faith who must nevertheless obey her spouse, I do not see how it can be described as an altogether independent, autonomous source of knowledge. I am inclined to think that not only those who follow the traditional presentation of the relations between philosophy and theology as developed by Augustine, Anselm, and Bonaventure, but also those who follow Thomas as well would agree that the only true philosophy is a Christian philosophy, one which is the *ancilla fidei*. I am also under the impression that behind the Teilhardian system is a half-conscious rationalism. The impression is confirmed by the naturalistic and Pelagianistic tendencies in the discussions on grace, and by a rather gnostic emphasis on the importance of cosmogonies for salvation.

Fr. Francoeur asks: Did Fr. Teilhard reject theological criticism? My reply is still, yes. My principal objection implies that an extension of a *merely* phenomenological method to matters primarily the object of theology or metaphysics is to reject the critical norms of these disciplines. It is not merely a question in *The Phenomenon of Man* of marking the "places where philosophers and religious thinkers . . . would be entitled to look for breaches of continuity"[13] in the movement toward Omega. It is rather a question of using theological and philosophical norms to guide one in forming (Omega), the soul, and the destiny of man in reading the meaning of

12. Cf. Journet, *Introduction*, 139ff; for the relations between theology and historical study, cf. 159–259.

13. *Phenomenon*, 29.

the phenomena. Fr. Teilhard, at least according to his professed intentions, stated in the Preface, intended to justify his conclusions on these points in the work at hand from a merely phenomenological point of view. This is an impossibility. And while such a work may "look like a philosophy,"[14] I should say it were rather a pseudo-philosophy.

Authorities

As to the authorities cited, I have already referred the reader to some rather serious reserves of Fr. D'Arcy on the method of Fr. Teilhard. As to the article of Fr. J.E. Bruns in the *Catholic World*, I rather think it has not escaped the influence of Hegel, dealing as it does with the idea of a possible synthesis of the Christian God up-above and the Marxist God up-ahead, and with the idea of the need for a metaphysics of genesis, i.e., becoming, to replace the old, static, worn-out metaphysics of being, a description hardly valid as it stands.[15] As to the articles of Vollert and Russo, and Msgr. de Solages,[16] I think they rather minimized the difficulty instead of denying it. Moreover, I did not say I found an explicit confession of monism in *The Phenomenon of Man*. What I did say was that I did not see how Fr. Teilhard prevented his phenomenology from leading to such. What is still not clear in any of these cited articles is how such a method as that practiced by Fr. Teilhard does not lead ultimately to such conclusions.

And if it is authorities that are desired, then I refer the reader to the lengthy and detailed essays written by such eminent theologians as P.M.L. Guerard des Lauriers, O.P., Msgr. R. Masi, P. Philippe de la Trinité, O.C.D., Msgr. C. Journet, Msgr. M. Alessandri.[17] These theologians arrive at substantially the same conclusions as I did in my review. Given the nature of the Pontifical Roman Theological Academy (as stated in the *Proemium* to these articles),[18] under whose auspices the articles were published, I should

14. *Phenomenon*, 30.

15. To borrow a phrase of Fr. Teilhard's "the noosphere" is already sufficiently charged with a rationalistic and agnostic, Hegelian mentality. This mentality is in no little wise responsible for the persecution of Christ's mystical members, now raging over a large part of the globe. It strikes me as not being very wise for Catholics to reinforce the adversary of Christ by proposing a synthesis of Christianity and Hegelianism.

16. The article of Solages, cited by Fr. Francoeur, appeared first in French in 1947 (prior to *Humani Generis*). For an evaluation of the persons and ideas which formed the theological background of Solages' article, cf. Eldarov, *Presenza della teologia*.

17. See *Divinitas* 3 (1959) 219–364, organ of the Pontifical Roman Theological Academy.

18. *Divinitas*, 219.

think that these views give some indication of the thinking of the church's Magisterium on the problems involved.

What is more, the one citation of church authority made by Fr. Francoeur in connection with the relations of science and theology is hardly *ad rem*. The text of the Holy Father cited by my fellow dialogist, does not deal with an important distinction I made in my review, viz., the formal aspect under which the man who is scientist finds God in the world. In my review I maintained that the scientist *as* scientist and the phenomenologist *as* phenomenologist are not concerned with adoration because they are not concerned with God in so far as they think formally in an empiriological context. This does not mean that the scientist cannot adore God and edify his fellow Christians by interpreting and understanding this world in a light higher than that of science.

The remark on the spirit of St. Francis is not at all apropos. St. Francis did not approach the world in the spirit of a romantic lover of nature; or as a naturalist. The approach of St. Francis was strictly that of the believer who, in his experience of God in prayer, comes to see the image of God in the creature and the creature in God. It is in this spirit that the *Canticle of Brother Sun* was written after the ecstatic experience on Mt. Alvernia in the fall of 1224. And while such an experience was not without great effect on the minds of Franciscan theologians, this effect is seen better in the views of St. Bonaventure on the relations of science, philosophy, and theology, expounded, e.g., in the *Proemium* to the *Sentences*, *De reductione artium ad theologiam*, *Collationes in hexaëmeron*, from which I cited a brief passage to indicate his general position. The spirit of Fr. Teilhard's thought, as it is put in *The Phenomenon of Man*, is too much the naturalist's to fit the equation of Fr. Francoeur.

Canonical Aspects

It should be noted that I did not in any way deal with the question of a possible violation of the Jesuit vow of poverty. I do not intend to broach that question now. My sole concern was the question of the *imprimatur* and the consequent lack of any rule of orthodoxy in a work which *de facto* deals with religious questions. Briefly, it is necessary for a religious priest to obtain the permission of his religious and ecclesiastical superiors to publish any work. In the case of works dealing with religion it is necessary to obtain the *imprimatur*. When a priest dies, his literary heirs inherit this obligation if they are Catholic, because they are not publishing their work, but a priest's. But even if these editors are not Catholic,[19] the fact that a work, especially of a priest, appears without *imprimatur* indicates that for the faithful there is no official seal of orthodoxy for the work in question. And when, as in the case of *The Phenomenon of Man*, the *imprimatur* has not only not been granted, but a Roman Congregation has found it necessary to forbid its general circulation among seminarians, the obvious conclusion for the loyal Catholic is that church authority at the present time finds in this work matters dangerous to faith.[20]

Hence, I think there has been some objective circumvention of the laws of the church in the manner of publishing this work. The manner of publication is not canonical, and even if all the editors were non-Catholic, the manner of publication would still be uncanonical for Catholic readers, there being no guarantee of orthodoxy in the works of a priest dealing with matters religious.

Conclusion

The entire tenor of Fr. Francoeur's reply manifests an apparent lack of appreciation for the theological basis of my central objection. Hence it is no surprise that he was unable to pinpoint the nature of my objections. I think it rather impossible for one "to clarify . . . serious misunderstandings" never really understood in the first place. For the rest it has not been my intention to question the personal orthodoxy or sanctity of Fr. Teilhard at all. I have

19. Some of these literary heirs, as Fr. Francoeur admits, are Catholics. They at least are bound by the laws of the church. There is also the consideration that the reputation of priests as teachers of orthodoxy is being used to promote at least one work in particular, whose orthodoxy and security in matters religious is not only not guaranteed, but is frowned upon by authority.

20. As to the reasons for the refusal of the *imprimatur*, Fr. Francoeur has missed the point, and in the process committed a historical error. The Scope's trial in Tennessee took place in 1925, twenty, not thirty years after Fr. Teilhard began writing (1905). At the time of this trial, principally a dispute between Protestant groups, the church was permitting theologians favorable to some theory of transformism to publish prudently their works. I do not think the defense of transformism by Fr. Teilhard in itself had much to do with the refusal of permission to publish, but only in so far as it was bound up with theories and principles of thought inimical to theology. The work in question, *The Phenomenon of Man*, was completed in its first redaction before 1940. Between 1940 and 1955, when it was finally published in French, the church permitted priests and theologians prudently to publish favorable views on evolution, so long as they did not preempt the right to decide the question definitively before the church did. Nevertheless, Fr. Teilhard's work has not received an *imprimatur*, indeed has been frowned upon by a Roman Congregation charged with the maintenance of orthodoxy in seminaries and universities.

the greatest sympathy for his objectives, especially apologetic, in writing this work, as well as for the many valid observations and contributions he makes to the cause of truth. For all that, I do not think his work is without the serious shortcomings I have noted. Until substantial revisions are made, especially in the method of procedure, or until that method as practiced by Fr. Teilhard is shown to be valid, I shall continue to regard this work as leading to confusion on matters fundamental to belief and, therefore, not without grave danger for the Catholic reader and misleading to the non-Catholic in the presentation of Catholic thought.

Pope Benedict XVI on Intelligent Design and Omniscience[1]

Intelligent Design

IN RECENT MONTHS THERE has been considerable discussion, some of it polemical and acrimonious, of the essay of the Cardinal Archbishop of Vienna which appeared in the *New York Times*, 5 July 2005. Unfortunately, some of the most acrimonious and negative criticism of the essay came not from non-Catholic scientists, but from Catholic clergy, some in high station.

In a catechesis, part of an ongoing series, this one explaining the "Great Hallel" (Ps 135) and the praise and thanks owing the Creator for his great wisdom and goodness reflected in all of his creation and so an intelligent project or design, the Holy Father briefly and precisely commented on what is popularly known as intelligent design. He did so in such wise as to make it clear, without naming names, that the position of Cardinal Schoenborn does indeed represent the perennial teaching of the church, solemnly proclaimed by Vatican I, and thoroughly rooted in sacred Scripture. The Holy Father confirms this first with a series of apt selections from *Genesis*, the *Psalms*, *Wisdom* and St. Paul to the *Romans*, and then from the teaching of St. Basil the Great, one of the 10 "primary doctors" of the church.

He notes that in virtue of this teaching synthesized by St. Basil one cannot claim as genuine science or as genuine scientific method an approach to the study of the things of this world which prescinds from or denies this great truth, for the rest imprinted in the hearts of all, believers and non-believers alike. This foolish attempt to study the universe as a kind of "force at the mercy of chance" is a direct denial of what all in some way can recognize, if they want to. What is even still worse is the attempt of some Catholic priests and theologians to claim on the basis of a single

1. This essay was originally published in the Roman journal *Christ to the World* 51 (2006) 55–60.

informal remark of Pope John Paul II that evolution of the species is more than an hypothesis and for all practical purposes evolution, and according to some of the more vociferous critics of the Cardinal of Vienna and now of the pope in a form which ignores "intelligent design", is part of Catholic faith. Loudly and clearly Pope Benedict is saying: this is not so today any more than it was so seventeen hundred years ago!

More exactly, the pope is saying the teaching synthesized by St. Basil early on in the history of the church entails a genuine obligation to give up any attempt to explain the world as independent of the Creator and as not reflecting from within itself the intelligence and goodness of its designer. It means above all to desist from any scandalous attempt to indoctrinate the young in this atheism by inducing them to think in so unscientific a way and to prevent them to come in contact with the truth about creation and "intelligent design." The refusal to do this is inspired by the atheism the critics have permitted to blind the eye of their mind and put to sleep the reason of their intelligence.

The talk, brief as it is, is found in a document which represents not a mere personal opinion, but an exercise of the pope's office as teacher of all by divine appointment of the Savior of the world. Hence, the teaching found in it is binding on all who believe and should be recognized as true by all men of good will. In effect, the pope is saying in the name of Jesus Christ, though whom all things in heaven and earth were made and designed to operate harmoniously in a certain way for a certain end, that notwithstanding physical and moral evil, before the subject of creationism and evolution is taken up by anyone at all, recognition, i.e., antecedent recognition of this great truth must already have occurred. Otherwise, one is convicted of approaching the subject, not reverently, in the spirit of prayer and devotion and thanks, but foolishly tricked by the bias of atheism to consider the universe as a kind of "force at the mercy of chance." It is this bias which falsifies the methodological premises of the scientist who does not in some way, at least in fact, acknowledge and submit to the truth of "intelligent design" and teach it via his study.

The Catholic objection to Neo-Darwinism is just this: that in fact it denies intelligent design by attempting to explain the world on the basis of change and necessity alone, viz., as though the universe were devoid of guidance and order, a force at the mercy of chance. Such a presentation of the universe is not objective science, but myth, not truth, but a fairy tale. No use of the human intelligence can claim scientific objectivity in any field of study, if it declares independence of God.

Omniscience of God

In connection with recent controversy surrounding evolution, creation and intelligent design, in part occasioned by the essay of Cardinal von Schoenborn of Vienna in the *New York Times*, a number of critics of the Cardinal, including members of the Catholic clergy, have been heard making the claim that "intelligent design" is neither true, nor a premise of the "scientific" enterprise. For intelligent design in the final analysis rests on the existence of an all-powerful Creator, all-powerful, because among other reasons, he is the omniscient God, who knows all and sees all. This cannot be so, since on such a premise "chance" cannot be the primary cause underlying the operation of natural processes according to the necessary laws proper to each. Or in other words the modern concept of science would have to be abandoned as "unscientific." Hence, these critics, clerical included, in order to avoid admitting even the possibility that the modern concept of science might be without objective foundation, confess they no longer believe in the "medieval" God of "non-scientific" minds, a mythical Creator who knows all and sees all and so designs the whole of creation as an intelligent work, for that reason capable of being studied rationally or scientifically.

In his catechesis during the General Audience of 9 November 2005, the Holy Father dealt clearly and simply with the false premise that scientific method is based on "chance and necessity", and not ultimately on the intelligibility and order reflected in all the works of the Creator. The denial of this, said the Holy Father, derives not from science as such, but from what St. Basil the Great calls an atheism in the heart, an atheism leading the nonbeliever to confuse empirical science and specifically his erroneous concept of its methodology based on chance, with science itself.

In his catechesis of 14 December 2005, entitled "God knows all, God sees all" (published in *L'Osservatore Romano* for 15 December 2005, 4–5) the Holy Father deals simply, directly and clearly with the tragic denial of divine omniscience, especially by priests, asserting as in the November catechesis, that the truth of this mystery, like the truth about intelligent design, does not depend on scientific demonstration, or on the plausibility of this or that scientific hypothesis, but on considerations prior to and independent of empirical science and its methodology of verification-falsification. The truth of these mysteries is so certain, that their denial in the name of some science is enough to invalidate the claim of "scientific" for such thinking and to leave such thought totally in the dark about reality. Whence, the glorification of "chance" as the explanation of life and destiny. Not a very happy outlook on life.

Bibliography

Behe, Michael J. *Darwin's Black Box*. New York: Free Press, 1996.

Bonaventure. *Opera Omnia*. Edited by PP. Collegii S. Bonaventurae. 10 vols. Florence: Ad Claras Aquas, 1882–1902.

———. *Breviloquium*. In vol. 5 of *Opera Omnia*, 201–91. Florence: Ad Claras Aquas, 1891.

———. *Christus unus omnium magister*. In vol. 5 of *Opera Omnia*, 567–79. Florence: Ad Claras Aquas, 1891.

———. *Collationes in Hexaëmeron*. In vol. 5 of *Opera Omnia*, 329–454. Florence: Ad Claras Aquas, 1891.

———. *Commentarius in IV libros Sententiarum*. In vols. 1–4 of *Opera Omnia*. Florence: Ad Claras Aquas, 1882–89.

———. *De reductione artium in theologiam*. In vol. 5 of *Opera Omnia*, 319–25. Florence: Ad Claras Aquas, 1891.

———. *Itinerarium mentis in Deum*. In vol. 5 of *Opera Omnia*, 295–313. Florence: Ad Claras Aquas, 1891.

———. *Quaestiones disputatae de mysterio Ss. Trinitatis*. In vol. 5 of *Opera Omnia*, 45–115. Florence: Ad Claras Aquas, 1891.

———. *Quaestiones disputatae de scientia Christi*. In vol. 5 of *Opera Omnia*, 3–43. Florence: Ad Claras Aquas, 1891.

Bruns, J. Edgar. "God Up Above – or Up Ahead?" *The Catholic World* 191/1,141 (1960) 23–30.

Carol, Juniper B., *Why Jesus Christ? Thomistic, Scotistic and Conciliatory Perspectives*. Manassas, VA: Trinity Communications, 1986.

Chesterton, G. K. *George Bernard Shaw*. New York: John Lane, 1909.

Collin, Rémy. *Evolution*. New York: Hawthorn, 1959.

Cuénot, Claude. *Teilhard de Chardin: A Biographical Study*. Baltimore: Helicon, 1967.

D'Arcy Martin C., *The Meaning and Matter of History*. New York: Meridan, 1959.

———. "Varieties of Human Love." In *Adventures of the Mind from the Saturday Evening Post*, edited by Richard Thruelsen and John Kobler, 206–18. New York: Alfred A. Knopf, 1959.

Denzinger, Heinrich. *Compendium of Creeds, Definitions, and Declarations on Matters of Faith and Morals*, edited by Peter Hünermann, translated and edited by Robert Fastiggi and Anne Englund Nash. San Francisco: Ignatius, 2012.

De Solages, Bruno. "Christianity and Evolution." *Cross Currents* (1951) 26–37.

Des Places, Édouard. *Syngeneia: la parenté de l'homme avec dieu d'Homère à la patristique.* Paris: Klinksieck, 1964.

Donceel, J.F. *Philosophical Psychology.* London: Sheed and Ward, 1955.

Doran, William R. "De corporis Adami origine doctrina Alexandri Halensis, Sancti Alberti Magni, Sancti Bonaventurae, Sancti Thomae." STD diss., Mundelein Seminary, 1936.

———. "St. Thomas and the Evolution of Man." *Theological Studies* 1 (1940) 382–95.

Dorlodot, Henri. *Le darwinisme au point de vue de l'orthodoxie catholique.* Brussels: Vromant, 1921.

Duhem, Pierre. *Le Système du monde.* 10 vols. Paris: Herman and Sons, 1913–59.

Eldarov, Giorgio M. *Presenza della teologia: saggio su una recente controversia alla luce dell'enciclica "Humani generis."* Padua: Il Messaggero di S. Antonia, 1954.

Fehlner, Peter Damian. "Martire della Carità–Uomo del Millennio: san Massimiliano Maria Kolbe." *Immaculata Mediatrix* 3 (2002) 345–76. Appears in volume six of the *Collected Essays of Peter Damian Fehlner, OFM Conv: St. Maximilian Kolbe,* as "Martyr of Charity–Man of the Millennium: St. Maximilian Mary Kolbe."

———. "Teilhard de Chardin: Ambiguity by Design." *The Homiletic and Pastoral Review* May (1960) 709–17. Appears in the present volume.

Francoeur Robert and Peter D. Fehlner. "Exchange on Teilhard de Chardin." *The Homiletic and Pastoral Review* June (1960) 34–47. These articles appear in the second appendix to this volume.

Galleni, Ludovico. "Evoluzione." In *Dizionario Interdisciplinare di Scienza e Fede,* ed. G. Tanzella Nitti and A Strumia, vol. 1, 575–90. Vatican City: Urbaniana, 2002.

Gilson, Étienne. *From Aristotle to Darwin and Back Again: A Journey in Final Causality, Species, and Evolution.* Notre Dame: Notre Dame, 1984.

———. *The Christian Philosophy of St. Augustine.* New York: Random House, 1960.

Grabmann, Martin. *I divieti ecclesiastici di Aristotele sotto Innocenzo III e Gregorio IX.* Rome: Pontifical Gregorian University, 1941.

Gregory IX, *Ab Aegyptiis Argentea* [1228]. In *Compendium of Creeds, Definitions, and Declarations on Matters of Faith and Morals,* edited by Heinrich Denzinger, n. 824. San Francisco: Ignatius, 2012.

Hildebrand, Dietrich von. *Trojan Horse in the City of God.* Chicago: Franciscan Herald, 1967.

Hoeres, Walter. *Kritik der Transzendental-philosophischen Erkenntnistheorie.* Stuttgart: Kolhammer, 1969.

Jaki, Stanley. *Genesis 1 through the Ages.* London: Thomas More, 1992.

John Duns Scotus. *De primo omnium rerum principio.* Edited and translated by Allan B. Wolter. Chicago: Franciscan Herald, 1966.

John Paul II. *Fides et ratio.* In *Acta Apostolicae Sedis* 91, 5–88. Vatican City: Vatican Press, 1999.

Journet, Charles. *Introduction a la Théologie.* Paris: Desclee, 1947

Koestler, Arthur. *The Sleepwalkers.* London: Hutchison, 1968.

Kuhn, Thomas S. *The Structure of Scientific Revolutions.* Chicago: University of Chicago, 1970.

Leroy, M.D. *L'evolution restreinte aux espèces organiques.* Paris: Delhomme and Briguet, 1891.

Livi, Antonio. "Metafisica." In *Dizionario Interdisciplinare di Scienza e Fede,* ed. G. Tanzella Nitti and A Strumia, vol. 1, 939–57. Vatican City: Urbaniana, 2002.

Lonergan, Bernard. *Method in Theology*. New York: Seabury, 1972.

Madariaga, Bernardo. *La Filosofía al Interior de la Teología*. Madrid: Cisneros, 1961.

Malevez, Léopold. "La méthode du P. Teilhard de Chardin et la Phénoménologie." *Nouvelle Revue Théologique* 79 (1957) 579–99.

Messenger, Ernest C. *Evolution and Theology*. London: Burns, Oates & Washburn, 1931.

———. *Theology and Evolution*. London: Sands & Co., 1949.

Mivart, St. George. *On the Genesis of the Species*. New York: Appleton, 1871.

Mondraganes, Pius M. "De impossibilitate aeternae mundi creationis ad mentem S. Bonaventurae." *Collectanea Franciscana* 5 (1935) 529–70.

Motherway, T.J. "The Creation of Eve in the Catholic Tradition." *Theological Studies* 1 (1940) 97–116.

Newman, John Henry. Citations are from the uniform edition published by Longmans, Green and Co., London, New York, Bombay. Date { } year of composition; date in [ ] uniform edition; date in ( ) edition used.

———. *An Essay in Aid of a Grammar of Assent*. {1870} (1898).

———. *An Essay on the Development of Christian Doctrine*. {1845} [1878] (1900).

———. *Lectures on Justification*. {1838} [1874] (1900).

———. *The Arians of the Fourth Century*. {1833} (1908).

———. *The Idea of a University, Defined and Illustrated*. {1852–9} [1873] (1909).

Oromi, Miguel. *Introducción a la Filosofía esencialista*. Madrid: Cisneros, 1961.

Paul VI. Allocution, July 11, 1966. In *Acta Apostolicae Sedis* 58 (1966) 649–55.

———. *Sollemni hac Liturgia [= Credo of the People of God]*. In *Acta Apostolicae Sedis* 60 (1968) 433–46.

———. *Mysterium Fidei*. In *Acta Apostolicae Sedis* 57 (1965) 753–74.

Pius XII. "Address to the Pontifical Academy of Sciences." In *Acta Apostolicae Sedis* 33 (1941) 504–12.

———. "Au moment": Address to the Pontifical Academy of Sciences. In *Acta Apostolicae Sedis* 47 (1955) 394–401.

———. *Divino Afflante Spiritu*. In *Acta Apostolicae Sedis* 35 (1943) 309–19.

———. *Humani Generis*. In *Acta Apostolicae Sedis* 42 (1950) 561–77, 960.

Portalie, Eugene. *A Guide to the Thought of St. Augustine*. London: Burns and Oates, 1960.

Quenetain, Tanneguy de. "Un livre qui boulverse notre vision du monde." *Réalités* 128 (1956) 40–44.

Reale, Vito. "Agostino di Ippona." In *Dizionario Interdisciplinare di Scienza e Fede*, ed. G. Tanzella Nitti and A Strumia, vol. 2, 1533–50. Vatican City: Urbaniana, 2002.

Russo, François. "The Phenomenon of Man." *America* 103 (1960) 185–89.

Sagüés, Joseph F. "De Deo creante et elevante." In *Sacrae Theologiae Summa*, vol. 2, 461–1010. Madrid: Biblioteca de Autores Christianos, 1955.

Sermonti, Giuseppe and Roberto Fondi. *Dopo Darwin: Critica all'evoluzionismo*. Milan: Rusconi, 1982.

Siri, Joseph. *Gethsemane*. Chicago: Franciscan Herald, 1981.

Solaguren, Celestino. "El Cristocentrismo cósmico de Teilhard de Chardin." *Verdad y Vida* 19 (1961) 131–43.

Suarez, Francisco. *De opere sex dierum*. Lyons: Gabriel Boissat and Associates, 1635.

Teilhard de Chardin, Pierre. *The Phenomenon of Man*. New York: Harper, 1959.

Testa, Emmanuele. "La Creazione del Mondo nel Pensiero del SS Padri." *Studii Biblici Franciscani* 16 (1965–6) 5–68.

Thomas Aquinas. *De aeternitate mundi*. Turnhout: Brepols, 2013.

————. *De Potentia*. Taurini: Marietti 1949.

————. *Quaestiones quodlibetals*. Taurini: Marietti, 1942.

————. *Summa Theologiae. Opera Omnia*. Vols. 4–12. Rome: Typographia Polyglotta S.C. de Propaganda Fide, 1888–1903.

Thompson, W.R. "Evolution and Taxonomy." *Studia Entomologica* 5 (1962) 549–70.

————. "Systematics: The Ideal and the Reality." *Studia Entomologica* 3 (1960) 493–49.

————. "The Work of Jean Henri Fabre." *The Canadian Entomologist* 96 (1964) 62–70.

Tresmontant, Claude. *Pierre Teilhard de Chardin: His Thought*. Baltimore: Helicon, 1959.

Vanzago, Luca. "Bergson, Henri." In *Dizionario Interdisciplinare di Scienza e Fede*, ed. G. Tanzella Nitti and A Strumia, vol. 2, 1584–95. Vatican City: Urbaniana, 2002.

Vatican I, *Dei Filius*. In *Compendium of Creeds, Definitions, and Declarations on Matters of Faith and Morals*, edited by Heinrich Denzinger, nn. 3000–45. San Francisco: Ignatius, 2012.

Vollert, Cyril. "Toward Omega: Man in the Vision of Teilhard de Chardin." *The Month* 23/5 (1960) 261–69.

Wildiers, N.M. *An Introduction to Teilhard de Chardin*. London: Collins, 1968.

Zahm, J.A. *Evolution and Dogma*. Chicago: D.H. McBride, 1896.

Index